Political Culture and Leadership
in Soviet Russia

bs historical trends
Leadership

Political Culture and Leadership in Soviet Russia

From Lenin to Gorbachev

Robert C. Tucker
Professor of Politics Emeritus
Princeton University

W · W · Norton & Company
New York   London

Printed in the United States of America.

Library of Congress Cataloging-in-Publication Data

Tucker, Robert C.
    Political culture and leadership in Soviet Russia.

    Includes index.
    1. Political culture—Soviet Union. 2. Political leadership—Soviet Union.
3. Soviet Union—Politics and government—1917-   I. Title.
JN6581.T82   1987   306'.2'0947   87-11025

This book was written under the auspices of the Center of International Studies, Princeton
University.

ISBN 0-393-02489-X

W. W. Norton & Company, Inc., 500 Fifth Avenue, New York, N. Y. 10110
W. W. Norton & Company Ltd., 37 Great Russell Street, London WC1B 3NU

3 4 5 6 7 8 9 0

Contents

In memory of

Raisa and Konstantin Pestretsov

Preface

While rich in specialized research, Soviet studies in the West are remiss in their failure so far to produce a general interpretation of Russia's historical experience in the seventy-year aftermath of the revolutions of 1917. This book aims to fill that gap.

Two ideas—political culture and leadership—form its analytical underpinnings. As here defined, a culture is a society's customary way of life, comprising both accepted modes of thought and belief and accepted patterns of conduct. Political culture is everything in a culture that pertains to government and politics. In Soviet Russia, very little does not so pertain.

Cultures being matters of habit and its transmission through a society's agencies of acculturation, they are relatively persistent through time although they do undergo changes, especially in the modern age. Movements under reform leadership can hasten cultural change when the need for it grows strong. And from time to time, in various societies, situations arise, on occasion through wars, in which socio-political revolutions occur. As distinct from coups or palace revolutions, these involve rapid and radical change in the society's way of life; as socio-political revolutions, they are cultural ones. Russia's Bolshevik Revolution belongs to this type.

In no instance of a revolution is the break with the past culture total. No matter how culturally innovative a revolution may be—in the sense of creating new institutions, beliefs, rituals, ideals and symbols—the national cultural ethos lingers on in many ways, and more persistently in some areas of life than in others. In time a process of adaptation occurs whereby elements of the nation's pre-revolutionary cultural past are assimilated into the revolutionary new culture, which thus takes shape as an amalgam of the old and new. This helps to explain why countries that undergo Communist revolutions tend to diverge in later developmental directions, for no two national cultural pasts are alike.

In Soviet studies the cultural approach has been slower to mature than some of us expected when we embarked on it in the later 1960s as the earlier 'totalitarian paradigm' lost its hold on many scholarly minds. This may be because it has to be combined with something else in order to yield the useful results that it can yield. For all by itself, culture or political culture does not *do* anything; people do. Thus analysis must take account of the culture-bearing human beings who act in ways that either help a culture to persist through time or to change, as the case may be. In particular, it must consider the minds and motives of those people who acquire political power or influence as leaders.

The study of leadership as a process has only recently begun to take its proper and central place in political science. This book is informed by a conception of the functions and forms of leadership that was set forth in the present writer's *Politics as Leadership* (1981) and is briefly summarized in chapter two below. It combines a cultural approach in Soviet studies with an examination of the parts that leaders have played in cultural change or, as in Brezhnev's time, its obstruction. Such a strategy is all the more apposite when one's subject is Russian Communism, which has been a leader-centred movement and polity from its revolutionary birth under Lenin at the opening of this century to the struggle for cultural renewal that has begun in Gorbachev's Russia as the century approaches its close.

The lengthy final chapter on the contemporary period is partly the product of a 'field trip' to Moscow that the writer was fortunate to take in May-June 1986 under a grant from the International Research and Exchanges Board. It provided the opportunity to discuss political culture and leadership in theoretical terms with scholars in the Soviet Academy of Sciences' Institute of State and Law, and to observe at close hand, if only for a short time, the extraordinarily interesting spectacle of a Soviet Russia in process of cultural change after the Brezhnev era's stagnation and growing crisis. This process was apparent in official words and acts, in meetings of film-makers and of writers, in new plays and films showing in Moscow's theatres, in press articles and thoughts expressed in formal and informal conversation.

The effort in the final chapter, written since then, to capture the content and texture of ongoing change—and resistance to change—became, in some measure, a test of the fruitfulness of the concepts advanced, and the soundness of positions taken, in earlier chapters written before Gorbachev's advent to power. It is for the reader to judge how helpful those concepts and those accounts of earlier periods have been in interpreting the present-day struggle over reform of the Soviet political culture handed down from the Leninist, Stalinist and post-Stalinist past.

Chapter one, originally prepared for a conference on political culture held in 1971 by the American Council of Learned Societies' Planning Group on Comparative Communist Studies, appeared in *Political Science Quarterly*, vol. 88, no. 2 (June 1973), 173-90. Chapter two, save for introductory remarks that I have added, is a shortened version of a chapter in the writer's *Politics As Leadership* (Columbia, Mo. and London, 1981). Chapter three appeared in *Bolshevik Culture: Experiment and Order in the Russian Revolution*, ed Abbott Gleason, Peter Kenez, and Richard Stites (Bloomington, Indiana University Press: 1985), 25-39. An earlier version of chapter four was distributed by the Kennan Institute of Advanced Russian Studies as an occasional paper, 'Stalinism versus Bolshevism? A Reconsideration,' along with comments by Professor Peter Reddaway. Chapter five appeared in *Stalinism: Essays in Historical Interpretation*, ed Robert C. Tucker (New York, W. W. Norton: 1977), 77-111. Chapter six appeared in *Foreign Affairs*, Winter 1981/82, 414-35; and an abbreviated version of Chapter seven appeared in *World Policy Journal*, Spring 1987. In editing the previously published essays for inclusion here, I have pruned some to minimize repetition. My thanks go to the various publishers for permission to reprint them.

As often in the past, Princeton University's Center of International Studies has provided much needed services in the preparation of the book. For support during periods of leave from teaching when the research and writing went on, and more recently since my retirement from teaching, I am indebted to the Kennan Institute for Advanced Russian Studies in the Woodrow Wilson International Center for Scholars, the National Endowment for the Humanities, the National Council for Soviet and East European Research, Indiana University's Institute for Advanced Study, and the American Council of Learned Societies.

I am grateful to the colleagues and former students with whom the ideas advanced in this book were discussed and debated as they arose and matured in my mind over fifteen years or more. To my wife, Evgenia Pestretsova Tucker, I am especially indebted for her encouragement, sage comments, and rare expertise in Russian.

1 Culture, Political Culture, and Soviet Studies

Among the less noticed centenaries of 1971 was that of Edward Tylor's *Primitive Culture*, the book that launched the anthropological concept of culture on its remarkable career. Like most important events in intellectual history, it was not so much a beginning as a further advance. Tylor's definition of culture—'that complex whole which includes knowledge, belief, art, morals, law custom, and any other capabilities and habits acquired by man as a member of society'—derived in part from Gustav Klemm, whose *Allgemeine Culturgeschichte der Menschheit* (1843-52) had in turn stated that it was Voltaire 'who first put aside dynasties, king lists, and battles, and sought what is essential in history, namely culture, as it is manifest in customs, in beliefs, and in forms of government'.[1]

The period since *Primitive Culture's* appearance has seen both a prodigious effort in the empirical study of cultures and a gradually expanding discussion of the culture concept itself. A critical review cites 164 definitions. Eschewing a further definition of their own, the authors observe that 'all cultures are largely made up of overt patterned ways of behaving, feeling, and reacting. But cultures likewise include a characteristic set of unstated premises and categories ("implicit culture") which vary greatly between societies.' Further, they summarize the main themes of the 164 definitions as: 'culture is a product; is historical; includes ideas, patterns, and values; is selective; is learned; is based upon symbols; and is an abstraction from behavior and the products of behavior.' Finally, they conclude

1

that although the anthropological concept of culture had become a fairly well delineated one, no full theory of culture had yet emerged. There are 'plenty of definitions but too little theory'.[2] I have the impression that their conclusion, drawn some decades ago, would still stand today.

Even though anthropology has far outgrown its origins as the ethnography of preliterate societies, the culture concept has proved too large for it. If man is the culture-bearing and culture-creating animal, then the idea of culture must play a central role in every one of the disciplines dealing with human-kind—psychology, history, and the several social sciences; and culture becomes, as Kroeber and Kluckhohn put it, 'a major concept in a possible unified science of human behavior'.[3] Such a science is a thing of the future, but the increasing penetration of the culture concept into the social sciences is very probably one of the signs of present progress in that direction.

Since the Second World War, the culture concept has come into American political science by two different routes. First, there were efforts to look at political phenomena in psychocultural terms, as instanced by Nathan Leites's 1948 article.[4] This work, in turn, was largely an outgrowth of wartime research that sought to bring culturological and psychological searchlights to bear upon the ways of the enemy. Ruth Benedict's *The Chrysanthemum and the Sword* is the best known single product of that research.[5] As the Second World War gave way to the Cold War, it seemed logical to seek psychocultural insight into the ways of thought and behaviour of Russian Communists. One of the results was a work by the British anthropologist Geoffrey Gorer, *The People of Great Russia*, explaining Soviet aggressiveness and the psychology of 'capitalist encirclement' by the fact that the Bolshevik leaders had presumably been subjected in infancy to the Russian folk practice of swaddling young children.[6] This 'swaddling' theory has no serious standing.

The idea of political culture is the second form in which the culture concept made its appearance in political science. This idea arose partly in reaction against the kind of psychocultural theorizing that tended to treat public political life as a simple extension or reproduction of the patterns of family experience prevalent in a particular culture. Such a reaction was in Gabriel Almond's mind when he argued that a society's political system is embedded in a political culture, comprising that society's pattern of orientations to political action, which is 'a differentiated part of the culture and has a certain autonomy'.[7] He wanted to underline the 'certain autonomy' of a society's political culture.

The political culture approach is now deeply embedded in the culture of American political science. If a critical stock-taking is in order, there are two questions about the notion and the approach that seem especially worth considering. They concern the scope of the concept of political culture, and whether we should think of political culture as comprising an autonomous realm within the total culture of a society.

II

Almond's original conceptualization of political culture was influenced by his intellectual purpose at the time, which was to create a typology of political systems. Because he approached political culture in terms of its relevance to this scholarly enterprise, he was led to give the phenomenon a subjective or psychological characterization—as the 'set of meanings and purposes' in which any political system is embedded. Most political scientists interested in political culture have followed his lead. The dominant definitional tendency is reflected in Verba's formula of 1965: 'The political culture of a society consists of the system of empirical beliefs, expressive symbols, and values which define the situation in which political action takes place. It provides the subjective orientation to politics.'[8]

In so defining political culture, political scientists have parted company with many anthropologists. Viewing culture as the socially learned and transmitted way of life of a society, these anthropologists have treated it as a behavioural as well as a psychological concept. Their culture concept covers what people culturally do as well as what they culturally feel and think. The anthropologists also take account of the important distinction between culture behaviour and culture norms. Linton distinguishes between 'real culture patterns' and 'ideal

ideal vs. actual patterns of behavior

culture patterns'. The former are "the limited range of behaviors within which the responses of a society's members will normally fall', while the latter are consensuses of opinion on the part of the society's members as to how people *should* behave in particular situations.[9]

There is no obligation lying upon political scientists to follow Linton's culture concept in their own conceptualizing of political culture. But is this deviation from his usage desirable? To some writers on political culture, it has not seemed so. For example, in his study of the effort of Castro's movement to transform the traditional political culture of Cuba, Richard Fagen views political culture as embracing 'patterned ways of life and action as well as the states of mind that sustain and condition these patterns'. Apart from pointing to some anthropologists' culture concept as authority for doing this, he points out that the new Cuban elite has not been aiming solely toward influencing ways of thinking or feeling about politics, but also at influencing behaviour.[10]

To epitomize the issue, Fagen observes that if a large number of people in a certain country habitually cheat on their income tax returns, this would not be taken by the proponents of the psychological definition as an item of that country's political culture. I should like to pursue the question with a comparable example spelled out in more detail. Let us assume that in a certain country, X, people in the great majority believe that it is wrong for government officials to accept bribes; and, further, that government officials habitually take bribes. On the psychological approach, the belief would constitute an item in X's political culture but the behavioural pattern would not. On the broader view of political culture, however, both the belief and the behavioural pattern would belong to X's political culture, the belief being (in Lintonian terms) an ideal political culture pattern and the bribe-taking practice being a real political culture pattern. Looking at the matter in these terms, we would be faced with a discrepancy within the political culture rather than one between political culture and conduct. Admittedly, it is ultimately a matter of scholarly expediency which position we take. But this seems to be one of those issues of expediency that carry significant implications for research orientation and for theory.

The question is occasionally discussed on the plane of explanation. Some defenders of the psychological definition have argued that the explanatory enterprise suffers when political culture is taken to include the political behaviour patterns—which may, in fact, be what one wants to explain by reference to the political culture. My question is this: does the scholarly value of the concept of political culture turn on its explanatory potency? Might not the central importance of a concept like that of political culture be that it assists us to take our bearings in the study of the political life of a society, to focus on what is happening or not happening, to describe and analyse and order many significant data, and to raise fruitful questions for thought and research—without explaining anything? May it not be, further, that political culture and its vicissitudes comprise a great deal of what it is that we should wish to explain?

Almond, it was noted earlier, postulated the existence of a political culture which 'is a differentiated part of the culture and has a certain autonomy'. It is the particular pattern of cognitive, affective, and evaluative orientations to political action prevailing in a society. Whether we accept this psychological characterization of the political culture or opt for the approach that includes patterns of behaviour, we need to raise the question of the political culture's autonomy. Given that a society's culturally patterned way of life includes its way of political life, should we conceptualize this 'way of political life' as a more or less autonomous realm of culture? Since the case for an affirmative answer is implicit in much of the existing literature on political culture, it may be justified to concentrate here upon the possible bases for doubt.

We may ask, first, whether the notion of an autonomous political culture may not itself reflect a cultural bias—the preconceptions of modernity in the West. One anthropological analysis of modern European culture supports such a view. Louis Dumont contends that the emergence of religion, economics, politics, art, etc., as relatively self-contained autonomous spheres of society is a feature of the evolution of culture in the modern West that makes it an 'exceptional development' and even an 'eccentric phenomenon' in the wide experience of mankind. He particularly mentions the birth of 'an autonomous world of political institutions and speculations' as an example of this deviation from the holistic cultural situation in which politics, religion, morality and so on blend and interpenetrate one another.[11] From such a point of view, the notion of political culture as a relatively self-contained autonomous sphere might appear as an ideological expression of the modern West's cultural exceptionalism.

In church-state cultures like Byzantium, Islam, and medieval Christendom, religion and theology so radically affected orientations toward political action that the very notion of 'political action' meant something different from what modern Western people may mean by it (imagine Thomas Aquinas reacting to Harold Lasswell's formula for all politics as 'who gets what, when, how'); the political culture itself inhered in the religious culture. Or to take an example from a different quarter, Geertz describes the traditional Balinese state as a 'theatre-state' which was pointed not toward governance *per se* but 'rather toward spectacle, toward ceremony, toward the public dramatization of the ruling obsessions of Balinese culture: social inequality and status pride. . . . To govern was not so much to choose as to perform. . . . Power served pomp, not pomp power.'[12] What becomes of the autonomy of the political culture in such a case?

Examples need not be multiplied, although we may observe in passing that when we view the Communist party-state as a cultural or political-cultural formation, we are dealing with a phenomenon that shows in its self-conception, and even in its institutional configuration, a suggestive resemblance to the classic church-state. The question bears upon the conceptual foundations of a comparative politics that would study political life in cultural terms. Conceivably, we could relinquish the concept of political culture in favour of what might be called simply a cultural approach to politics: an orientation toward the study of political institutions, ideologies, practices, values, etc., as phenomena embedded in the larger cultures of particular societies. Alternatively, or at the same time, we could retain the notion of a political culture—meaning by it the predominantly political aspects of a culture—but beware of treating it as something clearly differentiated from the larger cultural pattern and forming an autonomous sphere.

III

As a conscious research strategy employing the concept of political culture, the cultural approach to Communist politics is relatively new. In a different way, however, it is not new at all, but preceded our more customary academic modes of attack on the problem. Professor Samuel Harper's *Civic Training in Soviet Russia* might have been called (anticipating Fagen) *The Transformation of Political Culture in Russia*; and his *Making Bolsheviks* could appropriately have been subtitled 'A Study in Political Socialization'.[13] René Fülöp-Miller's *The Mind and Face of Bolshevism* was not simply the 'Examination of Cultural Life in Soviet Russia' that its subtitle proclaimed it, but an examination of Soviet Communism in its early years under the aspect of Russia's cultural transformation.[14] This list could be lengthened.

Yet, the cultural approach did not prevail when Communist studies (in the form of Soviet studies) took its rise as an academic field after the Second World War. Although some psychocultural studies, such as Gorer's, appeared, the dominant theoretical perspective was an adaptation of systems theory, perhaps best reflected in a work summarizing a collective postwar project of Harvard's Russian Research Center, *How the Soviet System Works*.[15] Soviet studies developed under the dual aegis of Parsonian social systems theory and the concept of totalitarianism as elaborated in the 1930s and after by Franz and Sigmund Neumann, Hannah Arendt, Carl Friedrich, and others.

Historical context merits consideration here. The cultural orientation was conspicuous in Soviet studies at a time when the object, Soviet Communism, was still engaged in a strenuous and loudly proclaimed effort to transform the ethos inherited from the Russian past, a time of attempted cultural revolution. Soviet studies became an academic field, however, during high Stalinism, when seeming constancies—like purge and terror—were salient in the object of study. By then something like a Soviet political culture had crystallized, containing elements taken over deliberately from the old Russian ethos that the early Communists wanted to extirpate, and the spirit of Soviet Communism had in many ways turned conservative. Not unreasonably, what seemed most in need of explaining was how the system worked.

The special interest of the earlier stages to culturally oriented political scientists is understandable. Every successful Communist revolution has been attended by a sustained and strenuous effort of the newly established regime to transform the way of life of the population; and where the revolutionary takeover process has been protracted—as in China, Yugoslavia, and Vietnam—the transformation of the culture has begun in the course of the revolution, on liberated parts of the national territory, and has constituted an integral part of the revolution. Although it brings with it an elaborate ideology, a new institutional set-up, and a host of characteristic new practices, the Communist movement should not be thought of, it seems, as simply imposing a ready-made, new 'Communist culture' upon the receptive (or non-receptive) populace. Rather, the new culture, or new political culture, is something that emerges in and through the transformative process over a period of years; something, moreover, in which the new cultural ingredients that Communism brings with it as a movement blend with elements of the pre-existing national cultural ethos. Indeed, some of these latter elements will already be a part of the movement's culture in the pre-revolutionary stage; for its leaders have not become denationalized in the course of their conversion to and immersion in Communism.

Does a cultural approach have less relevance to the later stages, when the Communist regime presides over an essentially non-revolutionary society, like Soviet society today? A part of the answer may be that we cannot really be sure what the 'later' stages will look like in different instances, as China's latterday 'Cultural Revolution' indicates. Second, even though a Communist movement may lose its culture-transforming *élan* as it undergoes eventual deradicalization (with the possible consequence that it has to confront a Marxist or other counter-cultural movement within its midst), the cultural approach to the politics is no more precluded in principle than is the cultural approach to the politics of other unrevolutionary societies. Third, we should not take it for granted that non-cultural approaches to the Soviet 'later stages' have been successful. The social-systems approach that so deeply influenced Soviet studies in the 1940s and early 1950s was in important ways a failure. It didn't satisfactorily explain how the system worked in Stalin's time. Its picture of a totalitarian social system made no conceptual provision for the Stalin autocracy as a dynamism of the system (a cultural approach was likely to be more cognizant of the revival of the tsarist autocratic tradition as a major fact in the evolution of Soviet political culture under Stalin). Moreover, concentrating as it did upon supposedly functional constancies, called 'operating characteristics' in *How the Soviet System Works*, that approach had a built-in perspective of stable totalitarianism, save in the event of violent upheaval from below. In no way did it point to the eventuality of regime-sponsored politico-cultural change after such a juncture as Stalin's death, nor did it provide tools for effective analysis of the process of change when it occurred in Khrushchev's time and now again in Gorbachev's.

There are different ways of arriving at comparativism in Communist studies via a cultural approach. One could, conceivably, try to construct a 'modal' culture via generalization from the features that Communism has shown when in power in different countries and then investigate divergences from type in concrete cases. Another method, which I find more attractive, is to historicize our comparative studies and make use of all that anthropology has to offer on the process of the transmission or 'diffusion' of cultures. Russia was not only the birthplace of modern Communism as a political movement; after the revolution this movement and this system offered itself to other countries as a mandatory model. Meanwhile, however, it had taken over certain elements from the Russian politico-cultural heritage. In so far as other Communist movements were doing, or would in future do, the same thing, despite all the efforts Moscow was making to prevent it, the seeds were being planted not only for future diversity of communisms but for collision of Communist cultures. The principle implicit in all this may be stated in general form: if Communism in practice tends to be an amalgam of an innovated cultural system and elements of a national cultural ethos, then divergences of national cultural ethos will be one of the factors making for developmental diversity and cultural tension between different movements.

The cultural approach is no panacea for Soviet studies, any more than it is for any other branch of scholarship concerned with human beings. If it promises certain intellectual advantages, it also involves serious problems. The problem of primary data, always a difficult one in this field, may be in some ways even more difficult for the student of Communism as a form of culture than for the exponent of other approaches. The historicizing of our studies may take us farther than ever from general theory even as it opens up avenues for analysis of specifics and for low-level generalization. The list of problems could be extended. The most one could say in favour of the cultural approach would be something similar to what Churchill said of democracy. A most inefficient form of government. The trouble is, all the others are worse.

NOTES

1. A.L. Kroeber and Clyde Kluckhohn, *Culture: A Critical Review of Concepts and Definitions* (New York, n.d.), 14.
2. *ibid.*, 308, 357.
3. *ibid.*, 70.
4. Nathan Leites, 'Psycho-cultural hypotheses about political acts', *World Politics*, I (1948), 102–19.
5. Ruth Benedict, *The Chrysanthemum and the Sword: Patterns of Japanese Culture* (New York, 1946).
6. Geoffrey Gorer and John Rickman, *The People of Great Russia: A Psychological Study* (London, 1949).
7. H. Eulau, S. Eldersveld, and M. Janowitz, eds, *Political Behavior* (Glencoe, 1956), 36. The article, entitled 'Comparative political systems', originally appeared in *The Journal of Politics*, XVIII (1956). My remarks on the background of Almond's innovation derive in part from a conversation with him in September 1970.
8. Lucian Pye and Sidney Verba, eds, *Political Culture and Political Development* (Princeton, 1965), 513.
9. Ralph Linton, *The Cultural Background of Personality* (New York, 1945), 46, 52.
10. Richard R. Fagen, *The Transformation of Political Culture in Cuba* (Stanford, 1969), 5–6. For further discussion of this issue in relation to Communist studies, see *Political Culture and Communist Studies*, ed Archie Brown (New York, 1984).

11. Louis Dumont, 'Religion, politics, and society in the individualistic universe', *Proceedings of the Royal Anthropological Institute*, London, 1971, 31–2.
12. Clifford Geertz, 'Politics past, politics present: some notes on the uses of anthropology in understanding the new states', Paper presented to the International Sociological Conference, Evian, September 1966, 12.
13. Samuel Harper, *Civic Training in Soviet Russia* (Chicago, 1929); Samuel Harper, *Making Bolsheviks* (Chicago, 1931).
14. René Fülöp-Miller, *The Mind and Face of Bolshevism* (New York, 1928).
15. R.A. Bauer, A. Inkeles, and C. Kluckhohn, *How the Soviet System Works: Cultural, Psychological, and Social Themes* (Cambridge, Mass., 1956). Significantly, though 'cultural' appeared in the subtitle, the word 'culture' is not in the book's index. The introductory chapter offered the study as a contribution to 'social systems analysis'.

2 Leadership and Culture in Social Movements*

I

We all often find ourselves in circumstances that call for deliberating before we take action. To cite a common example, as drivers we approach a stoplight that flashes from green to yellow before we reach the intersection ahead.

Shall we speed up and cross before the light turns red, or jam on the brakes and stop before it does? Our choice of an action will partly depend on our driving habits (our personal culture as drivers) and partly on how we perceive the circumstances and size up their meaning in relation to our purposes and concerns. Are we late for an important meeting and hence in a great hurry? If so, we may speed across on the yellow light to save time. Is a huge lorry bearing down on us from behind and perhaps unable to stop as quickly as our small car can? Again, we may reason that a quick stop would be dangerous and so decide to speed on. But what if we fail to see the lorry in our rear-view mirror? If so, we may decide, especially if our culture as drivers so dictates, to stop in accordance with the rules. In sum, our action will depend on our perception of the circumstances and our assessment of their meaning for us. This we may describe as our diagnosis or definition of the situation—the 'problem-situation' as we may call it.

When an individual defines a situation on his or her own and acts in it, leadership as an influencing relation is not involved.

* Reprinted from *Politics as Leadership* by Robert C. Tucker, by permission of the University of Missouri Press. Copyright 1981 by the Curators of the University of Missouri.

The need for leadership arises when circumstances take on meaning for whole groups of people in such a way that diagnosis of their meaning is called for followed by action by the group or on its behalf to meet the situation as defined. When groups are small, leadership may be informal and shift from one individual to another depending on the sorts of situations encountered. When groups are large and organized, there is usually a formal leadership structure: the high command of an army, the management of a corporation, the officials of a trade union, or the administration of a university. The leadership structure of a political community is its government.

We may divide leadership's activity into three interlocking phases. First, there is a diagnostic function. Leaders are expected to diagnose group situations authoritatively, wisely and in good time (needless to say, many leaders fail to meet the test of effectiveness here). Second, they must prescribe a policy, i.e., a course of group action or action on the group's behalf that will resolve the problem-situation. Third, leadership has a mobilizing function. Leaders must gain the group's support, or predominant support, for the definition of the group situation that they have advanced and for the plan of action that they have prescribed. We may describe these functions as diagnostic, policy-formulating, and policy-implementing.

Political problem-situations arise when circumstances take on meaning in relation to a political community's purposes and concerns. What are these? In practice, they are the community's purposes and concerns *as someone conceives them*. How any member or leader of the community conceives them will almost certainly be affected by his or her group affiliations. Contemporary societies are divided along economic, sectional, ethnic, party, educational, and other lines. Very many of the groups into which they are divided are organized and have leaderships dedicated to the promotion of one group's interests. Characteristically, these are equated in the minds of the group's members and leaders with the interests—that is, the purposes and concerns—of the political community as a whole. So, a political party will regard itself as the natural custodian of those larger concerns as well as of its own. Those who become national political leaders will usually retain group allegiances even as they seek to be 'leaders of all the people'.

These considerations go a long way towards explaining the contentiousness inherent in political life—the controversies that constitute its daily stuff. Leaders of different party affiliations or from different sectors of society will predictably differ in their definitions of political situations that arise. Leaders of the party in power, seeking reelection, will find the overall state of the society good, or at any rate far better than when the party took office, whereas leaders of the party that seeks to oust them will find the society in a serious problem-situation caused by poor policies of the present leadership and will proclaim the need for a new set of policies aimed at rectifying this unfortunate state of affairs.

An interpretation of politics in terms of leadership is not at all incompatible with a due regard for democracy's role in political life. Democracy may be defined from our perspective as the guaranteed possibility of meaningful participation by citizens in the process of political leadership. Such participation takes place not only, and perhaps not even primarily, in periodic voting by citizens in contested elections of new leaders. It likewise takes place by the direct participation of citizens in the diagnosing of collective problem-situations and the proposing of policies to meet them.

This, in turn, goes directly to the matter of freedom of assembly and all the other forms of freedom of expression, above all the rights of free speech and press. Without these, ordinary citizens cannot reliably and effectively participate in the public process of situation-defining and proposing of policy responses. Indeed, they cannot even effectively participate in the pre-leadership function of signalizing the existence of circumstances that take on meaning as problem-situations because of the way they impinge upon the citizens' purposes and concerns. Only rarely, as when war breaks out, do circumstances immediately take on import for the entire political community. In the usual course of things circumstances have differential impact, affecting initially and particularly the people of some locality, occupation, economic level, industry, age group, ethnic group, etc. Only when citizens are secure in the rights of free speech and assembly, the right to strike, and so on, can they act without hindrance to bring the circumstances and their concern over them to the attention of the general public and the authorities and to seek recognition of their own problem-situation as the political community's.

So far we have proceeded on the implicit assumption that when circumstances arouse the concern of sizeable groups of people in a political community, constituted leadership diagnoses the problem-situation involved and prescribes a policy response. But that assumption does not always hold true. Many sets of circumstances have meaningfully impinged upon the purposes and concerns of large numbers of people without being defined, at least for a long time, as problem-situations about which political communities should take action. Historical examples would include slavery, serfdom, the lack of suffrage for women and the poor, minorities' deprivation of civil rights, extremes of poverty, child labour, and the danger of chemical pollution.

When constituted leadership fails to define meaningful circumstances as a situation calling for action, non-constituted leadership may, at some point, start doing so. Individuals in the political community may independently diagnose heretofore accepted conditions as wrong and remediable. They may devise proposals for change and publicly urge their acceptance. Constituted political authority may not react positively to such initiatives, but numbers of people, especially from the group or groups directly affected by the circumstances in question, may respond, often eagerly, to the non-constituted leaders' diagnoses and prescriptions for action. When that happens, movements for change arise. In so far as they take part in and influence the political life of their societies, they merit the designation *socio-political*. If, as often happens, the movements become organized, the originally non-constituted leaders typically acquire constituted leadership roles within the directing organizations of the movements. And if the movements acquire state power, as has often happened, they become constituted leaders of states.

Socio-political movements for change are leadership phenomena in two related senses. First, they characteristically arise through leadership activity by individuals at a time when constituted authority is not providing leadership of their variety, but when receptivity to that type of leadership exists in the political community. Second, once in being, a socio-political movement can furnish leadership for change that is not being provided by constituted authority. Such leadership may or may not be successful. If successful, it may be so in different ways. It may, for example, succeed by provoking or pressuring constituted authority in the community to adopt, in some form or degree, the movement's diagnosis of the situation and its recipes for corrective action. Alternatively, it may carry through its programme by acquiring state power, whether legally or through violent revolution, and therewith the capacity to act for change from constituted leadership positions.

Political science, in my view, has overconcentrated on the workings of established polities and given too little systematic attention to socio-political movements. One source of this deficiency lies in the failure to develop an analysis of the political process within which such movements find a logical and important place. Another is the tendency of political scientists to see their topic as the study of power and the powerful and to focus primary attention upon the study of the state as the organization that—as Max Weber put it—monopolizes the legitimate use of coercion on a certain territory. Unless terrorist in their mode of operation, socio-political movements rarely possess much coercive power, and unless they become a government they may never monopolize it on a sizeable territory.

Yet movements have played a remarkably large role in political history and continue to do so. Very many have captured power by revolutionary politics. Some, upon achieving power, have created what have been called 'movement-regimes' that continue to pursue the politics of change from governmental positions. The roster of twentieth-century leaders whose names might not have bulked large in history but for their involvement in successful socio-political movements would include Lenin, Trotsky, Stalin, Mussolini, Hitler, Nehru, Nasser, Ben-Gurion, Nkrumah, Ben Bella, Castro, and de Gaulle. In many more cases, movements and their leaders have mattered in political life without forming governments.

From the leadership standpoint, the study of socio-political movements and their dynamics is integral to the study of the political process itself. Political science as 'state science' is of necessity, therefore, critically incomplete.

II

The study of movements for change properly begins with consideration of the conditions in which they arise. Our hypothesis is that they tend to arise when circumstances adversely affecting considerable numbers of people in a political community are going undefined as a problem-situation by constituted political authority despite the possibility of change (which can mean anything from the circumstances' amelioration to their abolition) and when, as a result, no action is being taken for change.

First among the many possible explanations of this phenomenon is time-honoured usage or convention, often called *culture*. A society's culture, as the anthropologist Linton describes it, is its customary, socially transmitted way of life, comprising both prevailing practices, or 'real culture patterns', and prevailing norms, beliefs, and values, or 'ideal culture patterns'. In any particular society at any given time, there will be greater or lesser discrepancies between real and ideal patterns, between the ways most people regularly behave and the ways they believe one ought to behave. Through socialization (or acculturation), the young are inducted into the culture by training and experience. They learn both the ideal culture patterns or accepted principles and, also, especially as they graduate into adulthood, the prevalent practices. Where discrepancies exist, socialization works toward training the new generation into acceptance of them. If slavery, for example, is an established set of practices in a particular society although incongruent with certain religious principles held by most people in that society, the generality of the society's members, slaves included, may be socialized into believing in the rightness of the institution so long as slaves are treated according to certain rules.

But human beings who have the opportunity to develop and realize their human potentialities are not fatally imprisoned by socialization into their society's culture. Many, it is true, grow up and remain conformists, but not all do. Through autonomous self-development some outgrow, transcend, and on occasion rebel against what psychologist Gordon Allport calls their 'tribal codes', in other words, their culture[1] In a slave-owning society, for example, some people eventually come to believe, contrary to their socialization, that slavery is wrong. Among these some may define slavery publicly as a problem-situation and call for emancipation as the policy response. If others follow their lead, an abolitionist movement emerges.

One possible avenue of escape from the socialization that one receives in one's own culture is access to another culture whose ways of living and believing differ from those learned at home. Some persons socialized into one culture may be exposed to a different one by travel or study abroad and be influenced by its ways. Alternatively, a person may 'visit' via books a culture distant from him in space or time. An exemplar of escape from home culture through foreign study is the eighteenth-century Russian, Alexander Radishchev. Russia was then an agrarian society whose economy was based on serfdom in a form hardly distinguishable from slavery for a large portion of the peasant population. Radishchev was one of the highborn young Russians who went abroad for advanced education. In Leipzig University, where he studied between 1766 and 1771, he came under the influence of French Enlightenment thought. Later he was inspired by the American Revolution. He became a passionate opponent of serfdom. In the 1780s he wrote an anti-serfdom tract, *Journey from Petersburg to Moscow*. With the help of friends, he produced 650 copies of it on his own printing machine. Some were sold in a bookshop. For this crime he was condemned to death. Empress Catherine, who directed the investigation of the case, commuted the sentence to ten years of Siberian exile. From a leadership standpoint, the *Journey* was Radishchev's definition of Russian serfdom as intolerable, from which it followed that the serfs should be freed. No anti-serfdom movement emerged, however. It is interesting to compare his attempt at non-constituted leadership and its fate with that of Harriet Beecher Stowe, a non-constituted leader of the American abolitionist movement. Her *Uncle Tom's Cabin*, a definition of American slavery as intolerable, published in book form in 1852, is reckoned among the causes of the Civil War.

The cultural conformity that militates against the recognition of problem-situations on the part of constituted authority may be powerfully reinforced by the economic self-interest of a dominant social group—such as pre-Reform Russia's serf-owning nobility and Antebellum America's slave-owning class—in preserving things as they are. So, the circumstance that Empress Catherine defined as a problem-situation was not the serf culture but rather Radishchev's outraged protest against it, and her policy response as a constituted leader was, logically, the punishment of the offender.

Repression, which can be seen as leadership for non-change, is commonly a complacent society's response to difficult conditions that the dominant minority or majority does not wish to recognize as a problem-situation save in so far as people protest against them or strive, through a movement, to change them. Cultural conformism, economic self-interest, and the wish for an untroubled conscience can intermingle as motivations here.

maintain leadership by preventing change

III

Social scientists sometimes discuss movements without emphasizing the role that leadership normally plays in their inception. Thus, a sociologist writes, 'A social movement occurs when a fairly large number of people band together in order to alter or supplant some portion of the existing culture or social order.'[2] This description fails to bring out the dynamics involved in the formation of social movements. The question is, when *do* people band together for such purposes, and how does the process typically take place?

It is my contention that it typically occurs through successful leadership activity of a sort not being undertaken by constituted authority. A person or persons show initiative as non-constituted leaders along some path not being taken by constituted authority. They define a set of circumstances that deeply concern people as an urgent problem-situation, or—if that has been done already by others, in or out of government—they define the situation in a novel way. They propose a course of collective action to meet the situation as defined. And they seek the support of others for their view of

the leader

what the situation is and what should be done about it. If they succeed in all this, if people respond to their diagnosis and their plan of action, a movement begins to form.

What determines their success or failure in rallying sufficient support to start a movement? Among the obvious determinants are: the depth and breadth of the concern that exists in the political community over the circumstances in question; the cogency of the newly proffered diagnosis of the situation and proposed plan of action to the minds of people directly affected by the circumstances; the degree to which constituted authority is showing some leadership on its own part in the matter; and the presence or absence in the society of the freedoms of speech, press, and organizing that are requisite for the unhampered development of a social movement. Depending chiefly on these factors and their interrelationship, a movement may remain small and on the fringes of society, may grow to larger size, or may become so large that it merits the name *mass movement*.

Once a movement starts, an organization usually emerges to give it direction, and those who initiated the movement as non-constituted leaders become the constituted leaders of it. Alternatively, a small organizational base, often in the form of a political party, may antedate the movement's growth to sizeable proportions. Organizational structure, doctrine, ideology, ritual, on occasion uniforms and insignia, and in general all that can be summed up under the heading of the movement's *culture* make their appearance. But in the beginning is the leadership act. A 'leaderless movement' is virtually out of the question. It could only mean a movement in which all of the members acted as leaders in unison.

For purposes of analysis, socio-political movements may be divided into two broad categories: movements for reform and movements for revolution. Reform politics is broader than movement politics. Reform leaders have often appeared as heads of government or in other constituted roles of leadership, such as legislative or judicial posts, and have furnished leadership for reform without initiating political movements. In other cases, however, of which Roosevelt's New Deal administration, and now Gorbachev's administration in Moscow, may offer illustrations, constituted leadership can generate something resembling a reform movement.

Reform politics is perhaps as diverse in motivation as in manifestation. No single characteristic motive for reform leadership can be specified. It may be a moral belief, a power drive, or a search for glory. It may be a complex combination of these, which appears to have been the case with Woodrow Wilson as a reform leader in the presidency of Princeton, the governorship of New Jersey, and the presidency of the United States. Still another possible motivation is pragmatic concern for the continued stability of a political order that would be endangered by failure to change certain conditions.

When, for example, Alexander II assumed the throne of Russia in 1855 following the long, repressive reign of his father, 'Iron Tsar' Nicholas I, and in the midst of a losing war in the Crimea that dramatized Russia's backwardness *vis-à-vis* her adversaries, France and Great Britain, the new tsar defined Russia's situation in terms of the urgent need for modernizing reforms starting with the emancipation of the serfs. Moral considerations may also have influenced him, for he told the novelist Ivan Turgenev that he had been impressed by the latter's *Sportsman's Sketches*, a book about rural Russia that carried strong abolitionist overtones. Early in 1856, Alexander told assembled representatives of the Moscow nobility, 'It is better to abolish serfdom from above than to await the time when it will begin to abolish itself from below. I request you, gentlemen, to consider how this may be achieved.'[3] The situation was thus diagnosed as one of urgent pragmatic need for a far-reaching reform in order to forestall a revolutionary upheaval that would otherwise be likely. The outcome was the Emancipation Decree of 1861, which inaugurated a series of further reforms that, together with the abolition of serfdom, changed much in Russian society without, however, dismantling the autocratic, centralized, and bureaucratic system of government.

For various reasons, as noted above, conditions that arouse deep and anguished concern in many people, as serfdom did in Russia, can long go undiagnosed by constituted political authority as a problem-situation calling for remedial action. It may be the concern itself, or overt expression of it, as in Radishchev's *Journey from Petersburg to Moscow*, that official leadership sees as the problem and seeks to solve by repressive means. In historical contexts of this kind, we have hypothesized, some individuals may act as non-constituted leaders in ways that spark socio-political movements for change. In many instances, these are reform movements.

Leaders of reform movements have a characteristic way of defining the collective situation. To their minds, it presents a wrong and remediable discrepancy between the political community's principles (its 'ideal culture patterns', to revert to Linton's terminology) and its customary practices, its 'real culture patterns', or some particular set of them. We have noted that discrepancies of this kind commonly exist in political communities; they may be glaring. Thus it may be an accepted article of belief that citizens should have the right to vote, but in practice some section of the population, such as women or members of a minority group, may be deprived of voting ability. The principle of equality before the law may coexist with various forms of inequality in practice. Through socialization, most individuals, especially as they move into the adult world, learn to take the discrepancies for granted; and special patterns of belief often evolve in support of them. For example, the set of real culture patterns in South Africa termed *apartheid*, although in conflict with certain ethico-religious principles professed by many South Africa whites, is backed by the principles of a special apartheid doctrine also professed by many of these same people.

A proposition must be added now to the analysis of a sociocultural system offered by Linton. A human society is something beyond the total complex of ideal and real culture patterns constituting a community's way of life and thought, even when allowance has been made for the existence of subcultures. There is always a core belief, a central motif, in which the ideal culture patterns are embedded, and I propose to call this the society's *sustaining myth*. The term *myth* is not being used here in the frequently encountered derogatory sense in which it means an untruth. Such myths are the sources in which people find meaning in membership in their society; thus, in a manner of speaking, the myths *are* the society as a mental fact. A sustaining myth is a notion or concept of that society as a common enterprise. It represents what is distinctively valuable about the society from the standpoint of its members. America, for example, might be characterized, in terms of its sustaining myth, as a community of free and equal self-governing citizens pursuing their individual ends in a spirit of tolerance for their religious and other forms of diversity.

With some individuals, the socialization processes that dispose persons to live in peace with discordances between ideal and real culture patterns, and especially between their society's sustaining myth (in their understanding of it) and prevalent practices, do not work effectively. Precisely because the sustaining myth is deeply meaningful to them, the clash of certain practices with it comes to seem intolerable. These are persons of what we may describe as the 'reform mentality'. They are inclined to define the rift between principle and practice, between the society's sustaining myth and the ways in which some members of it are behaving toward other members, as a wrong situation that can and should be eliminated by *altering the practices in question*. They became abolitionists of slavery, fighters for suffrage for groups of the population that are denied voting rights, seekers of change in the big-city ghetto conditions that breed crime and violence, and so forth. They devise ways of dramatizing the issue and of persuading people, or the government perhaps, to change established patterns of action or inaction.

If these leadership activities elicit a considerable public response, a reform movement comes into existence. Those who give it active support will, in many cases, be persons whose concern over the practices to which the leader objects is not hard to arouse because these practices cause them grief, perhaps by injuring their dignity, perhaps by restricting their career opportunities, perhaps by denying them work or keeping them in poverty. Some who join the movement, however, will be non-disadvantaged individuals moved by moral commitment. If the movement grows and shows signs of success, still others may become active in it for self-seeking motives. To paraphrase what Crane Brinton said of revolutionaries in *The Anatomy of Revolution*, it takes almost as many kinds of people to make a movement for change as it does to make a world.

Dr Martin Luther King, Jr, is a notable exemplar of the reform leader in recent American history, and the civil rights movement in which he became prominent exemplifies the phenomenon of reform movements. The phase in which King became active as a leader started in Montgomery, Alabama, on 1 December 1955, when a black woman, Rosa Parks, refused a bus driver's order to move to the rear of the bus in accordance with the then prevalent practice of segregated seating arrangements. Mrs Parks was arrested for violating Montgomery's segregation ordinances. King, then pastor of a local Baptist church, joined with other leaders of Montgomery's black community in defining those circumstances as a wrong situation that could and should be corrected. In response they proclaimed a Montgomery bus boycott as a non-violent form of mass opposition to bus segregation. An earlier study of Gandhiism, in 1950, had helped to incline King's mind toward the tactics of non-violently confronting upholders of practices deviant from America's professed principles; and the wrongness of segregation in principle had been declared by the US Supreme Court when, on 31 May 1954, it ordered school desegregation 'with all deliberate speed'. King's role of leadership in the ensuing 382-day Montgomery bus boycott, which was supported by the local black citizens en masse, propelled him to national prominence as a leader of the civil rights movement.[4]

That King was a man of reform mentality is clear from his pronouncements in the anti-discrimination movement. This mentality spoke, for example, in his letter from the Birmingham, Alabama, jail, in which he said, 'One day the South will know that when these disinherited children of God sat down at lunch counters they were in reality standing up for the best in the American dream and the most sacred values in our Judeo-Christian heritage, and thus carrying our whole nation back to great wells of democracy which were dug deep by the founding fathers in the formulation of the Constitution and the Declaration of Independence.'[5] King was recalling Americans to the ideal culture patterns laid down in the charter documents of their democracy. He was protesting the deviation of some practices from American society's sustaining myth as he understood and professed it.

Reformers are characteristically outraged by contradictions between what their political community professes and some of the practices it condones. But effective leaders of reform mentality are rarely persons in whom anger is the salient emotion. They typically possess and can persuasively convey to others a vision of what the society would be like, how it would look, *if* its ideals were realized in practice. Such a vision of community was notable in King. He kept referring to the 'dream' and the 'American dream'. This was a vision of American society as it would be if its sustaining myth were lived up to by all. His dream America contained, too, the vision of a new black community within American society. This was expressed in a Montgomery sermon in which he said to the people assembled in the church, 'If you will protest courageously, and yet with dignity and Christian love, when the history books are written in future generations, the historians will have to pause and say, "There lived a great people—a black people—who injected new meaning and dignity into the veins of civilization."'[6] The mobilizing power of such a vision, so communicated, was shown in King's tragically shortened career as a reform leader.

Reform leadership might seem, almost by definition, non-conservative because it is leadership for change, and conservatism is often viewed as an attitude of opposition to change. Yet conservatism has more than one meaning. It may mean attachment to the socio-political status quo, comprising both the generally accepted norms and the complex of prevailing practices. Discrepancies between the one and the other may be ignored, or they may be rationalized in a variety of ways. Another possible meaning of conservatism, however, is attachment to the political community's sustaining myth and ideal culture patterns as its foundation, its real constitution (whether or not set forth in a constitutional document). Reform leadership, which status-quo conservatives may see as dangerously radical, is in fact conservative in this latter sense: it would make ideal culture patterns practically more meaningful at the expense of making changes in the ways in which people, or some people, factually behave. In so far as reform leadership and the movements it generates are effective, moreover, the consequence may be to consolidate a social order whose stability would be threatened by failure to confront and reduce the gap between ideals and everyday realities. That is why the true revolutionary almost always fears the reformer as one who, underneath it all, is a conservative enemy of the revolutionary cause.

REFORMER VS. REVOLUTIONARY LEADERSHIP

IV

The revolutionary and the reformer both seek social change. One possible basis for distinguishing the one from the other is tactics. The reformer, it could be argued, characteristically seeks change by gradual and peaceful tactics that emphasize persuasion, whereas the revolutionary seeks change by extremist tactics that include violence. But there are objections to this reasoning. First, revolutionaries often adopt reformist tactics for a particular purpose at a given period, preparatory to the use of extreme means when conditions are ripe. In *Left-Wing Communism: An Infantile Disorder*, Lenin lectured the Communists of the world on the necessity of such flexibility. Second, some reform leaders, even though they eschew and abhor violence, have adopted tactics of non-violent confrontation to which upholders of established practices will predictably respond violently. Such was the case with Gandhi's march to the sea in the Salt Campaign of 1930, and again with peaceful civil rights demonstrations that took place under the leadership of Martin Luther King. So, just as revolutionary politics may adopt reformist tactics for a particular time and purpose, reform politics may use non-violent tactics that the reform leaders know are likely to provoke violence and thereby dramatize for the political community at large the very situation to whose presence they desire to call general attention.

Leadership for reform and leadership for revolution are best differentiated according to their divergent ways of apprehending and defining the collective situation. The reform leader, we have suggested, espouses the political community's sustaining myth, its professed ideal culture patterns, and defines the deviation of certain practices from those patterns as a wrong situation that can and should be corrected by changing the practices. Revolutionary leadership, on the other hand, sees and defines the collective situation as so irremediably wrong that the only possible solution is a fundamental reconstitution of society.

REFORMER = w/in framework

Revolutionary consciousness begins in estrangement, in a person's feeling of not being a part of the existing society, of not sharing its sustaining myth. The ideal as well as the real culture patterns are rejected. Indeed the former, along with the sustaining myth, will be the object of the revolutionary's special scorn because, as he sees it, the function of the myth and of the ideals is ideological—to obfuscate the realities of the collective situation by giving people the illusion that it is remediable. In seeking to mobilize a movement, therefore, a revolutionary leader will be particularly concerned to break the hold of the society's proclaimed principles upon the minds of people in the movement's hoped-for constituency.

As much as the reform leader, the revolutionary leader is possessed of a vision. But whereas the reformer's vision is of present society as it would be if its sustaining myth were made real, or more real, in the lives of its members, the revolutionary has a vision of a society founded on radically different principles. A revolutionary mind of great creative power will be one that forms or adumbrates a new concept of social living that may, if a revolution takes place, become the sustaining myth of a new society. The radically different principles advanced by a revolutionary leader may be past ones that have been forsaken, for example the principles of a true Islamic society as envisaged by the Iranian religious revolutionary Ayatollah Khomeini. Alternatively, they may be principles conceived and presented as unprecedented in human experience.

An archetypal revolutionary leader in the modern age, with an archetypal revolutionary mind, is Karl Marx. The *Communist Manifesto* of 1848 by Marx and Friedrich Engels is a classic concise public presentation of their position and played a part in creating the most influential socialist movements of the nineteenth and twentieth centuries. Let us examine it not simply as the statement about past, present, and future history that it appears to be, but as a leadership act, a document that sought to perform the diagnostic, action-prescribing, and support-mobilizing functions of leadership as described above.

The meaningful circumstances that the *Manifesto* diagnoses as a problem-situation are experiences that were widely endured by the industrial working class, or proletariat, during the Industrial Revolution and after: subsistence-level wages, inhumanly long working days, terrible working conditions, child labour, pauperism, ruined families, and despoiled lives. The *Manifesto*'s proffered definition of the collective situation explains those circumstances of working-class misery by the dynamics of capitalist production through exploitation of wage labour. It follows for Marx and Engels that the proletariat cannot end its misery by any other means than revolutionary mass action to overthrow the system that causes the misery. On this basis they prescribe proletarian class war against the bourgeoisie as the collective response to the situation. 'The proletarians have nothing to lose but their chains', concludes the *Manifesto*. 'They have a world to win. WORKING MEN OF ALL COUNTRIES, UNITE!' Those later writers who have wondered why Marx and Engels would exhort the workers to revolt against the exploiters in a rising that they treat as absolutely inevitable simply fail to comprehend the minds of Marx and Engels as men who were not only thinkers but would-be leaders of a movement. As such they found it natural to couple their definition of the proletarians' situation with a prescription of what should be done.

The community whose situation the *Manifesto* seeks to define is not a nation-state—as with much conventional constituted political leadership—but a social class. This class it views as universal, as mankind itself *in statu nascendi*, on the ground that masses of people in all modern bourgeois societies are being proletarianized and that all non-bourgeois societies are becoming, or are fated to become, bourgeois. What the *Manifesto* purports to diagnose is thus the human situation, and this in the context of all past history as a progression of humanity through one form of class-divided society to another, each time via a social revolution that marks the ascendancy of a new mode of productive labour. Capitalist wage labour figures in this sequence as the last exploitative mode prior to the last revolution, which by socializing the means of production will create a classless, stateless, worldwide community of man where human productive activity will not be exploited for gain.

Such is the *Manifesto*'s vision of a radically new society, a community of producers, whose basic culture pattern, real and ideal alike, will be free creativity of associated human beings producing according to their abilities and receiving according to their needs. As revolutionaries, Marx and Engels pour scorn on the ideal culture patterns of the society they would abolish—upon 'bourgeois notions of freedom, culture, law, etc.', upon 'bourgeois individuality, bourgeois independence, and bourgeois freedom'. They deride that society's libertarian sustaining myth as its 'religious and political illusions', as ideological sham and hypocrisy. They criticize socialist reformers, like the Owenites in England, who wished to attain communitarian ends by peaceful means of persuasion, as obstructors of revolutionary class war.[7] And in a passage elsewhere that conveys the essence of the reform mentality with total clarity by polemicizing against it from a revolutionary's point of view, Marx decries the reformist socialism that 'only idealizes society, takes a picture of it without shadows and wants to achieve its ideal athwart the realities of present society'.[8]

The initiatives by which founding leaders help bring movements into being by their persuasive new ways of diagnosing collective situations and prescribing courses of action in them naturally do not exhaust the range of movement leadership, whether for reform or for revolution. Once movements arise and become organized, with ideologies and established patterns of political action to promote their ends, the movement leaders, like any other, must go on functioning as leaders in changing constellations of circumstances by further diagnosing problem-situations and further prescribing responses to those situations. Grand diagnoses that take all human history as their context, such as Marx's, are no more than momentous starting points in movement leadership, even for Marxist movements. Sometimes movement leadership consists in a revisionist redefining of the collective situation by leaders who, like Eduard Bernstein in the German Social Democratic movement of the end of the nineteenth century, find meanings in new sets of circumstances that indicate, at least to them, the need for new ways of thought and action by the movement. What started as a movement for revolution can in this manner undergo transformation into a movement for reform.

It can happen, alternatively, that a mind of uncompromisingly revolutionary orientation will diagnose circumstances themselves as the problem and prescribe action to change the circumstances in the interest of realizing the movement's original revolutionary goals. In such a case, the needs of the movement as a revolutionary one have been uppermost in the leader's mind in his definition of what the circumstances mean. A historic exemplar is Lenin in his seminal pamphlet of 1902, *What Is To Be Done?*, which can be seen as the key act of leadership that brought Russian Communism into being as, initially, a current within the larger, already existing Russian Marxist movement.

Here Lenin took as his starting point the threat that 'Economism', a Russian Marxist counterpart to Bernsteinian revisionism in Germany, presented to Russian Marxist revolutionism. The underlying source of the danger, according to the pamphlet's way of diagnosing the situation of the working-class movement around the turn of the century, was the workers' spontaneous tendency toward 'trade-union consciousness', meaning an orientation on improving workers' conditions economically, ignoring the need for revolutionary overthrow of the capitalist system. This was implicitly a definition of the situation deviant from Marx's position that capitalist conditions themselves must revolutionize the workers.

From it Lenin drew the conclusion, as a policy response, that the need of the movement was to 'combat spontaneity' through revolutionary propaganda and agitation, which in Russia's police-state conditions would have to be conducted clandestinely by small groups of professional revolutionaries acting as missionaries of revolutionary conciousness among all groups of the tsar's subjects with grievances against the existing regime; and that this required, as a prime condition of success, the creation of a small, close-knit, conspiratorially organized political party capable of acting as the conscious vanguard of large masses of the people in their movement toward an ultimate revolutionary settling of accounts with tsarism.

That turning point in history was itself a consequence, in part, of Lenin's creative situation-defining activity in movement politics. Russia's February Revolution in 1917 swept away tsarist rule and created a democratic Provisional Government in which the Bolsheviks did not participate. In the early aftermath, while Lenin remained in Switzerland, Bolshevik leaders in Petrograd, including Stalin, did not diagnose the new set of circumstances prevailing in the country as revolutionary. Their minds were in the grip of a stereotype according to which a 'bourgeois-democratic' revolution like Russia's February one must be separated by a considerable time interval from a socialist one. So, as they saw it in March 1917, the situation was for the time being post-revolutionary, and Bolshevism's proper policy response was to exert all possible pressure upon the Provisional Government to take Russia out of the World War.

Lenin, however, still in Swiss exile, was of a different mind. In an article of 1915, as if anticipating the present occasion, he had set forth a general conception of what constitutes a 'revolutionary situation'. There are, he said, three main symptoms: a crisis 'up above', in the policy of the ruling class; an unusual aggravation of the privation and tribulations of the oppressed classes; and a substantial rise, for these reasons, in the level of mass activity.[9] Now, from afar, he interpreted the circumstances of free, war-weary, and incipiently turbulent Russian society in those terms. Immediately upon arriving in Petrograd in early April, he issued a set of 'theses' on party policy that were in contradiction with the party leadership's definition of the situation hitherto in force. The 'thèses' diagnosed Russia's situation as revolutionary and on that basis prescribed for the Bolshevik movement a revolution-oriented policy of opposition to the Provisional Government under the slogan, 'All Power to the Soviets!'[10] By dint of hard persuasion, Lenin overcame the initial reluctance of various other leading Bolsheviks to view the situation in that light and rallied the party's support for his position.

Here we see how an act of leadership can be self-fulfilling: it can help bring about the very situation that the leader has diagnosed as already existing. The militant new political stance that the Bolshevik Party adopted under Lenin's influence proved to be one of the factors that converted the latently revolutionary situation of Russian society into the actually revolutionary one that obtained in the autumn when, following Lenin's urgings, the party launched the successful coup by which it took power. Leadership in this case decisively contributed to one of history's mighty lurches.

NOTES

1. Gordon W. Allport, *Becoming: Basic Considerations for a Psychology of Personality* (New Haven, 1955), 71.
2. William Bruce Cameron, *Modern Social Movements* (New York, 1966), 7.
3. W.E. Mosse, *Alexander II and the Modernization of Russia*, rev. edn (New York, 1962), 41–2. For Alexander's remark to Turgenev, see p. 41.
4. This summary of the facts follows the account given by Lerone Bennett, Jr, in 'When the man and the hour are met', in *Martin Luther King, Jr.: A Profile*, ed C. Eric Lincoln (New York, 1970), 7–39.
5. Cited by Haig Bosmajian, 'The letter from Birmingham Jail', in *ibid.*, 136. In 'The conservative militant', his contribution to this collection, August Meyer writes that King 'was capitalizing on the basic consensus of values in American society by awakening the conscience of the white man to the contradiction between his professions and the facts of discrimination' (153).
6. Lerone Bennett in *ibid.*, 17.
7. The citations from the *Manifesto* in this and the previous paragraph appear in *The Marx-Engels Reader*, ed Robert C. Tucker, 2nd edn (New York, 1978), 475, 485, 487, 499, and 500.
8. *The Class Struggles in France* in *ibid.*, 592.
9. Lenin, 'The symptoms of a revolutionary situation', in *The Lenin Anthology*, ed Robert C. Tucker (New York, 1975) 275.
10. For Lenin's 'April theses', see *ibid.*, 295–300.

3 Lenin's Bolshevism as a Culture in the Making

There are good grounds for regarding early Bolshevism as a millenarian movement. If we do so, the insights of recent anthropological scholarship into the nature of millenarian movements as new communities or new cultures-in-the-making become highly pertinent to the study of early Bolshevism. As one anthropologist has expressed it, 'The hypothesis that millenary activities predicate a new culture or social order coming into being...is a fair one. Certainly it is more scientific to regard these activities as new cultures-in-the-making, or as attempts to make a new kind of society or moral community, rather than as oddities, diseases in the body social, or troublesome nuisances to efficient administration—though of course they may be all these as well. Finally, of course a millenarian movement is a new religion in the making. New assumptions are being ordered into what may become a new orthodoxy.'[1]

Millenarian movements, sometimes also called *cults* and by the anthropologist Anthony F.C. Wallace *revitalization movements*, typically draw their followers from among the disadvantaged or distressed groups in a society. In his interpretation of early Christianity as a millenarian movement, John G. Gager emphasizes the central role of a 'messianic, prophetic, or charismatic leader' in such a movement, and points out that the movement's adherents envisage the coming of a heaven on earth via the displacement or radical reversal of the existing social order.[2] Thus we are dealing with what is in essence a revolutionary, albeit also it may be a religious, phenomenon. From the anthropological point of view, the crucial fact is that there arises in the movement itself, within the pre-millenial here-and-now, a new community with a certain set of beliefs, values, and practices that may be destined to become foundation stones of a new established culture *if* the movement achieves wordly success.

A full-scale analysis of early Bolshevism as a millenarian movement with Lenin as its prophet or charismatic leader is beyond the scope of the present chapter. It is addressed to the more limited task of examining the mental structure of Lenin's Bolshevism, particularly as expressed in *What Is To Be Done?*, as an implicit design for the new socio-political world, the party–state political culture, which came into being in the aftermath of the October Revolution of 1917.

I

We have Lenin's word for it, in *'Left-Wing' Communism: An Infantile Disorder* (1920), that Bolshevism arose in 1903 'as a current of political thought and as a political party'.[3] The apparent reference was to the conflict over paragraph one of the Party Rules at the Russian Social Democratic Worker Party's constitutive Second Congress, in the aftermath of which the term 'Bolshevism' began to be used for the faction that Lenin led and the party concept that it represented. But Lenin's account of Bolshevism's origin leaves out the part he himself played in originating the current of thought and founding the party. If 1903 was the year of Bolshevism's birth as a current and a movement, the act of conception took place in 1902 in Lenin's mind as expressed in *What Is To Be Done?*, which formulated the 'hard' concept of party membership that caused the contention at the Second Congress and the resulting division of the Russian Social Democrats between Lenin-supporting 'Bolsheviks' and Martov-supporting 'Mensheviks'.

In appearance a treatise on how to make a revolution, especially under the then-prevailing police state conditions of Russia, the pamphlet advanced the thesis that the right kind of revolutionary party organization was a necessity in order that a mass revolutionary movement might develop and a revolution occur. Such a party should be small in numbers and composed chiefly of full-time professional revolutionaries thoroughly versed in Marxist theory, totally dedicated to the party's goal of realizing the Marxist revolutionary project, and so skilled in the art of conspiracy, of underground political activity, that they could evade the Okhrana's equally skilled effort to detect and apprehend them. They would work in small groups under centralized direction of the party's leadership, developing the revolutionary mass movement under party guidance which would eventually sweep away the tsarist autocracy.

All this underlay Lenin's Archimedean phrase, 'Give us an organization of revolutionaries, and we will overturn Russia!'[4] Revolutions do not simply come, he was contending, they have to be made, and the making requires a properly constituted and functioning organization of revolutionaries. Marx proclaimed the inevitable and imminent coming of the world proletarian socialist revolution. Lenin saw that the coming was neither inevitable nor necessarily imminent. For him—and this was a basic idea underlying the charter document of his Bolshevism, although nowhere did he formulate it in just these words—there was no revolution outside the party. *Nulla salus extra ecclesiam.*

So strong was his emphasis upon the organizational theme, so much was his treatise concerned with the organizational requisites for the revolutionary taking of political power, that it has been seen by some as in essence a prospectus for Bolshevism as a power-oriented 'organizational weapon'. Such was the thesis of a book of that title, which argued that 'Bolshevism calls for the *continuous* conquest of power through full use of the potentialities of organization', and that 'it is Lenin, not Marx, who is communism's special hero, for it was Lenin's form of organization, with its implications for strategy, that gave birth to communism as a distinct trend within Marxism'.[5] Again, Merle Fainsod saw in *What Is To Be Done?* the main vehicle of 'the organizational concepts of Lenin' and 'the seminal source of the organizational philosophy of Bolshevism'.[6] True enough, but how adequate? I wish to argue that to reduce Lenin's Bolshevism to the striving for total party power through organization, and *What Is To Be Done?* to organizational philosophy, is to miss its essential meaning as the document that prefigured the appearance in Russia after 1917 of the Soviet culture, in other words, as a new socio-political world in the making.

Marx had seen in the modern proletariat a revolutionary class, a 'dehumanization which is conscious of itself as a dehumaniz-ation and hence abolishes itself'.[7] From the start a revolutionary class 'in itself', its destiny was to become a revolutionary class also 'for itself', in consciousness. This must come about through the developmental dynamics of the capitalist production process. To the proof of this proposition Marx devoted *Capital*. He was mistaken in the belief that the proletariat was inherently a revolu-tionary class and must necessarily become more and more revolutionized by capitalism's inner laws. Upon Marx's mis-take—whether or not he realized it was that—Lenin based Bolshevism. It rested upon the sound but radically un-Marxist (in the Marx—Engels sense) proposition, for which he could and did cite Karl Kautsky as authority: 'The history of all countries shows that the working class, exclusively by its own effort, is able to develop only trade union consciousness, i.e., the conviction that it is necessary to combine in unions, fight the employers, and strive to compel the government to pass necessary labour legislation, etc.'[8]

Revolutionary consciousness, on the other hand, comprised understanding of Marxist theory, belief in the need for and desirability of a socialist revolution, commitment to the Marx-ist revolutionary project. Initially the prerogative of an educated minority, it could be brought to workers only 'from without', by the efforts of the revolutionary Social Democrats as an organized body of the elect, the 'conscious' ones. The mission of the revolutionary party was to propagate political (that is, revolutionary) consciousness among the working class, spontaneously awakening to the need for a struggle but which on its own, spontaneously, would not acquire political consciousness of the Social Democratic kind. Thus, Lenin was laying the foundation of a party of missionaries engaged in propagating the Marxist faith.

To grasp his Bolshevism as a mental structure, it is of utmost importance to see that he was concerned to spread revolu-tionary political consciousness not simply among the workers as a class but among—in his own words, repeated over and over in *What Is To Be Done?*—'all classes'. The argument by which he sought to establish the necessity of an all-class approach was a tortured one:

Class political consciousness can be brought to the workers *only from without*, that is, only from outside the economic struggle, from outside the sphere of relations between workers and employers. The sphere from which alone it is possible to obtain this knowledge is the sphere of relationships of *all* classes and strata to the state and the government, the sphere of the interrelations between *all* classes. For that reason, the reply to the question as to what must be done to bring political knowledge to the workers cannot be merely the answer with which, in the majority of cases, the practical workers, especially those inclined toward Economism, mostly content themselves, namely: 'To go among the workers.' To bring political consciousness to the *workers*, the Social Democrats must *go among all classes of the population*; they must dispatch units of their army in *all directions*.[9]

On this shaky basis (shaky from the standpoint of Marx's Marxism), Lenin kept stressing the theme of 'all classes' and 'all strata'. 'We must "go among all classes of the population" as theoreticians, as propagandists, as agitators, and as organizers....The principal thing, of course, is *propaganda and agitation* among all strata of the people'.[10]

Never before, it seems, had such an explicitly 'all-class' approach been promoted by a Marxist revolutionary; never had Marxism's proletarian class emphasis been accompanied by and overlaid with such a concern to draw elements of all strata into the movement. Very likely this gave expression to the *narodnik* (Populist) revolutionary outlook that Lenin had imbibed, as he showed at various points in *What Is To Be Done?*, from those Russian revolutionaries of the sixties and seventies whom he so greatly admired. For all his doctrinaire Marxism and insistence that class struggle is a motor force of history, he was bound to oppose the idea of a separate proletarian class culture. His 'all-class' Bolshevism would make this Marxist *narodnik* the principled foe of the Proletcult that he became. His anti-Proletcult resolution of 1920[11] was prefigured in *What Is To Be Done?*

However weak the Marxist *logic* of going among 'all classes', the real basis for doing so was strong. Lenin was sensitively aware of the discontents and grievances that many individuals in all strata of Russian society harboured against the tsarist order. Although the working class was, as he said, the 'ideal audience' for the Social Democratic political pedagogues, being most of all in need of the 'political knowledge' that they had to impart, there were millions of working peasants and artisans who 'would always listen eagerly' to the party agitators' political exposures of Russian conditions. There were aroused university students, unhappy *zemstvo* employees, outraged members of religious sects, and mistreated teachers, all of whom must be made conscious of the meaning of such facts of Russian life as 'the brutal treatment of the people by the police, the persecution of religious sects, the flogging of peasants, the outrageous censorship, the torture of soldiers, the persecution of the most innocent cultural undertakings, etc.' Especially could their indignation be aroused if news about these matters were brought to them vividly and regularly by an all-Russian party paper, smuggled in from abroad, which would function as a 'collective propagandist and collective agitator'.[12]

The organizational concepts of *What Is To Be Done?* belong in the frame of this reasoning about the teaching of anti-regime political consciousness as the prime function of the revolutionary party, its way of preparing for the eventual overthrow of the tsarist state by mass revolutionary action under the party's guidance. The revolutionaries would form a sort of brotherhood (an 'order of sword-bearers', the impressionable Stalin would later call it) functioning conspiratorially and under centralized leadership as Marxist-trained political tutors of large numbers of non-party people receptive to their message. Their medium of operation would be worker study-circles, trade unions, and other local groups, in which they would form nuclei of revolutionary consciousness—party cells. Here Lenin drew upon his own experience of underground propaganda work as one of the organizers in 1895 of the short-lived St Petersburg Union of Struggle for the Liberation of the Working Class, and upon the larger experience of 'the magnificent organization that the revolutionaries had in the seventies,...which should serve us all as a model...'.[13] The all-Russian party paper, drawing its material from revolutionaries working in these clandestine circles and being distributed by them, would constitute an organizational training ground in revolutionary work.

Such was Lenin's plan for an organization that 'will combine, in one general assault, all the manifestations of political opposition, protest, and indignation, an organization that will consist of professional revolutionaries and be led by the real political leaders of the entire people'.[14] He admitted that the plan was at best, so far, a 'dream', but invoked the authority of Pisarev for the idea that 'the rift between dream and reality causes no harm if only the person dreaming believes seriously in his dream, if he attentively observes life, compares his observations with his castles in the air, and if, generally speaking, he works conscientiously for the achievement of his fantasies'.[15]

To understand Lenin's political conception in its totality, it is important to realize that he saw in his mind's eye not merely the militant organization of professional revolutionaries of which he spoke, but the party-led popular *movement* 'of the entire people'. The 'dream' was by no means simply a party dream although it centred in the party as the vanguard of conscious revolutionaries acting as teachers and organizers of a much larger mass following in the movement. The dream was a vision of an anti-state popular Russia raised up by propaganda and agitation as a vast army of fighters against the official Russia headed by the tsar; and of this other, popular Russia as an all-class *counter-community of the estranged*, a mass of people trained to revolutionary consciousness by its party tutors and dedicated to the goal of a revolution that would rid Russia of its 'shame and curse', as Lenin called the autocracy.

Of course, the dream was not realized, despite Lenin's determined, persistent efforts in the ensuing fifteen years to make it come true. His fantasy picture of a collective of like-minded revolutionaries functioning harmoniously in a centralized organization remained just that. For the actual Bolshevik Party as it evolved under Lenin was and remained a faction-ridden grouping of ever disputatious Russian revolutionaries. Nor did he realize his dream of forming under the party's leadership a great popular following that could and would destroy the tsarist order in a victorious mass revolution and thereby become 'the vanguard of the international revolutionary proletariat',[16] making Russia the spearhead of world revolution. Prior to 1917, the party acquired nothing like a mass popular following.

Yet it was this party that managed to take over and hold on to political power in the new time of troubles unleashed by the World War. That momentous turn of historical circumstance gave Lenin the opportunity to attempt, from positions of power, from above, to translate his old dream into socio-political reality. Then it turned out that what in fact he had done, albeit unwittingly, in *What Is To Be Done?* was to sketch out the prospectus for a new culture: the tutelary party—state that he sought to construct and set on its course during his few remaining years.

II

Is the rise of the Bolshevik party—state, the single-party system, to be explained as a consequence of the adversities experienced by the fledgling revolutionary regime in the time of the Civil War when it was beset by hostile forces? In *The Revolution Betrayed*, Trotsky argued that such was the case. During the Civil War, he wrote, the (socialist) opposition parties were forbidden one after another. 'This measure, obviously in conflict with the spirit of Soviet democracy, the leaders of Bolshevism regarded not as a principle, but as an episodic act of self-defense.'[17] Citing that statement as his authority, Isaac Deutscher later reformulated the argument in more forceful terms: 'The idea that a single party should rule the Soviets was not at all inherent in the Bolshevik programme. Still less so was the idea that only a single party should be allowed to exist.'[18]

A Bolshevik only from 1917 and a unique political personality among Bolshevik leaders thereafter, Trotsky was a dubious source of authoritative testimony on this critically important point. Whether or not the idea that 'a single party should rule' inhered in the Bolshevik Party's programmatic declarations, it was present in the Bolshevism that prevailed in history, namely, Lenin's. When he wrote *The State and Revolution* while in hiding during the summer of 1917, seeking to show the Marxist propriety of seizing power by violent means and establishing a 'dictatorship of the proletariat', Lenin revealed in a single lapidary sentence that his Bolshevism envisaged this dictatorship in the form of a party–state: 'By educating the workers' party, Marxism educates the vanguard of the proletariat, capable of assuming power and *leading the whole people* to socialism, of directing and organizing the new system, of being the teacher, the guide, the leader of all the working and exploited people in organizing their social life without the bourgeoisie and against the bourgeoisie.'[19] On this crucial point, the treatise, which was largely a tissue of quotations from Marx and Engels, made no reference to those authority figures. There was none to make. It was not classical Marxism but Lenin's Bolshevism that conceived the proletarian dictatorship as a state in which a political party would have the mission to 'lead the whole people to socialism' as their teacher, leader, and guide.

We have Lenin's further, later testimony to the fact that the party–state as a system had been latent in his Bolshevism from the start. In 1920, when the system was in its third year, he described in *'Left-Wing' Communism* how it worked. After observing that 'no important political or organizational question is decided by any state institution in our republic without the guidance of the Party's Central Committee', he explained by the example of the trade unions, as formally non-party bodies with a mass membership at that time of over four million, that Communists made up the directing bodies of the vast majority of the unions and carried out the directives of the party in their trade-union activity. There were other mass organizations under party leadership, such as the non-party worker and peasant conferences, he went on, as well as the soviets and their congresses. Then he continued:

Such is the general mechanism of the proletarian state power viewed 'from above,' from the standpoint of the practical implementation of the dictatorship. We hope that the reader will understand why *the Russian Bolshevik, who has known this mechanism for twenty-five years and seen it develop out of small, illegal and underground circles*, cannot help regarding all this talk about 'from above' *or* 'from below,' about the dictatorship of leaders *or* the dictatorship of the masses, etc., as ridiculous and childish nonsense, something like discussing whether a man's left leg or right arm is of greater use to him.[20]

In Lenin's mind, the Soviet system of rule by the Communist Party was not a post-revolutionary innovation, and not (as Trotsky said) 'in conflict with the spirit of Soviet democracy'. It was, rather, the institutionalization *in power* of a set of party—mass relationships that originated in the party's prehistory, in the experience of the underground circles in which he had been active around 1895 in St Petersburg. The party—state of 1920 was the party-led movement of the early years in open ascendancy as a socio-political formation in Russia.

As such it was, in one very important aspect, a system of power, as Lenin was frank to acknowledge when he wrote here:

Without close contacts with the trade unions, and without their energetic support and devoted efforts, not only in economic, but *also in military* affairs, it would of course have been impossible for us to govern the country and to maintain the dictatorship for two and a half months, let alone two and a half years.[21]

In practice, he went on, these contacts call for propaganda, agitation, and frequent conferences with influential trade union workers, and also for

a determined struggle against the Mensheviks, who still have a certain though very small following to whom they teach all kinds of counter-revolutionary machinations, ranging from an ideological defense of (*bourgeois*) democracy and the preaching that the trade unions should be 'independent' (independent of proletarian state power!) to sabotage of proletarian discipline, etc., etc.[22]

Lenin's arrogation of all power to the Bolsheviks in the new Russia, his resolute orientation toward making the Soviet state a Bolshevik-ruled party—state, is not to be explained by an urge to power for power's sake, but by an urge to power for the sake of leadership of the society by the sole political force (as he saw it) in possession of the Marxist truth as guidance for politics. The one-party system appeared a legitimate political formation on account of the teaching role that Lenin considered the party to be uniquely qualified to play. The party-state in all its spheres was to be a tutelary state, with the party as political pedagogue in non-party organizations such as the trade unions:

The conquest of political power by the proletariat is a gigantic forward step for the proletariat as a class, and the party must more than ever and in a new way, not only in the old way, educate and guide the trade unions, at the same time not forgetting that they are and will long remain an indispensable 'school of communism' and a preparatory school in which to train the proletarians to exercise their dictatorship, an indispensable organization of the workers for the gradual transfer of the management of the whole economic life of the country to the working *class* (and not to the separate trades), and later to all the working people.[23]

Viewing matters so, Lenin was bound to take the position that he did in the trade-union controversy of 1920—1. He could not accept the view of the Workers' Opposition that the workers, through their unions, should take over management of the economy. No, there must be a long preparatory period during which they would be 'schools of communism' in which the party would be teacher. The Workers' Opposition view was 'a deviation towards syndicalism and anarchism', as he put it, for

Marxism teaches...that only the political party of the working class, i.e., the Communist Party, is capable of uniting, training and organizing a vanguard of the proletariat and of the whole mass of the working people that alone will be capable of withstanding the inevitable traditions and relapses of narrow craft unionism or craft prejudices among the proletariat, and of guiding all the united activities of the whole of the proletariat, i.e., of leading it politically, and through it, the whole mass of the working people.[24]

One can imagine the scathing comment that a resurrected Marx would have made about the failure of his disciple from the Volga to understand some fundamentals of what 'Marxism teaches'.

In Lenin's Bolshevism, however, the workers after the revolution required party tutelage. Responding to Trotsky's platform for statification of the trade unions, he said (of the unions) that 'this is not a state organization, not an organization for coercion, it is an educational organization, an organization for enlistment, for training, it is a school, a school of administration, a school of management, a school of communism'.[25] The local soviets, too, were, in Lenin's eyes, fundamentally a school, a training ground: 'Only in the soviets does the mass of exploited people really learn, not from books but from their own practical experience, how to construct socialism, how to create a new public discipline, a free union of free workers.'[26] Indeed, all the non-party mass organizations of the Soviet system were conceived as party-taught, party-led, and party-organized schools in a tutelary state, Lenin's pedagogical polity.

III

Thus Lenin's Bolshevism remained in power essentially what it had been from the start, an orientation on party tutelage of a popular movement toward a revolutionary goal. The goal having been attained in a negative way—the destruction of the tsarist order—it now turned into the goal of constructing a socialist society in a new Russia defined officially as Soviet in its political organization but not yet socialist as a society.

Socialism connoted a highly cultured society. In the heady atmosphere of 1917, when he was obsessed with the need to nerve the party leadership for a seizure of power in what he sensed was but an interregnum, Lenin had conjured up, perhaps in his own mind as well as in others, a vision of Russia as ripe for early, indeed virtually immediate socialist transformation.[27] By 1919–20, he took a much longer view. The transformation of Soviet Russia into a socialist country would be the work of a generation, if not more. Consequently, Lenin's Bolshevik Marxism came to make provision for a 'transition period' not envisaged in classical Marxism, a post-revolutionary period of transition *to* socialism.[28] What was to be done under these conditions was what had seemed to him in 1902 the thing needing to be done: the organization of revolutionaries, as a vanguard, as organized Marxist consciousness, must assume a tutelary role of leadership of the entire people, excluding interference by other parties misguided in their socialism, specifically the Mensheviks.

So the concept of a movement remained central in Lenin's Bolshevism. He saw the new society of the Soviet but not-yet-socialist republic as a *society in movement* save that now it was a constructive movement for the creation of socialism and ultimately communism. Such a thought had been in his mind, in an anticipatory way, before the taking of power. He had written in *The State and Revolution* that '*only* socialism will be the beginning of a rapid, genuine, truly mass forward movement, embracing first the *majority* and then the whole of the population, in all spheres of public and private life'.[29]

A *locus classicus* of his subsequent thinking along these lines is his speech of 2 October 1920 to the Third All-Russia Congress of the Communist Youth League. To build communism (he could just as well have said socialism) involved a lengthy learning process, he argued; it meant first of all, 'learning communism'. This was not at all a matter simply of mastering Marxist theory, nor was it a matter of acquiring a 'proletarian culture' in a class sense of the term. For 'only a precise knowledge and transformation of the culture created by the entire development of mankind will enable us to create a proletarian culture'. Learning communism meant, moreover, acquiring the skills needed for the economic revival of Russia along modern technical lines, on the basis of electrification, for which purpose mass literacy and technical knowledge were requisite. Hence the Communist Youth League must become fundamentally a teaching organization, from whose practical activity any worker 'can see that they are really people who are showing him the right road'. In conclusion, Lenin said that the generation of people now at the age of fifty (he was fifty then) could not expect to see a communist society. 'But the generation of those who are now fifteen will see a communist society, and will itself build this society. This generation should know that the entire purpose of their lives is to build a communist society.'[30]

A human society is not merely a large collection of people living in an organized way on a certain territory and interacting with one another on the basis of some institutionalized division of functions. Such a grouping of people does not form what may properly be called a 'community' or 'society' without a sense of common involvement in a meaningful enterprise, some consciousness of group membership transcending, though probably including, a common language and symbols. This is the society's sustaining myth. In a certain sense the myth *is* the society; or to put it otherwise, the society has its real existence in its members' minds. Lenin, despite the opposition he had shown in the intra-Bolshevik controversies of earlier years to the ideas of Bogdanov, Lunacharsky, and others concerning a 'usable myth' for socialism,[31] was himself engaged here in an historic act of mythologizing. He was putting into words the central, sustaining myth of Soviet society, laying the foundation of Soviet Communism as a culture. In the Leninist canon, to be a Soviet citizen was to be a member of a goal-oriented all-Russian collective of builders of socialism and communism.

There were different grades of membership. To belong to the Communist Party or the Communist Youth League was, by his definition, to be a *conscious* builder, one dedicated to the collective purpose as a personal life-purpose. It was to be a member of the leadership cohort in the constructive movement for the post-revolutionary transformation of the society into a socialist one. As Lenin put it to the Communist Youth League: 'You must be foremost among the millions of builders of a communist society in whose ranks every young man and young woman should be. You will not build a communist society unless you enlist the mass of young workers and peasants in the work of building communism.'[32] Enlisting was basically an educational enterprise: the transmitting of literacy, technical skills, and above all political consciousness, including dedication to the goal, to millions of not-yet-conscious builders of the new society.

As an heir of the nineteenth-century Russian Westerners, Lenin considered the learning of Western ways, the adoption of the organizational and technological achievements of what to him were the more cultured countries, to be a most important part of the learning process comprised in the building of communism. Thus his enthusiasm for the adoption of America's 'Taylorism' in Soviet Russia. Thus his injunction, at the very time when Germany imposed a 'Tilsit peace' on Russia at Brest-Litovsk, to learn from the Germans.

Yes, learn from the Germans! History is moving in zigzags and by roundabout ways. It so happens that it is the Germans who now personify, besides a brutal imperialism, the principle of discipline, organization, harmonious cooperation on the basis of modern machine industry, and strict accounting and control. And that is just what we are lacking. That is just what we must learn.[33]

Toward the end, he decided that learning to work co-operatively was the crux of socialism's construction in Russia. He elaborated this theme in 'On Cooperation', one of the set of last articles that constituted his valedictory to the party and country. Going back to the 'old cooperators' (he mentioned Robert Owen in this connection but might just as well have chosen Fourier, whose projected *phalanstères* excited the imagination of Lenin's old idol Chernyshevsky), he proposed that 'the system of civilized cooperators is the system of socialism'. To enlist the whole population of Russia in co-operative societies was thus the main content of the building of socialism. State financial backing for co-operatives would be one way of doing so, but chiefly it was a problem of educational work, of 'culturalizing' (*kul'turnichestvo*). A whole historical epoch, comprising one or two decades at a minimum, would be required to carry out the 'cultural revolution' needed in order to educate the Russian peasant to the advantages of the co-operative way:

But the organization of the entire peasantry in cooperative societies presup-poses a standard of culture among the peasants (precisely among the peasants as the overwhelming mass) that cannot, in fact, be achieved without a cultural revolution.... This cultural revolution would now suffice to make our country a completely socialist country; but it presents immense difficulties of a purely cultural (for we are illiterate) and material character (for to be cultured we must achieve a certain development of the material means of production, must have a certain material base).[34]

Such was Lenin's final word on what it would mean to build a socialist society. His heavy emphasis upon 'educational work' as a long-range process of persuasion in the setting of a party-led movement of the entire people to socialism was in keeping with his Bolshevism's master theme, enunciated over twenty years before. It was still a matter of 'consciousness' overcoming popular 'spontaneity' by a pedagogical process. Now it had reached the point of conceptualizing Soviet Russia as the scene of a culture-building culture. Needless to add, the programme for a cultural revolution presented in 'On Cooperation' had nothing to do with the politico-cultural witch hunt that Stalin sponsored under the name of 'cultural revolution' in 1928–31. That episode in the later history of Soviet Russia had as little claim to being the cultural revolution conceived by Lenin as Stalin's terroristic collectivization of the peasants had to being the 'cooperating of Russia' envisaged by Lenin.

When Soviet studies emerged as a branch of academic scholarship in the 1940s and after, it became customary to treat Soviet Communism as, in essence, a system of power, or total power. *How Russia Is Ruled*, by Merle Fainsod, stands as a monument to that understanding of the object of study, but it is only one of many. Although it had come or was coming true at the time when these works appeared, the image of the object as a system of power was wanting in historical accuracy. Soviet Communism had been designed by its principal founder as in essence a new culture containing *within* itself a system of party–state power. From Lenin's movement 'dream' of 1902 to his post-revolutionary dream of a society in party-led movement toward socialism and communism there was continuity. Both before and after 1917, he and others tried to translate the dream into socio-political reality. The conquest of real political power in the Revolution made a huge difference by creating all sorts of possibilities for success in the culture-building effort that had not existed before 1917. Nevertheless, the venture was showing itself to be beset with enormous difficulties while Lenin still lived, and the appearance in the year of his death of Stalin's *Foundations of Leninism*, where the mass organizations that Lenin conceived as 'schools of communism' were characterized mechanistically as 'transmission belts' of party rule, was a symptom of a process then in full swing: the conversion of the tutelary state designed but at most only partially realized under Lenin into the system of total power that it became under Stalin.

NOTES

1. Kenelm Burridge, *New Heaven, New Earth: A Study of Millenarian Activities* (New York, 1969), 9.
2. John G. Gager, *Kingdom and Community: The Social World of Early Christianity* (Englewood Cliffs, N.J., 1975), 21.
3. *The Lenin Anthology*, ed Robert C. Tucker (New York, 1975), 553.
4. *What Is To Be Done?*, in *The Lenin Anthology*, 79.
5. Philip Selznick, *The Organizational Weapon: A Study of Bolshevik Strategy and Tactics* (New York, 1952), 17, 41.
6. Merle Fainsod, *How Russia Is Ruled*, rev. edn (Cambridge, Mass., 1963), 39.

7. Marx and Engels, *The Holy Family: A Critique of Critical Criticism* (1845), in *The Marx-Engels Reader*, ed Robert C. Tucker, 2nd edn (New York, 1978), 132.

8. *What Is To Be Done?*, in *The Lenin Anthology*, 24. In 1902 Kautsky denied that socialist consciousness is the necessary result of the proletarian class struggle, and wrongly asserted that this denial was in accord with Marx's position. For Lenin's citation of Kautsky, see *ibid.*, 28.

9. *ibid.*, 50.

10. *ibid.*, 52.

11. For the resolutions's text, see *ibid.*, 675–6. Proletcult was a group committed to propagating a 'proletarian culture'.

12. *ibid.*, 43, 55, 102.

13. *ibid.*, 85. The reference, he explained, was to the *Zemlia i Volia*.

14. *ibid.*, 60.

15. *ibid.*, 106.

16. *ibid.*, 22.

17. Leon Trotsky, *The Revolution Betrayed* (New York, 1972), 96. The book originally appeared in 1937.

18. Isaac Deutscher, *Stalin: A Political Biography*, 2nd edn (New York, 1967), 224.

19. *The State and Revolution*, in *The Lenin Anthology*, 328.

20. *'Left-Wing' Communism*, in *The Lenin Anthology*, 553, 572–3. Italics added.

21. *ibid.*, 572–3.

22. *ibid.*, 573.

23. *ibid.*, 574–5.

24. 'Draft Resolution on the Syndicalist and Anarchist Deviation in our Party', in *ibid.*, 497–8.

25. 'O professional'nykh soiuzakh, o tekushchem momente i ob oshibkakh t. Trotskogo', V.I. Lenin, *Polnoe sobranie sochineniia*, 5th edn, 55 vols (Moscow, 1958–65), vol. 42, 203.

26. 'Tezisy po II kongressu Kommunisticheskogo Internatsionala', in *ibid.*, vol. 41, 187–8.

27. See especially his essay 'Can the Bolsheviks retain state power?' (September 1917), where he wrote: 'The big banks are the "state apparatus" which we *need* to bring about socialism, and which we *take ready-made* from capitalism; our task here is merely to *lop off* what capitalistically mutilates this excellent apparatus, to make it even *bigger*, even more democratic, even more comprehensive. Quantity will be transformed into quality. A single State Bank...will constitute as much as nine-tenths of the *socialist apparatus*.' *The Lenin Anthology*, 401.

28. Marx foresaw an immediate post-revolutionary period of transition 'between capitalist and communist society', but envisaged society in this transition period as already rudimentarily communist (or socialist, a word he used interchangeably with communist). On this, see his

remarks in 'Critique of the Gotha Program' (*The Marx-Engels Reader*, 531, 538). Lenin's Bolshevism inserted a period of transition *to* socialism after the political revolution of October 1917 by which his party took power.

29. *The Lenin Anthology*, 382.
30. 'The tasks of the youth leagues', in *The Lenin Anthology*, 664, 666, 673, 674.
31. For the use of this phrase and a discussion of 'collectivism' as socialist myth, see Robert C. Williams, 'Collective immortality: the syndicalist origins of proletarian culture, 1905–1910', *The Slavic Review*, vol. 39, no. 4 (September 1980), 392–5.
32. *The Lenin Anthology*, 667.
33. 'The chief task of our day' (1918), in *ibid.*, 436–7.
34. *ibid.*, 710..3.

4 Between Lenin and Stalin: The Breakdown of a Revolutionary Culture

After seizing the reins of government amidst the turmoil of 1917 and proclaiming a revolutionary 'Republic of Soviets', Lenin and his Bolshevik followers forged a single-party regime during the Civil War of 1918–20. Their draconian policies caused those years to go down as the time of 'War Communism'.

In 1921, under Lenin's urging, the ruling party declared a retreat in the march to communism. It adopted the New Economic Policy (NEP), under which a money economy was restored, nearly 25,000,000 peasant proprietors were permitted to farm their holdings on nationalized land and sell their produce after paying a state tax, and small-scale entrepreneurs, the 'Nepmen', were given a free hand in light industry and the service trades. An era of normalcy and relative prosperity ensued.

Stalin's rise to dominance of the post-Lenin regime in 1928–9 brought an end to the NEP and the start of a new time of radical change. Proclaiming the need swiftly to transform NEP Russia into a socialist Russia, he led the party–state into a breakneck, war-oriented industrialization drive under the Five-Year Plan and a revolutionarily rapid collectivizing of the peasantry by coercive means. Then, through the terroristic Great Purge of 1934–9, in which millions were imprisoned and untold numbers perished, he transformed the Bolshevik Party into a submissive instrument of his will and created a police-based autocracy more absolute than that of the tsars. The Stalinist 1930s brought into being a militarized as well as industrialized party–state, a Soviet society hierarchically divided into a privileged bureaucratic serving class, a subordinate industrial working class, a collective-farm peasantry likewise under state control, and a large under-class of forced labourers in a far-flung concentration-camp empire. When Stalin turned sixty in December 1939, the controlled press acclaimed him as the heroic 'Builder of Socialism', under whose direction Lenin's designs for the transformation of NEP Russia into a socialist Russia had been realized.

Now, nearly a half century after, there is still no scholarly consensus on the meaning and causation of those events. Were they predetermined by, and a fulfilment of, Lenin's Bolshevism, as some Western scholars have believed, following Stalin's own view of it while reversing the moral plus and minus signs, or was this 'Stalinism' the very antithesis of what 'Leninism' stood for, as Stalin's exiled arch-rival Trotsky argued in his 1937 book *The Revolution Betrayed?* Otherwise formulating the question, was Stalin's transformative decade a resumption and culmination of the Bolshevik Revolution of 1917–21 or in basic ways a negation of it?

To illustrate how deeply divided the scholarly mind is over this issue, we may note the contention of the author of an informative recent study that the Russian Revolution was a 'single process' running from 1917 through the First Five-Year Plan (i.e., to the start of 1933). On her view, the policies Stalin pursued in the early 1930s represented the original Bolshevik Revolution's fulfilment, and the Great Purge was not integral to this extended revolutionary process but rather 'a monstrous postscript, added under the stress of impending war'.[1] Other scholars would argue, or have done so, that the Great Purge was, in all its monstrosity, a part of the extended revolutionary process, and would offer in evidence the fact that periodic party purges—bloodless, it is true—were prescribed by Lenin, who himself initiated the first 'general purge' of the party following its Tenth Congress in 1921. Still others, the present writer included, believe that there were two revolutions rather than one, that Stalin's transformative decade, although it had roots as well as its historical precondition in Lenin's Bolshevism, was not a predetermined outcome and continuation of the latter but a revolution with a distinctive character and dynamic of its own.

How shall we adjudicate this difficult historical issue? I submit that a necessary preliminary step is to reopen the question of what happened in Bolshevism, its politics and political culture, between Lenin and Stalin, in the interim after Lenin died in 1924 and before Stalin achieved uncontested primacy in the still oligarchical Bolshevik regime in 1929, and to seek in this way to cast fresh light on the Stalin phenomenon in its nascence. In so addressing the task, I shall view Lenin's Bolshevism as a revolutionary culture that grew by accretion from its early beginnings around the turn of the century to Lenin's last period of activity under the NEP.

II

- adjustment of strategy
- War Communism
period

Lenin's Bolshevism was a complex of ideal and real culture patterns, that is, beliefs about proper political courses of action for a Marxist revolutionary party to follow (ideal patterns) and courses of actions that were in fact regularly pursued (real patterns). In more familiar terms, it comprised, on the one hand, a set of theoretical ideas and doctrines (an ideology) concerning the policies, the strategy and tactics, that the revolutionary Marxist party should pursue in its quest for power, and with the power, once it was taken in 1917; and, on the other hand, the patterns of action that were followed, or action-tendencies.

To cite an example, we may mention the Red Army's attempted march on Warsaw in 1920. This gave expression to a action-tendency that corresponded to a doctrinal belief (ideal revolutionary cultural pattern). The belief held that it was legitimate from a Marxist standpoint for the Bolsheviks, now in power in Russia, to take steps, including armed action, to assist proletarian revolutions in countries of advanced capitalism which were (supposedly) ripe for them. When a Polish army invaded the Ukraine in 1920 and then fell back under the Reds' counter-attack, Lenin persuaded the party leadership to dispatch the Red Army across Poland in hope of reaching Germany's borders and thereby provoking the revolution for which that advanced country seemed ripe.

Lenin was a believing Marxist. Yet it was characteristic of him—and this was a source of his creativity as a revolutionary thinker—to adapt classical Marxist tenets to the needs of revolutionary practice as he saw them. The result was a Marxism-according-to-Lenin (or 'Marxism—Leninism', as it became known officially in Russia after he died) in which party doctrine was shaped and reshaped according to practical revolutionary imperatives. Thus Lenin argued in *What Is To Be Done?* that the working class's inability to acquire revolutionary consciousness by its own devices made it incumbent upon a Marxist revolutionary party to go among the workers, as well as other strata, as missionaries of such consciousness in order to prepare the populace to rise in revolt upon the advent of a revolutionary situation. Hence, party propaganda and agitation among the workers developed as a real culture pattern in underground Bolshevik Party practice. No matter that according to Marx it was capitalism's dynamics as a mode of production that would drive the industrial working class to overthrow capital's yoke.

When the World War finally propelled Russia into a revolutionary situation following the deposition of the tsar in the February Revolution of 1917, Lenin, in addition to giving practical guidance to his fellow Bolsheviks, went back to the Marxist texts to adapt the creed to the necessities of revolutionary action in that national crisis. He wrote *The State and Revolution* in 1917 in order to show, on the authority of Marx and Engels, the Marxist propriety of the party's seizing power by armed action and setting up a 'revolutionary dictatorship of the proletariat' (in Russia's case, of the 'proletariat and peasantry') that would quell by violence its internal enemies from among the old regime's supporters.

On the ground that Marx and Engels had meant by a dictatorship of the proletariat something quite different from the repressive single-party state that Lenin and his followers were creating in Russia, Marxist Social Democrats like Karl Kautsky in Germany (with whom Russia's Mensheviks had affinity) contended that it was un-Marxist for Lenin's party to seize power, suppress opposition, and rule by force and violence. In *The Proletarian Revolution and the Renegade Kautsky* (1918), Lenin thunderingly replied that it was not only proper but mandatory for true Marxists to take power by violent means and then wield the instruments of repression against their revolution's numerous class enemies. This, too, was his thesis in an essay of 1919, never completed, on the proletarian dictatorship. It described this dictatorship as 'the continuation of the class struggle in new forms' and called the state, as a weapon of the proletariat in its class struggle, 'a special form of cudgel, *rien de plus*'.[2]

Thus during 1917–20 Lenin's Bolshevism came to stand for revolution from above in the specific sense of action by the revolutionary government to repress internal enemies. In the writings just cited, this idea was formulated as a doctrinal belief. The belief was institutionalized in real culture patterns that emerged during the Civil War. The Bolsheviks set up in the Cheka a political police whose mission was to suppress opposition to their regime. One means of suppression, specified in the Red Terror decree of 5 September 1918, was the creation of concentration camps as centres for the isolation of 'class enemies' (but not yet forced labour). Nor were elements of the revolution's proclaimed class constituency—the workers and peasants—excluded by social status from the category of class enemies. Workers and sailors were crushed by force when they rose in rebellion on the island of Kronstadt in Petrograd harbour in early 1921, raising the banner of 'Soviets without Bolsheviks!' A small minority of relatively well-off peasants called 'kulaks' were defined as 'village bourgeoisie', and a governmental proclamation of June 1918, signed by Lenin, declared 'merciless war' against them. He proposed that an anti-kulak decree specify that owners of grain who did not send surplus grain to state depots be declared 'enemies of the people', have their property confiscated, and be expelled forever from the community.[3]

Lenin made it a Bolshevik tenet that terror was a legitimate form of governmental action under a proletarian dictatorship. The belief was embodied in real cultural patterns in Bolshevik practice during War Communism: summary justice, the taking of hostages, shooting on the spot, and imprisonment of people categorized as class enemies. In Lenin's Bolshevism these were rightful forms of revolution from above. Nor did be abandon his belief in terror's legitimacy after War Communism gave way to the NEP and Soviet law codes were drawn up. In a letter of 1922 to Justice Commissar D.I. Kursky about the criminal code then being drafted, he wrote:

The courts must not eliminate terror.... It must be grounded and legalized in principle, without duplicity and embellishment. The formula must be as broad as possible because only revolutionary legal consciousness and revolutionary conscience will set conditions, broader or narrower, of application in practice.[4]

Still, as we have seen in the previous chapter, Lenin during the NEP gravitated to his fundamental orientation on the Marxist party's educative mission, to the notion of politics as pedagogy and persuasion in relation to the party's worker and peasant constituency. Even at the height of War Communism, he stressed the need to 'live in peace' with the middle peasants, who constituted the great majority of Russia's overwhelmingly peasant population, between a minority of poor peasants and farmhands on the one hand and a still smaller one of kulaks on the other, and warned that anyone who took it into his head to deal coercively with the middle peasant would 'make a mess of everything'. To deal by persuasion with the middle peasant was, he explained, partly a matter of improving his economic conditions by providing tractors as an inducement to co-operative farming: 'If tomorrow we could supply one hundred thousand first-class tractors, provide them with drivers—you know very well that this at present is a fantasy—the middle peasant would say, "I am for the *kommunia* (i.e. for communisin).'[5] Inevitably, therefore, the 'co-operating' of Russia by political pedagogy and persuasion was linked in Lenin's Bolshevism with industrializing.

Reasoning so, he conceived the building of socialism in backward Russia as a long-range project that would proceed by evolutionary, not revolutionary means. He could not have been more explicit on this point. Revolution he defined as 'a change which breaks the old order to its very foundations, and not one that cautiously, slowly and gradually remodels it, taking care to break as little as possible'. War Communism represented a 'revolutionary approach' to building socialism, whereas the NEP signified a 'reformist approach' whose method should be 'not to *break up* the old social-economic system—trade, petty production, petty proprietorship, capitalism—but to *revive* trade, petty proprietorship, capitalism while cautiously and gradually getting the upper hand over them, or making it possible to subject them to state regulation *only to the extent* that they revive'.[6]

In evolving the programme of socialism's construction in Russia as a long-range evolutionary process proceeding by means of persuasion and necessitating progress in industrializing as a prerequisite of building a socialism of co-operatives, Lenin was intensely aware of popular cultural inertia as an obstacle to social change of the kind desired. Far more than Marx, whom he took as his mentor in theory, Lenin was a culture-conscious revolutionary. He showed it in his concept of 'cultural revolution' as a pedagogical process of overcoming habitual ways of individualistic thinking and living on the part of the vast peasant majority. He showed it in what he said about 'the force of habit' as the major problem with which the ruling party of Bolshevik revolutionaries must deal. 'The dictatorship of the proletariat', he wrote in 1920, 'means a persistent struggle—bloody and bloodless, violent and peaceful, military and economic, educational and administrative—against the forces and traditions of the old society. The force of habit in millions and tens of millions is most formidable force.'[7]

No Bolshevik was more keenly cognizant than Lenin of the fact that the revolutionary party had come to power in a land peopled largely with men and women who were comfortable in the established culture, comprising not only individual economic ways but Orthodox religiosity, the old village ethos, old modes of thought and conduct. They had been responsive in 1917 to the Bolsheviks' call for power to the soviets not because they wanted to make a break with their old Russian culture but because they craved the 'peace, land and bread' that the Bolsheviks proferred in their revolutioneering slogans and that the Provisional Government was fatally hesitant to offer. They were not socialists, as peasants afterward showed in their saying 'Long live the Bolsheviks, down with the Communists!' The 'Bolsheviks' were those who had encouraged them to seize the landowners' estates and parcel them out among themselves; the 'Communists' were those who now (under War Communism) wanted to take that land away from them and organize them in collectives, which were abhorrent to most of them.

So, the revolutionaries-in-power had a great problem of propagating their revolutionary culture and, indeed, of deciding, partly on the basis of their Marxist texts but largely by interpreting situations at hand and evolving courses of action in response to them, what that culture should be as a set of norms and goals to realize in practice. Lenin was the principal setter of guidelines for the party; it was his Bolshevism that prevailed—so long as he lived.

The upshot is that Lenin's Bolshevism was a composite revolutionary culture, an amalgam of ideal and real culture patterns that evolved over time from the start of the century to his actions, writings and speeches of the revolutionary and Civil War period and, finally, under the NEP. His Bolshevism was a body of disparate and even conflicting elements developed over a quarter of a century. Even in his own mind and politics it formed at best an uneasy synthesis with a fundamental theme—the party's pedagogical role *vis-à-vis* the revolution's popular constituency—recurring.

It would not prove transmissible to his followers *in toto*. Despite all they shared of his Bolshevism as a revolutionary culture, they were a disparate lot with Bolshevik minds of their own, differing political personalities, differing cultural predispositions, clashing power interests, and differing views of Soviet Russia's situation at home and abroad. The Leninist synthesis was bound to break down as they struck out on their own after Lenin died. No matter how strongly and sincerely they stressed the need to 'follow the path of Lenin', they were going to take divergent paths. Leading individuals and factions would, in each instance, stress certain parts of Lenin's Bolshevism, disregard or de-emphasize others, and transmute still others into something new—claiming all the while that they were upholding Leninist orthodoxy, as Stalin for example did in his lectures of 1924 on *The Foundations of Leninism*.

III

No period of Soviet history is so revealed in published materials and so open to documented study as the post-Lenin

1920s, and none is the subject of so voluminous a scholarly literature. Yet, we still lack an adequate analysis of the rifts that appeared then in the Bolshevik leadership.

In part this is because scholarship has concentrated very heavily on the power contest, giving second place to differences over policy. A further reason is that in addressing the policy differences, scholars have not done so in political-culture terms. The clashing tendencies in the leadership have not been identified as divergent offshoots of Lenin's Bolshevism as a culture. One consequence is that scholarship has found it difficult to conceptualize Stalin's form of Bolshevism in its birth-time.

To some extent, the Bolshevik leaders met the test of the new period in a unified way. Lenin's death at the age of fifty-three accentuated their problem of solidifying the party's bonds with the nation. Its unifier and unique authority figure had passed away during what was still the regime's historical adolescence. Hence, a governing party committed to transforming old Russia's cultural ways found itself under pressure to adapt to them to a greater degree than it had done while Lenin lived. One means of adaptation was the creation (to the dismay of Lenin's widow, Krupskaya, and some other leading Bolsheviks) of a civic cult of Lenin replete with the mausoleum in Red Square featuring his embalmed body, a Lenin Institute to publish his writing, 'Lenin corners' in all sorts of Soviet institutions, and so on.[8] This had overtones of an old Orthodox Russia that had preserved saints' bones as holy relics and made cult figures of deceased and living tsars. The Lenin cult became a key part of a Soviet political culture that blended new and old. No one would have been more thoroughly disgusted by it than the cult's object.

The party at that time, although 'ruling', was an island of state power in a sea of worker-peasant Russia still wedded to the old culture. The workers in whose name the party ruled were in various ways still close to their village pasts. The party itself, moreover, was changing in composition by taking in large numbers of new members, notably in the 'Lenin levy' declared at the time of Lenin's death as a dramatic means of promoting ties between the party and the people. Unlike the one-time undergrounders of pre-1917 party vintage, now called 'Old

Bolsheviks', the incoming new members were not likely to be culturally alienated from old Russian ways; some were mainly career-seekers under the new political dispensation. They brought into the party habits of mind and forms of feeling derived from their non-Bolshevik cultural upbringing, including, in some instances, strong Russian national feeling and the anti-Semitism that not infrequently accompanied it.

Conflicting power interests in the prolonged period of supreme-leadership vacuum were a further spur to accommodation to established Russian cultural ways. Although the regime was oligarchical, not autocratic in mode of decision-making, Lenin's adult life as the party's builder and central dynamo of leadership had engraved in its own political culture the role of a supreme leader (*vozhd'* in Russian), and there was no designated or obvious successor to him in it. As a contender for the vacant role, Stalin was especially minded to cater to Russian nationalist feeling in the party by espousing, as he did, the programmatic idea that Soviet Russia could go it alone in constructing a socialist society, the idea of 'socialism in one country'. He was not the only leading figure to do so, but the way in which he advocated the idea, as will be shown below, was especially calculated to appeal to the new party generation—to which, significantly, he dedicated his lectures on *The Foundations of Leninism*.

A further reason for the continuing lack of an adequate analysis of the political divisions in post-Lenin Bolshevism is that our understanding of them has been unduly influenced by the thinking of the only well-informed protagonist in the intra-party conflicts of the mid-1920s who was later free to write about them abroad: Trotsky. His account distinguished three factions in the post-Lenin leadership: the party left (or left opposition, of which he himself and others, including Zinoviev and Kamenev, were foremost representatives), the party right led by Alexei Rykov (Lenin's successor as premier in the Soviet government), *Pravda*'s editor Nikolai Bukharin, and the trade-union chief Mikhail Tomsky, and the party centre led by Stalin and his confederate Molotov. But Trotsky's scheme was two-dimensional: there were, according to it, three factions but only two policy lines, those of the left and the right.

The third faction, which Trotsky called 'bureaucratic centrism', had no line of its own. Stalin was an 'empirical' power politician, an opportunist devoid of original ideas, incapable of abstract thinking, the party's 'outstanding mediocrity'. In tactical alliance with the rights, he adopted their pro-peasant orientation in the fight against the left opposition. When the latter went down to defeat in late 1927, his rightist zagzag gave way to an 'ultra-left zigzag' in industrializing and an 'adventurist collectivization'.[9] Trotsky's two-dimensional scheme entered our historiography. Thus, Isaac Deutscher held that Trotsky's view of Stalin as a centrist acting under alternate pressures from right and left 'properly described Stalin's place in the inner party alignments of the nineteen-twenties, but fitted the realities of later years less well'.[10] That Trotsky's view properly described the Stalin of the mid-1920s will be disputed here.

IV

The left opposition, a congeries of groups, had numerous leading figures. Trotsky was outstanding among them. Earlier, he rose to fame during the Civil War as war commissar and organizer of the Red Army. Under War Communism he espoused revolutionary statism in a more extreme form than Lenin's. In the party's heated debate of 1920 over the place of trade unions in the new system, his platform of 'statification' of the unions lost out to Lenin's programme of making them party-guided 'schools of communism' for the workers. Trotsky at that time advocated militarized labour and coercion to work. In *Terrorism and Communism* (1920) he wrote that it was impossible to advance from bourgeois anarchy to socialist economy 'without compulsory forms of economic organization', and further: 'Repression for the attainment of economic ends is a necessary weapon of the socialist dictatorship.'[11] These lines may have found an appreciative reader in the party rival who was to become his nemesis and have him hounded to death in Mexico in 1940.

Under the NEP Trotsky and others on the party left moved in the direction that Lenin's Bolshevism did, and certainly away from the idea that repression for economic ends was a

necessary weapon of social transformation. But that left room
for serious policy differences which became apparent in their
early post-Lenin duel with the combined forces of the party
right and Stalin's faction. The left Communists were truer to the
strain of revolutionary internationalism in Lenin's Bolshevism,
and less adaptable to the change-resistant popular ethos than
the right leaders were. This found expression in their opposition to the new doctrine of 'socialism in one country'.

In 1924 it was plainly evident that the socialist revolutions on
which the Bolsheviks had counted during and soon after the
World War were not going to materialize in the near future.
Trotsky, as he had shown by advising against Lenin's proposal
to dispatch the Red Army through Poland in 1920, was anything
but the adventurist in external affairs that his party opponents
painted him as being. Yet, he and his fellow leaders on the left
refused to detach the domestic Soviet developmental process
and its prospects from the further progress of international
Communist revolution, however delayed the latter might be.
They would not depart from the Marxist view that socialism or
communism was a world-wide stage of development. They kept
faith with Lenin's position, restated by him at the Tenth Party
Congress, that Russia's revolution could never have final
success without support by socialist revolution in 'one or
several advanced countries'.[12]

The left leaders fully accepted the need, meanwhile, for
efforts toward socialism's construction at home. They did not
take the sanguine view of the peasantry that the rights did, and
wanted a relatively rapid industrialization at a rate exceeding
the 6 per cent annual growth rate of Russian capitalism before
the war by two, three or more times. The right, as they saw it,
stood for 'economic minimalism' (in Trotsky's phrase) or
'tortoise-pace' industrialization (in Bukharin's).[13] Their recipe
for financing the desired rate of industrializing was a tax on the
better-off minority of the peasantry, and they would encourage
the peasant poor to form farming collectives. Paraphrasing
Marx's term in *Capital* for the forceful measures, including
enclosures, that set capitalism going at its dawn—'primitive
capitalist accumulation'—Trotsky, followed by the left's prominent economist, E. Preobrazhensky, called the proposed
taxation policy 'primitive socialist accumulation'. To the rights

this raised the spectre of an estrangement between the party and the peasantry, and they assailed Trotsky ferociously, albeit without foundation, for harbouring designs for a coercive 'second revolution'. In the heat of party polemics, Bukharin, who as the party's best known theoretician was in the forefront of the debate, called 'primitive socialist accumulation' a formula for disaster through economic adventurism.

Less purist in their adherence to the revolutionism in the Leninist revolutionary culture, the rights recognized, first of all, that Lenin had banked in vain on the early spread of proletarian revolution in advanced European countries. They (not Stalin) originated the project of Russia's going it alone in building up a socialist society, an idea that has been traced to Rykov.[14] This meant downplaying world revolutionary politics even though, in fidelity to Lenin's Bolshevism, the eventuality of world-wide Communist revolution was not abandoned as an ideological precept. In private one figure then sympathizing with the rights, Abel Yenukidze, gave it as his opinion that Lenin himself, had he lived longer, would have rectified his mistake of 1917 concerning the imminence of revolutions abroad; and he told an American journalist acquaintance, Reswick, that when world revolution failed to materialize, 'it was up to us to uncook the *kasha*', meaning to make far-reaching concessions to the change-resistant populace in the economic field.[15]

Because isolated Soviet Russia was still a backward peasant land, the process of building a socialist economy and society would necessarily have to be very slow and gradual. So, the rights put heavy emphasis on the later Lenin's envisagement of a generation-long effort, via cultural revolution, to achieve the 'co-operating of Russia'. And with a view to the state's capacity to offer the peasant consumer goods in return for his surplus produce, they strongly favoured the maintenance of balance in industrialization policy between light and heavy industries. Thus Lenin's project of instilling new attitudes in the peasant and providing him with material incentives for co-operative farming was uppermost in the rights' thinking. There was, moreover, a traditional Russian institution, the village council or *mir*, still present all through rural Russia in the 1920s, and the rights believed that the regime could rely on it as a basis for their 'agrarian-co-operative socialism', as Bukharin called it. Rykov told Reswick that

if we, a backward people, stop playing at world revolution and organize our national life on the pattern of our traditional rural *mir*, the capitalist world will have no cause to fear us. On the contrary, it will be to their interest to supply Russia with arms or even to join us if we are attacked by Japan or Germany.[16]

In their concept of a socialism based on the *mir* the rights were visualizing a further form of Bolshevism's blending with old Russian culture. On this account, and because they advocated socialism in one country, they may be seen as exponents of a moderate form of national Bolshevism.

Between them and the less culturally adaptable Bolsheviks on the left, for whom revolutionary internationalism was vital to Bolshevism as a creed, the political antagonism was bound to be the deep one that—to Stalin's great advantage—it was. Yet, divided as they were, both the right and left positions were within the Bolshevik movement's mainstream. Each accused the other of deviating from Lenin's guidelines, but neither deserved the other's harsh indictment. The lefts wanted a faster tempo of economic development, partly because they were more inclined to see war as relatively imminent, hence the time span for industrializing as more limited. But it never occurred to them to crush peasant resistance to collectives by brute force in a revolutionary collectivization from above, driving an unwilling peasant majority into collective farms before productive resources were available for large-scale farming.[17] That would be Stalin's way.

Had Lenin remained alive and vigorous for another five years or so, his unifying powers as *vozhd'* probably would have kept the party leadership from disintegrating into warring factions as it did. Since it was his programme that the rights were developing further in their socialism of the village *mir*, it is likely, too, that he would have supported them up to a point. As for the international prospect, his last article, 'Better Less, But Better' (1923) showed him pinning hopes on national independence movements in countries of the East like India and China, and Soviet Russia's *rapprochement* with them, rather than on early socialist revolutions in Europe.[18]

Subsequent Russian and world history would have been different if Lenin had lived longer. But history turns on what does or does not happen. His death at an early age helped it to take the course that it did under a successor-leader whom he was carefully preparing in his last months to purge from party power because he saw him, belatedly, as dangerously deviant in an ultra Russian nationalist direction from Bolshevism as a political culture.

V

Stalin, who in his lectures of 1924 on *The Foundations of Leninism* duly echoed Lenin's position that Russia's socialist revolution could never have final success without support from socialist revolution in one or more advanced countries, soon afterward discarded that view and joined the rights in preaching the possibility that Soviet Russia could proceed all the way to a socialism in international isolation. There was a difference, however, in the way in which he advocated the new doctrine and the way they did.

They laboured over the knotty problem of the *how* of socialism's construction in Soviet conditions; he did not. Beyond echoing on occasion their hopeful view of the peasantry, he devoted little attention in his speeches to the specifics of the socialism-building process. He identified himself with the 'one country' idea and it with himself, by espousing it in a strident spirit of Soviet Russian national pride. He harped on Russia's capacity to blaze the trail to socialism for all mankind just as, in 1917, she had set the world an example by being the first country to carry through a proletarian political revolution.

His message was well calculated to appeal to the large numbers of newer party members and some older ones who were infected with what a delegate from the Ukraine, V.P. Zatonsky, protestingly called 'Red Russian patriotism' in his address to the Tenth Party Congress. By transforming Russia from a backwater of Western Europe into the forefront of a world movement, Zatonsky said, the Revolution had awakened a national movement in the party, many of whose members tended not simply to take pride in being Russian but to see the new multi-national state not as the confederation of equal peoples that it claimed to be, but as a new 'Russia one and indivisible'.[19]

Because Stalin was himself a minority person, born as Iosif Djugashvili in a Transcaucasian tsarist colony, Georgia, and had risen to prominence before 1917 as a Bolshevik authority on the nationalities, Lenin chose him to be commissar for nationality affairs in his government. It was Stalin's unnecessarily high-handed way of supervising his native Georgia's incorporation into the new Soviet state in 1921-2 that opened Lenin's eyes to the fact that his commissar for nationality affairs was, underneath, a Russian Red patriot with a strong leaning toward an aggressive Russian nationalism that would make the Soviet federation into a new 'Russia one and indivisible'. Such Great Russian chauvinism (Lenin's term for this Russian nationalism) was beyond the bounds of the internationalism that for him was one of the Bolshevik culture's ideal patterns and, so far as feasible, something to be practised in real politics as well.

Coming as it did on top of other events that led him to see in Stalin a potential danger to the party's cause, the Georgian affair stimulated Lenin to dictate, at the close of 1922, some notes on the nationalities question. These were part of his preparation to unseat Stalin from his powerful post as the party Central Committee's general secretary at the forthcoming Twelfth Party Congress. In the notes he characterized some leading Bolsheviks who were Russified minority represen-tatives (Stalin, his fellow Georgian Sergo Ordzhonikidze, and the Polish-born chief of the Cheka, Feliks Dzerzhinsky) as men who were overdoing it on the side of 'true-Russianism' (that is, Russian nationalism), and he bluntly denounced Stalin as a 'rude Great Russian Derzhimorda'.[20] Lenin's notes were circulated at the Twelfth Congress in April 1923. But because he was unable to attend that congress, having suffered in the previous month the stroke that ended his active political life, Stalin managed by astute playing on the division between Trotsky and the right leaders to survive in power. Had not Lenin's health conclusively failed just when it did, Stalin would have suffered a crushing setback during the congress and Soviet history might have followed a different course from the one it later took under his influence.

His 'true-Russianism' made of him a national Bolshevik of very different complexion from the moderates on the party right who wanted to adapt policy to the village *mir* in organizing a socialism of co-operatives and to subtly downplay international revolution as a policy goal. Even at the height of his tactical alliance with the rights, Stalin gave indication of this divergence from their national Bolshevism by the studied way in which his speeches stressed *eventual* resumption of revolution abroad. Soviet Russia could construct a fully socialist society in isolation, he held, but its revolution could never be 'final', that is, irreversible, until revolutions occurred in some other countries. This would give Soviet Russia support from abroad that would render her secure against the danger of foreign intervention and defeat in war.

So Stalin, in his way, kept faith with international Communist revolution as a paramount, if deferred policy goal. But his way of keeping faith was very different from that of Lenin and the party left, who envisaged the future revolutions occurring in one or more 'advanced' countries, that is, Western European ones. Stalin's perspective, on the contrary, was revolution in 'neighbouring countries'. The capitalist encirclement, he averred, must be replaced with a 'socialist encirclement'.[21] The further growth of the international Communist revolution was implicitly equated with Soviet Russia's future aggrandizement, its takeover of bordering lands (as occurred during Stalin's accord with Hitler in 1939–41 and after World War II). Hence Stalin's form of national Bolshevism, quite unlike that of the rights, was an *imperial* Bolshevism, an amalgam of Bolshevik revolutionism with Great Russian imperialism.

Just as Stalin differed from both left and right in his foreign policy orientation of the mid-1920s, being expansionist where the rights were not and imperialist in his Communist revolutionism where the lefts were not, so he differed from both in internal policy thinking. Unlike the rights, he did not think of adapting the Bolshevik culture to so traditional an institution as the village *mir* (which was to disappear from the countryside during and after collectivization in the early 1930s); and unlike the lefts (and Lenin), for whom substantial progress in industrializing was the prerequisite of socialism in the countryside, he envisaged a revolutionarily rapid collectivization as a prerequisite of the war-oriented industrialization that he wanted in order to prepare Russia for the new European war in which its aggrandizement could occur. He declared in 1931 that Russia must prepare for the test of war in ten short years. An industrialization favouring heavy and war industries would be made possible, as he saw it, by driving the peasantry into collectives that, as state-controlled institutions, could extract the wherewithal to finance an all-out build-up of industry by importing machinery, engineers and others from abroad, as Peter the Great—to whom he referred approvingly in a major speech of 1928—had done in the eighteenth century.

Stalin's realization that such a collectivization would be quite unlike the gradual transformation of the countryside that Lenin had designed was implicit in such statements as the following that he made in 1926: 'Building socialism in the USSR means overcoming our own bourgeoisie by our own forces in the course of a struggle.'[22] 'Our own bourgeoisie' meant not only the Nepmen in the towns but the bulk of the peasants, including the middle peasants, in the villages. A coercive collectivization meant the forcible abolition of the NEP, going against the current of prevailing NEP culture. Although Trotsky at one time called it 'a leftist paroxysm of Stalinist policy', it was not even remotely a part of the left programme. As Trotsky pointed out elsewhere, nothing like it had been proposed or even suggested in the left Communists' dissident platform of 1927. 'Abolition of the NEP in the countryside—could such a thing have entered the minds of any of us, even in the heat of controversy?' he asked in his foreign-based *Bulletin of the Opposition*, and he explained soon after that 'The practical possibilities of collectivization are determined by the presence of technological productive resources for large-scale agriculture and the peasantry's degree of readiness to shift over from individual to collective farming.'[23]

Such was Stalin's Bolshevism in its birth-time as a policy orientation in his own mind during the 1920s. Although it had a potential constituency, it was not, like the left and right programmes, the publicly known policy position of a party faction. For if the secretive Stalin took even such close factional associates as Molotov, Voroshilov and Kaganovich into his confidence concerning his contemplated courses of action, evidence of that is still lacking; and as for the larger party public, it was kept in the dark unless some perspicacious souls divined Stalin's position from occasional delphic statements by him such as those with which a later historian can work with the benefit of hindsight about what came after. This peculiar Bolshevism, differing as it did from that of the left and that of the right, was very much Stalin's own.

But does it have, as he himself insisted over and over and unquestionably believed, valid title to the term 'Bolshevism', or should it be set apart under the heading of 'Stalinism' and seen as something quite outside the political-culture world of historic Bolshevism? No doubt Lenin would have relegated it to the outer darkness. Trotsky subsequently did when he gave up his view of Stalin as a centrist and characterized 'Stalinism' as a regime of Soviet 'Bonapartism'. Bukharin did too when, in Aesopian statements that he published as editor of *Izvestia* in 1936, before his arrest and arraignment in the great purge trial of 1938, he hinted that Stalin's political programme was akin to fascism.[24]

Wayward as it was from Lenin's point of view, Stalin's position has some claim to be considered by the historian as one form that Bolshevism took in the post-Lenin period. The claim rests on the fact that during the revolutionary period Lenin's Bolshevism came to include revolution from above as an integral pattern, both 'ideal' in the sense of doctrinally justified and 'real' in the sense of practised. It meant the continuation of revolutionary action from positions of state power, the wielding of this power as a 'cudgel' against the revolution's numerous enemies.

There was, of course, a hugely important difference between Lenin's kind of revolution from above and Stalin's. For Lenin the cudgel was for use against the revolution's class enemies, although these included kulaks, an offshoot of its worker-peasant constituency, and even workers if they should act as malingerers or show signs of being rebellious. Whereas Stalin, in collectivizing by terror and forcibly abolishing the NEP, was wielding the state cudgel against the great majority of the proclaimed popular constituency and not simply against the kulaks whose liquidation as a class was the slogan of his collectivizing revolution from above. Yet even here Lenin cannot be absolved of responsibility for what was going to happen under Stalin. For he had left the notion of 'class enemy' ominously elastic in Bolshevik theory and practice during the Civil War. So elastic that Stalin in the later 1930s would stretch it to include the great numbers of Bolsheviks arrested in his purges.

Revolution from above, as practised for example by Peter the Great in his attempted modernizing of Russia in the first half of the eighteenth century and earlier by Ivan the Terrible in his vendetta against the landowning magnates and others, was a recurrent pattern in tsarist Russia's history. It was a pattern familiar to anyone who took the trouble to read history books available in the Moscow of the 1920s. And Stalin, far from being the purely pragmatic politician, uninterested in ideas, that Trotsky contemptuously dismissed him as being, was one who read books about old Russia's history at that time and found models for emulation in some of the early tsars and cues for policy in some of their revolutionary actions from above. No matter that Lenin would have been horrified: revolutionary action from above was one of the patterns that he had prescribed to Marxists in the polemical treatises that he bequeathed to the Bolshevik movement between 1917 and 1921.

What can be said, then, of Stalin's position as it emerged in his mind in the 1920s? An analysis in terms of political culture must find a place for it as a nationalistically and imperialistically wayward form of Bolshevism, a Bolshevism of the radical right.

NOTES

1. Sheila Fitzpatrick, *The Russian Revolution* (Oxford and New York, 1982), 3.
2. *The Lenin Anthology* (New York, 1975), 490. See this source also for *The Proletarian Revolution and the Renegade Kautsky*.
3. V.I. Lenin, *Polnoe Sobranie Sochinenii*, 55 volumes (Moscow, 1958-65), vol. 36, 316.
4. *ibid.*, 45, 190.
5. *ibid.*, 32, 186, 188.
6. 'The importance of gold now and after the complete victory of socialism' (1921), *The Lenin Anthology*, 512.
7. *'Left-Wing' Communism—An Infantile Disorder*, in *The Lenin Anthology*, 569.

8. For a full account, see Nina Tumarkin, *Lenin Lives! The Lenin Cult in Soviet Russia* (Cambridge, Mass., 1983).
9. 'A test of the three factions', *Writings of Leon Trotsky: 1932-33 (New York, 1972)*, 85; Leon Trotsky, *Stalin: An Appraisal of the Man and His Influence* (New York, 1967), xv.
10. *The Prophet Outcast. Trotsky: 1929-1940* (London, 1963), 95.
11. Cited by Baruch Knei-Paz in *The Social and Political Thought of Trotsky* (Oxford, 1978), 266–7.
12. *The Lenin Anthology*, 504.
13. Trotsky, 'A test of the three factions', 85.
14. N. Valentinov, *Doktrina pravogo kommunizma* (Munich, 1960), 16. For Bukharin's role in the debate and a full account of his life and thought, see Stephen F. Cohen, *Bukharin and the Bolshevik Revolution: A Political Biography 1888-1939* (New York, 1973).
15. William Reswick, *I Dreamt Revolution* (Chicago, 1952), 164.
16. *ibid.*, 255.
17. Alexander Erlich, *The Soviet Industrialization Debate 1924-28* (Cambridge, Mass., 1967), 37, 178.
18. *The Lenin Anthology*, 745.
19. *Desiatyi s"ezd VKP (b). Mart 1921 goda. Stenograficheskii otchet* (Moscow, 1960), 202–3. 'Russia one and indivisible' was a slogan of extreme nationalists among the Whites in the Civil War.
20. For these and other details on the conflict between Lenin and Stalin, see Robert C. Tucker, *Stalin As Revolutionary 1879-1929: A Study in History and Personality* (New York, 1973), ch. 7. 'Derzhimorda' is a colloquial Russian term for a police bully, derived from the name of a character in Gogol's play *The Inspector General*.
21. Stalin, *Sochineniia* (13 vols, Moscow, 1946-52), V, 109 and VIII, 263. These statements were made in the early and mid-1920s.
22. *ibid.*, IX, 21. The occasion was a speech to the Executive Committee of the Communist International.
23. *Biulleten' oppozitsii*, no. 15–16 (September-October 1930), 18; and no. 14 (August 1930), 27.
24. For Bukharin's statements, see 'Stalin, Bukharin and history as conspiracy', in Robert C. Tucker, *The Soviet Political Mind: Stalinism and After*, 2nd edn (New York, 1971), 75–6.

5 Stalinism as Revolution From Above

Western scholarship has been tardy in fixing analytic attention upon Stalinism. A bulky historical literature on the Stalin period and many biographies and memoirs dealing with the man Stalin coexist with a dearth of interpretive discussion of the 'ism', by which I mean not alone the body of thought but the entire Stalinist phenomenon as an historical stage in the development of the Russian and other Communist revolutions and of Communism as a culture.

To some degree, this situation shows the impact of Soviet thought patterns upon our scholarship. From the mid-1920s, it became a firm article of doctrine in Soviet Russia that the only legitimate 'ism' was Marxism-Leninism. Stalin himself never countenanced the use of 'Stalinism' because of the deviational implications it would consequently have carried. The events of the Stalin-led revolution from above of the 1930s were officially described as Marxism-Leninism in action—the natural and logical unfolding of the original Leninist revolutionary impulse and programme. There was a strong tendency in the Western sovietological literature of the 1940s and 1950s to give credence to this claim.

Stalin and his party allies of the mid-1920s employed (or as Trotsky maintained, concocted) the term 'Trotskyism' as the emblem of a system of political heresy against Leninism. For Trotsky and his followers, however, the heresy was the political line that Stalin and his associates were pursuing and the ideological tenets, such as 'socialism in one country', which they were using in justification of the line. So it is in the Trot-skyist polemical literature that we find the earliest interpretive and critical discussion of Stalinism. In this interpretation, Stalinism appeared as the practice, and its reflection in theory, of a conservative bureaucratic takeover of the Bolshevik Revolution, a Soviet Thermidor, of which Stalin himself was merely the representative figure and symbol.[1]

In contradistinction to the first of the two positions just mentioned, I hold that Stalinism must be recognized as an historically distinct and specific phenomenon which did *not* flow directly from Leninism, although Leninism was an impor-tant contributory factor. In contradistinction to the second, I will argue here (1) that Stalinism, despite conservative, reac-tionary or counter-revolutionary elements in its make-up, was a revolutionary phenomenon in essence; and (2) that notable among the causal factors explaining why the Stalinist revolution occurred, or why it took the form it did, are the heritage of Bolshevik revolutionism, the heritage of old Russia, and the mind and personality of Stalin.

The NEP Russia that emerged from the Bolshevik Revolution of 1917-21 could be described as a society with two uneasily coexisting cultures. There was an officially dominant Soviet culture comprising the Revolution's myriad innovations in ideology, governmental structure, political procedures, economic organization, legal order, education, the intellectual pursuits, values, art, daily life and ritual. Side by side with it was a scarcely sovietized Russian culture that lived on from the pre-1917 past as well as in the small-scale rural and urban private enterprise that flourished under the NEP. It was a Russia of churches, the village *mir*, the patriarchal peasant family, old values, old pastimes, old outlooks, along with widespread illiteracy, muddy roads, and all that Trotsky had in mind when he wrote that: 'Essentially the Revolution means the people's final break with the Asiatic, with the Seventeenth Century, with Holy Russia, with icons and cockroaches.'[2] The coexistence of cultures was competitive in a one-sided way: it was the declared objective of the new one to transform the old one, so that, as Lenin declared in addressing the Moscow Soviet on 20 November 1922, 'out of NEP Russia will come socialist Russia'.

While upholding the historical correctness of the Bolshevik decision to take power in 1917 and to pursue the revolutionary political course that it did subsequently, Lenin in 1921 and after redefined the movement's objective and strategy in the new situation marked by retreat at home and delay of other Marxist revolutions abroad. The transcending of the NEP was to take place within the framework of the NEP, by evolution not revolution.[3]

History, as we know, did not go the way that Lenin charted; it went the Stalinist way. This was radically different from the path delineated in those Lenin articles of the final period that Bukharin, in the essay that he published in *Pravda* in January 1929 for the fifth anniversary of Lenin's death, described as 'Lenin's Political Testament'. Stalinism in its time of self-assertion and triumph, the 1930s, was a revolution in exactly the sense that Lenin had defined it in warning against a revolutionary approach to the further building of Soviet socialism: 'a change which breaks the old order to its very foundations, and not one that cautiously, slowly and gradually remodels it, taking care to break as little as possible'. Instead of transcending the NEP evolutionarily, Stalin's revolution from above abolished it revolutionarily, by decree and by force. Instead of proceeding gradually and by means of persuasion, it proceeded at breakneck speed and wielded state power coercively to smash popular resistance by terrorizing the population. Instead of taking care to break as little as possible, it broke the spirit along with the bodies of a great proportion of the generation that had come of age during the first phase of the Revolution a decade before. It also consumed a very heavy proportion of those party leaders and members who had, in the 1920s, been Stalinists in the simple sense of supporters of the general secretary and his 'general line' in the fight with the opposition.

The rural revolution called 'mass collectivization' illustrates these points. In the space of a few years and at the cost of untold suffering and a famine whose toll of lives ran into many millions, a countryside with about twenty-five million peasant farmsteads functioning on nationalized land was transformed into one in which the great majority of those peasants were organized into some 200,000 collective farms (*kolkhozy*) while many more were employed as hired workers on state farms (*sovkhozy*). In the *Short Course* of party history (1938), which Stalin edited personally, the collectivization is described as 'a profound revolution, a leap from an old qualitative state of society to a new qualitative state, equivalent in its consequences to the revolution of October 1917'. The *Short Course* goes on: 'The distinguishing feature of this revolution is that it was accomplished *from above*, on the initiative of the state, and directly supported *from below* by the millions of peasants, who were fighting to throw off kulak bondage and to live in freedom in the collective farms.'[4]

It was indeed a state-initiated, state-directed and state-enforced revolution from above—as was the Stalinist revolution as a whole—but the *Short Course* lied when it spoke of mass peasant support from below. Historical evidence available to us now in great abundance attests that not alone the ones classified as kulaks, whose 'liquidation as a class' was proclaimed as the banner of the collectivization drive, but the mass of middle peasants and even some of the rural poor were sullenly opposed to the rural revolution and joined the *kolkhozy* only under duress or because of fear. The claim in Soviet publicity of Stalin's time and after that the collectivization was Lenin's 'co-operative plan' in action is groundless. Not only was there no patient, long-drawn-out educational effort ('cultural revolution') to prepare the peasantry's mind for voluntary acceptance of co-operative farming, and no antecedent industrialization sufficient to produce the 100,000 tractors that Lenin had foreseen as a powerful inducement to the peasants to farm co-operatively. Still more important, the *kolkhozy* were socialist co-operatives only in their formal facade.

The rural revolution from above of 1929-33 proceeded simultaneously with the heroic phase of the Stalinist industrial revolution from above: that state-directed, frantic, military-oriented industrialization drive whose very slogan, 'Fulfil the Five-Year Plan in Four', reflected the gap between what actually happened and the Plan as officially adopted in 1929.[5] The relationship between these two processes presents a highly complex problem on which scholarly opinion has evolved as new factual information has become available. It was at one time widely believed that the forcible mass collectivization was a necessity for the desired high-speed super-industrialization in that the *kolkhoz* system enabled the Soviet state to extract other-wise unobtainable (or uncertainly obtainable) agricultural surpluses to finance such basic needs of industrialization as the importation of foreign machinery and technicians and to supply the urban population with food and industry with raw materials.[6] Such, indeed, appears to have been the underlying conception on which Stalin acted at the time; collectivization was envisaged as the pre-condition of a form of industrialization geared to the priority of heavy industry and war industry over the consumer goods industries whose greater development would have been a *sine qua non* of a Soviet industrialization within the frame of a continued rural NEP. In the event, however, the economic consequences of collectivization were so catastrophic that researches by Western scholars, supported by archival data published in 1968 and 1969 by the Soviet historian A.A. Barsov, have reached the conclusions that (1) 'mass collectivization of Soviet agriculture must be reckoned as an unmitigated economic policy disaster', and (2) 'the oppressive state agricultural procurement system, rather than serving to extract a net contribution from agriculture as a whole, should be credited with preventing the collectivization disaster from disrupting the industrialization drive'.[7]

II

Only two major aspects of the Stalinist revolution from above have been discussed here. Any adequate account, even of fundamentals, would have to consider also the state-building process which went on *pari passu* with mass collectivization and industrialization: the expansion of the bureaucratic state apparatus, the huge growth of the system of forced labour, the concomitant growth of the politico-economic police empire which administered it, and the extreme centralization of state power. Something more will be said about this below. Concentrating for the present on collectivization and industrialization, I want to ask why they took place in the Stalinist way.

According to a view which draws part of its inspiration from Trotsky's thinking and which achieved wide influence owing to its espousal by Isaac Deutscher, Stalinist industrialization-cum-collectivization was a forced response to a 'grave social crisis' of the later 1920s. Citing Stalin's statistics, Deutscher states that in January 1928, in particular, government grain purchases fell short by two million tons of the minimum needed to feed the urban population.[8] Emergency measures were applied by the government to extract grain that was being withheld from the market. The peasants were not, for the most part, politically motivated against the Soviet regime, but were driven by economic circumstances in that the small farms produced only enough to meet the peasants' own food needs while the 'big farmers' with surpluses were charging prices beyond the ability of the town population to pay and also were demanding concessions to capitalist farming. In this dilemma, yielding to the peasants would antagonize the urban working class and refusal to yield would also bring a threat of famine and urban unrest. A 'radical solution' was demanded, and Stalin, having until the very last moment shrunk from an upheaval, acted 'under the overwhelming pressure of events' and embarked upon the second revolution in an 'unpremeditated, pragmatic manner'. He was 'precipitated into collectivization by the chronic danger of famine in 1928 and 1929'.[9]

Such, in Deutscher's classic version, is the 'circumstantial explanation' (as we may call it) of the initial phase of the Stalinist revolution from above. It is followed by Carr and Davies with specific reference to the collectivization drive. Having shown that party policy, including that of the lefts such as Trotsky and Preobrazhensky, had always envisaged a gradualistic approach in collectivization, Carr and Davies find the explanation for the abandonment of gradualism in favour of 'direct assault' in 'the now chronic and irremediable crisis of the grain collections' and 'the dire need for grain to feed town and factories'. They go on: 'In this desperate impasse, the leaders snatched eagerly at the growing belief in the prospects of collective agriculture and in its capacity to meet the needs of a planned economy.' And echoing Deutscher, they declare that 'The sudden decision reached at the end of 1929 was neither preconceived nor premeditated.'[10] This restated Carr's earlier argument (likewise an echo of Deutscher's) that in the summer of 1929 the system of official grain collections had effectively broken down and: 'A third successive annual crisis of the grain collections loomed ahead. The problem of supplying town and factories had become completely intractable. Gradualism was not enough.' Then, too, Carr had referred to 'the haphazard and impulsive character of the final decision'. [11] Elsewhere, referring to the industrial revolution from above, Carr mentions the so-called war scare of 1927 after the severance of diplomatic relations with Soviet Russia by Great Britain, and goes on to say that 'the security motive in the drive to catch up with the west by rapid industrialization should not be overlooked'. [12]

The circumstantial explanation has been offered in a still more extreme form by Alexander Gerschenkron in his thesis that the economic crisis at the end of the NEP era was also a 'political crisis of the first magnitude'. He explains: 'Inability to maintain the food supplies to the cities and the growing resistance of the millions of the peasants, strong in their intangible diffusion, seemed to spell the doom of the Soviet dictatorship.' A threat existed to the continuation of the Soviet regime in these conditions, Gerschenkron asserts, and 'It was under the pressure of that threat that Stalin underwent a radical change of mind and embarked upon the gamble of the First Five-Year Plan.' [13]

In Deutscher's version of the circumstantial explanation, as has been noted, Stalin, the political leader of the revolution from above, appears as a great improviser who responded to the pressure of extremely adverse national circumstances in 'an unpremeditated, pragmatic manner'. In consonance with this view, Deutscher calls Stalin a man of 'almost impersonal personality'. [14] All this received later elaboration in Carr's characterization of Stalin as 'the most impersonal of great historical figures'. To show what he calls 'the essentially impersonal character of Stalinist policy', Carr states that no element of personal conviction, nor any originality of conception, was involved when Stalin took leadership of the industrial revolution from above. The aims he ruthlessly pursued were those 'dictated by the dynamic force inherent in the revolution itself'. His qualities, like his convictions, were those of his milieu; they 'mirrored the current stage of the historical process'. His role in Soviet history was that of 'the great executor of revolutionary policy' with 'no vision of where it would lead'. [15]

In seeming inconsistency with the image of an all but mindless political improviser conjured up by the description of Stalin cited above, Deutscher does allow that the man who led Soviet Russia in the revolution from above acted on certain ideas. But he maintains that these were borrowed from others. 'The ideas of the second revolution were not his', Deutscher writes. 'He neither foresaw it nor prepared for it. Yet he, and in a sense he alone, accomplished it.'[16] Whose ideas were they then? Deutscher does not directly say, although some pages later he notes that Yuri Larin 'a second-rate economist, once a right-wing Menshevik', had propagated the idea of a 'second revolution' in the countryside as early as 1925.[17] We are left to infer that the ideas in question were those of representatives of the left opposition like Preobrazhensky, who had propounded in the early 1920s the idea of 'primitive socialist accumulation', that is, industrialization through exploitation, chiefly, of the rural economy. Yet Deutscher also declared, and rightly so in this instance, that 'There was no question, in the view of the left Bolsheviks, of driving the peasants into collective farms by force. The switchover from private to collective farming was to be carried out gradually, with the peasants' own consent.'[18] The strange upshot is that Stalin is treated both as a leader who acted under relentless pressure of circumstances *without* preconceived ideas, and as one who acted *with* or *on* certain ideas which, however, were not his own. But those whose ideas these presumably were did not think, in the Stalinist way, of collectivization as a revolutionary leap which the state would accomplish by coercive means. In short, whatever ideas Stalin took from the erstwhile left opposition, the idea of a revolution from above was not one of them.

III

It is a central thesis of this chapter that the circumstantial explanation, notwithstanding a certain specious plausibility, is fatally flawed, and that we shall not attain a tenable view of Stalinism in its fundamental aspect as revolution from above until this is understood. The circumstantial explanation is flawed, first, in the unproven nature of its assumption that collectivization in the terroristic form that it took was the only realistic alternative for the Soviet regime in 1929, much less a *sine qua non* of its survival as Gerschenkron suggests. Even allowing that the regime was faced in 1927-8 with something like a peasant 'grain strike' (to use the loaded *Short Course* terminology), there is no serious evidence of incipient political rebelliousness in the countryside at that time; and there *is* evidence of general peasant acceptance of the Soviet regime, whatever the specific grievances that caused peasants to grumble or to withhold grain from the market in expectation of more return. Nor, as already indicated earlier, has it been shown, nor is it true, that the terroristic collectivization was a necessity for the results achieved in the industrialization effort during the Plan years. As for the security motive to which Carr referred, growing out of the external tensions of 1926-7, a recent and careful scholarly review of the facts, while it indicates that the war scare was more than a mere sham and contrivance of intraparty conflicts of the time and probably enjoyed a certain credence on the part of various Soviet leading figures, also concludes that 'the war scare was in fact grossly and crudely manipulated by Soviet politicians in 1927'.[19] There were, as I would put it, grounds for Soviet concern about external relations in Europe, although not at that time grounds for serious fear of an oncoming coalition war against the USSR; but the *possibility* of war was brandished as a justification for the developing Stalinist orientation in internal policy.

The circumstantial explanation of forced mass collectivization hardly squares with the now demonstrated conclusion, cited earlier from Millar, that this course proved in practice an 'unmitigated economic policy disaster', nor is it cogent that a policy which directly and indirectly produced the worst famine in Russia's famine-plagued history, that of 1932-4 which cost a conservatively estimated five million lives,[20] was necessitated by the need to avert a famine. Although historical 'might-have-beens' are just as difficult to establish as are arguments of the 'there-was-no-other-possible-course' type, the insistently emerging conclusion from scholarly researches based on the more abundant data now available from Soviet sources is that 'a continuation of the New Economic Policy of the 1920s would have permitted at least as rapid a rate of industrialization with less cost to the urban as well as to the rural population of the Soviet Union'.[21] In effect, informed and thoughtful historical hindsight is confirming the basic economic realism of the programme for a balanced industrialization policy within the frame of a continuing NEP that Bukharin presented in his *Pravda* article of 30 September 1928, 'Notes of an economist'.[22] The Bukharinist non-revolutionary alternative for Soviet industrialization policy at the close of the twenties, an alternative inspired in large part by the Leninist thinking of 1921-3 discussed earlier here, was real. Had it been adopted, it could well have worked; had it worked poorly, the cost to Soviet economy could not have compared with that which had to be paid for the Stalinist solution. Such, also, is the position of an influential school of post-Stalin Soviet politico-economic thought whose 'scarcely veiled endorsement of Bukharin's industrialization strategy' has been persuasively argued and documented by Moshe Lewin.[23]

At this point, a modification of the circumstantial explanation might suggest itself: if Stalinism was not the necessary or sole practicable course that it once seemed to be, it was nevertheless so *perceived* at the time by the decision-makers, who after all had to act without foreknowledge of the whole sequence of effects, including catastrophic consequences, which their decisions would bring about. The difficulty with such a hypothetical fallback position (and this may explain why still living adherents of the circumstantial explanation have not taken it) is that numerous Bolshevik minds in Moscow and around the country, including some and possibly even a majority in the Politburo, *did not perceive the Stalinist course as the only possible action to take in the circumstances then obtaining*. Bukharin, in a clandestine conversation of July 1928 with Kamenev which became widely known in party circles, clearly foresaw the catastrophic consequences of Stalin's contemplated rural revolution from above. It was, he said, a ruinous policy course signifying a return to War Communism, a course leading to civil war, to an uprising that would have to be drowned in blood.[24]

The hypothetical fallback position cannot save the circumstantial explanation because it leaves open and unexplained the fact that the ruling party was divided in its appraisal of the circumstances in 1928-9 and that an influential section of Soviet political opinion opted for a course in agrarian policy and industrialization that would have been evolutionary, in accordance with the later Lenin's counsel, rather than revolutionary. The inevitable next question—why did the evolutionists go down to defeat in the party struggle, or why did Stalinism win?—cannot be answered by reference to the social-economic circumstances over which the quarrel raged in Bolshevik circles. It can only be answered by reference to the factors that determined the *Stalinist response* to the circumstances and its political victory. The circumstances as such cannot furnish the explanation of the revolution from above.

IV

One influence conducive to a Stalinist revolutionary response among Bolshevik politicians was the other Lenin—the revolutionary Lenin of the War Communism period and the heritage of Bolshevik revolutionism that he symbolized. It is understandable that Bukharin, involved as he was in a political struggle against Stalin and the policies he was advocating in 1928-9, treated Lenin's last writings as his 'political testament', and that is certainly what Lenin himself intended them to be. But for the Bolshevik movement and party, Lenin's political testament was the entire corpus of his thought and writing, the whole record of his revolutionary leadership of the movement up to, during, and after the October Revolution; and Lenin's political testament in this more comprehensive sense, or Leninism as a whole, contained very much that Stalin had good claim to as an authoritative text and warrant for the policies followed in the revolution from above.

The idea of a process of revolution from above, as has been shown in the foregoing chapter, has a Leninist pedigree. When Lenin contended in *The State and Revolution* in 1917, and in such subsequent works as *The Proletarian Revolution and the Renegrade Kautsky*, that the doctrine of proletarian dictatorship was the core idea of Marxism and that Marxism called for a seizure of power followed by dictatorial rule by violence against the internal bourgeoisie and associated social forces, he was saying: the revolution does not end with the party's taking of power; that is only a momentous point of historical transition beyond which the party continues its revolutionary destruction of the old order from above, that is, by wielding the coercive instruments of state power against the revolution's class enemies. Leninist revolution from above meant the use of state power for the continuation of class war *after* the revolutionary party has achieved such power and formed its government under the title of 'proletarian dictatorship'.[25] Whether Lenin ever used the phrase 'from above' in arguing this notion of the proletarian dictatorship as a continuing revolutionary struggle from the vantage-point of state power is of no consequence; the idea was unmistakably present in his thought.

It is true that already in 1919, at the height of the Civil War and War Communism, we find intimations in Lenin of the transition to the later reformist approach to the building of socialism that has been described earlier in these pages. This transition was associated with the idea that the fundamental obstacle to socialism was the body of habit left over from the past and that the revolutionizing of habit—in other words, of culture—was *au fond* an educational task rather than one to be resolved by coercive means. In his article of May 1919, 'A great beginning', Lenin hailed a workers' initiative of voluntary unpaid Saturday work (the Communist *subbotnik*) as a development of enormous historical significance, and observed in this connection that 'the dictatorship of the proletariat is not only the use of force against the exploiters, and not even mainly the use of force'.[26]

But it would not be proper to discount on this evidence the Lenin for whom state power, once in the hands of the revolutionary party, should be used as a cudgel against the class enemy. When Stalin in December 1926 rhetorically asked the Comintern Executive what the building of socialism meant in class terms and answered that 'Building socialism in the USSR means overcoming our own Soviet bourgeoisie by our own forces in the course of a struggle', he was simply drawing upon the Lenin and Leninism of the Civil War period and earlier, the Leninism in which the fundamental question for a Marxist seeking to create socialism was *Kto-kogo?*, or who will vanquish whom in the class war? To this Leninism of *Kto-kogo?*

he did subsequently add one proposition that was original with him: that the internal class struggle intensifies with the society's advance toward socialism. He was drawing upon the Leninism that had stood during 1918-21 for forcible food requisitioning from the peasant (*prodrazvërstka*), for stirring up of class war in the villages by means of the committees of the poor (*kombedy*), for the belief (to cite Lenin) that the proletarian dictatorship should mean 'iron rule' and not a 'jellyfish proletarian government', and for the ruthless resort to terror as an instrument of dictatorial rule. *This was Stalinist Leninism*, and the authenticity of Stalinism's claim to it is not seriously diminished by the important fact that what Leninism stood for in Lenin's own mind, as a conception of how to build socialism in Russia, underwent great modification in 1921-3.

Nor was this Leninism Stalin's only. A considerable proportion of his generation, men who had become Bolsheviks when Bolshevism was still an anti-regime revolutionary movement and who politically came of age, as Stalin himself did, during the era of War Communism, shared his outlook to some degree. I am not speaking here about general ideas alone or about Leninism simply as a system of political belief, but about the ingrained habits of mind, ways of defining and responding to situations, styles of action, common memories, mystique, etc., that collectively constitute the culture of a political movement in so far as a given age cohort of its membership (and leadership) is concerned. As its name indicates, War Communism had militarized the revolutionary political culture of the Bolshevik movement. The heritage of that formative time in the history of Soviet culture was martial zeal, revolutionary voluntarism and *élan*, readiness to resort to coercion, rule by administrative fiat (*administrirovanie*), centralized administration, summary justice, and no small dose of that Communist arrogance (*komchvanstvo*) that Lenin later inveighed against. It was not simply the 'heroic period of the great Russian Revolution', as Lev Kritsman christened it in the title of the book about War Communism that he published in the mid-1920s, but above all the *fighting* period, the time when in Bolshevik minds the citadel of socialism was to be taken by storm.[27]

War Communism had given way to the NEP in 1921 as a matter of official party policy, and in the ensuing new period there emerged, again under Lenin's political and ideological leadership, something that could be called 'NEP culture'. This NEP culture comprised a many-sided new way of Soviet life which found expression in institutions, ideas, habits of mind and conduct. Among its elements were the restored monetary economy, the emergent system of Soviet legality, the new stress on a voluntary bond between workers and peasantry, the primacy of persuasion and educative methods in the regime's approach to the people, the previously mentioned Leninist notion of gradualism and cultural revolution, and a general atmosphere of relative social normalcy. But we must beware of inferring from the familiar history-book linear scheme of development from War Communism to NEP society that NEP culture *displaced* the culture of War Communism in the minds of the generation of Bolsheviks who were moving into political leadership in the later 1920s. It certainly did in some, indeed many instances; NEP culture had its powerfully persuasive proponents not only in Lenin but also in Bukharin, Rykov and numerous others, some representing the gifted party youth. But we have the weighty testimony of such men as Valentinov, Piatakov and Stalin himself that the militant, voluntarist political culture and mystique of War Communism lived on among very many Communists. And from about 1927 on, some sensitive minds among the exponents of NEP culture became apprehensively aware of an impending new social cataclysm, a second storming of the citadel as it were.[28] To this it needs to be added that Lenin himself had provided possible cues for such a response in the military imagery that he had used more than once in speaking of the NEP itself: as a forced 'retreat' which would in good time be followed by a 'subsequent victorious advance'.[29]

In seeking to refute the 'circumstantial explanation' of the initial phase of the Stalinist revolution, it is not my intent to deny historical significance to the circumstances facing the Soviet regime in 1927-9, most notably the grain-collection difficulties. The point is that these circumstances did not carry a single unmistakable definition of the situation and implicit prescription for policy. That widely different definitions of the situation and widely different policy prescriptions were possible is proved by the fierce debates and deep policy differences that emerged at the time. My argument is that the Stalinist definition of the situation in terms of class war with the kulak forces and the Stalinist policy response in the form of forcible grain requisitioning and then mass collectivization represented, in part, an appeal to the Bolshevik *mores* of War Communism, and that this orientation proved potently persuasive largely because of the surviving strength of those *mores* among the Bolsheviks and not by any means only, as some have thought, because of Stalin's formidable organizational power as General Secretary. From this viewpoint, the great struggle over party policy in 1928-9 between Stalinism and Bukharinism was a fight between policies conceived in the spirit of the revolutionary culture of War Communism and the evolutionary NEP culture—and the former prevailed.

It must be added that Stalin himself should not be seen in all this as a man of organizational power only. It is true that the socialism-in-one-country concept originated with the rights and that Stalin on numerous occasions in the mid-1920s echoed their version of it, stressing NEP, for example, as the medium of the movement toward socialism and the peasant's amenability to such a movement. This has helped to foster the image of him as an improviser with hardly any policy ideas of his own at that time, or as one whose policy ideas were purely Bukharinist. Against such a view, two points need to be made. First, given the exigencies of the joint Stalin–Bukharin factional battle against the left opposition, which was pressing the need for rapid industrialization, it was politically impossible for Stalin to take issue openly with the rights' policy position, or even to fail to concur in it, before the vanquishing of the Trotskyist left at the end of 1927. Secondly, a close reading of the record shows that the Stalinist position, although not brought into the open as a policy platform before 1928, found expression, *sotto voce*, in various Stalin pronouncements of the NEP period, at the very time when he gave to many the appearance of being a Bukharinist in theory and policy.

One such pronouncement, the statement of 1926 about building socialism through 'overcoming our own Soviet bourgeoisie by our own forces in the course of a struggle', has already been cited as an example of the Stalinist Leninism of *Kto-kogo?* Other evidence includes: Stalin's *Pravda* article of

7 November 1925 in which he defined the present period as an *analogue of the pre-October period of 1917*, that is, the prelude to a new revolutionary storm and a studied restatement of this theme, with added detail, in 1926. Moreover, there was a significant theoretical difference between Bukharin and Stalin in their ways of arguing the socialism-in-one-country notion. Bukharin dwelt particularly upon the content of this socialism as an 'agrarian-cooperative socialism' of the kind projected in Lenin's last articles; Stalin's emphasis fell heavily on the 'one country' theme in a spirit of truculent Soviet Russian nationalism. A Great Russian nationalist tendency may be seen, moreover, as an ingredient of the Civil War syndrome in Soviet culture, this war having been fought not alone against the Whites but also against their foreign supporters and foreign interventionists.

V

But if the surviving spirit of War Communism influenced the way in which the drives for collectivization and industrialization were conceived and carried out, it does not follow that the Stalinist revolution repeated 1917-21 or that the new Stalinist order which took shape in the 1930s was a revival of the system of War Communism. To be sure, the start of the new decade saw such reminders of the heroic period as food rationing, and other resemblances appeared. As Moshe Lewin has pointed out, however, the early Stalinist process showed many distinctive traits that differentiated it from its pre-NEP predecessor: the feverish industrial expansion, the emergence of anti-egalitarian tendencies in contrast to the egalitarianism of the Civil War period, the rise of new elites combined with the loss of the relatively independent political role of the lesser leadership ranks at the earlier time, and the political muzzling of the party rank and file in relation to the leadership itself.[30] Still other, major differences call for mention: the *kolkhoz* system itself, which bore small resemblance to the agricultural communes initiated during the Civil War period; the use of police terror as a prime instrument of government in a manner sharply differentiated from the Red terror sponsored by Lenin via the original Cheka; and the interrelationship between internal and external policy. *The underlying basic fact confronting us is that when the Russian revolutionary process resumed in the Stalinist stage, it had a different character from the revolutionary process of destruction of the old order and makeshift creation of the new that marked the earlier, 1917-21 stage; and this change of character is to be understood in terms of a reversion to a revolutionary process seen earlier in Russian history.*

It has been argued here that the idea of revolution from above had a Leninist pedigree. While that is important for an interpretation of Stalinism, it must now be stressed that the phenomenon of revolution from above has a range of forms, and that the Leninist form—revolution from above as a victorious revolutionary party's violent use of the 'cudgel' of state power to repress its internal class enemies—represented only one element in Stalinism as a complex and many-sided revolution from above. Where the Stalinist phenomenon went far beyond the Lenin heritage lay in its constructive aspect. Leninist revolution from above was essentially a destructive process, a tearing down of the old order from the vantage-point of state power; Stalinist revolution from above used destructive or repressive means, among others, for what was, both in intent and in reality, a constructive (as well as destructive) process. Its ideological banner was the building of a socialist society. But, in substance, Stalinist revolution from above was a state-building process, the construction of a powerful, highly centralized, bureaucratic, military-industrial Soviet Russian state. Although this state was proclaimed 'socialist' in the mid-1930s, it differed in various vital ways from what most socialist thinkers—Marx, Engels and Lenin among them—had understood socialism to mean. Stalinist 'socialism' was a socialism of mass poverty rather than plenty, of sharp social stratification rather than relative equality, of universal constant fear rather than emancipation of personality, of Russian chauvinism rather than brotherhood of man, and of a monstrously hypertrophied state power rather than the decreasingly statified commune–state delineated by Marx in *The Civil War in France* and by Lenin in *The State and Revolution*.

It was not, however, by mere caprice or accident that this happened. Stalinist revolutionism from above had a prehistory in the political culture of Russian tsarism; it existed as a pattern in the Russian past and hence *could* be seen by a twentieth-century statesman as both a precedent and legitimation of a political course that would, in essentials, retrace the historical pattern. Confronted in the aftermath of the two-century-long Mongol domination with hostile and in some cases more advanced neighbour-states in possession of portions of the extensive territories that had made up the loosely confederated Kievan *Rus'*, the princes—later tsars—of Muscovy undertook the building of a powerful 'military-national state' capable of gathering the Russian lands under its aegis. Given the primacy of the concern for external defence and expansion and the country's relative economic backwardness, the government proceeded by remodelling the social structure, at times by forcible means, in such a way that all classes of the population were bound in one or another form of compulsory service to the state.

A salient expression of the tsarist pattern of revolutionism from above was the legalized imposition of serfdom upon the Russian peasantry in the sixteenth to seventeenth centuries, the peasant's attachment by law to the soil, together with the system of *barshchina* (the *corvée*) under which the peasant was bound to contribute a certain number of days of work on the landowner's (or state's) land during the agricultural year. The Stalinist rural revolution from above was in essence an accelerated repetition of this tsarist developmental pattern. It has been noted above that the *kolkhoz* as it emerged from the collectivization process was a co-operative only in its formal facade. Underneath, it bore a far from superficial resemblance to the landed estate in the period of serfdom; and it is a highly significant fact that the *kolkhoz* was actually perceived by many Russian peasants as a revival of serfdom. Westerners who travelled in rural Russia in the early 1930s have reported that it was a common peasant practice to refer to 'V.K.P.' (the initials of *Vsesoiuznaia Kommunisticheskaia Partiia*, the All-Union Communist Party) in the esoteric meaning of 'Second Serfdom' (*Vtoroe Krepostnoe Pravo*).[31] Two features of the *kolkhoz* system gave special point to this perception. One was that the *kolkhozy* came to operate according to arrangements under which the peasant owed the *kolkhoz* an annual obligatory minimum, specified by Soviet law, of 'workday units' (*trudodni*); this was a return to *barshchina*. Second, when the internal passport system, an institution of tsarist Russia, was revived in Soviet Russia by a governmental decree of 31 December 1932, as a means of bureaucratic control over the movements of Soviet citizens, the farm population was not issued passports. The deprivation of passports attached the peasant to the soil of the *kolkhoz* or *sovkhoz* as his serf ancestor had been attached to the soil of the landed estate.

The culminating phase of tsarism as a dynamic political superstructure engaged in the transformation of Russian society and development of its economic base for state-ordained purposes came in the long reign of Peter I, that 'crowned revolutionary' as Herzen later called him. Now the pattern of revolution from above emerged most distinctly, one of its prominent aspects being an industrial revolution from above aimed at building a powerful Russian war-industrial base. Intensifying serfdom, Peter employed state-owned serfs along with prisoners-of-war and others for industrial projects as well as the construction of canals on lakes Ladoga and Onega, etc.; and on occasion moved entire townships of people to the construction sites of the new enterprises in what are described as 'Peter's forced labour camps'.[32]

Again, the parallel with the Stalinist industrial revolution from above is striking, the major difference being the greatly expanded scale of the use of forced labour in the Stalinist case. To what has been said above about the relation between collectivization and industrialization, something of importance here needs to be added. During the First Five-Year Plan, the slogan about 'liquidation of the kulaks as a class' was used as a pretext for deportation of peasant families *en masse*—a process made all the more massive by the extreme looseness with which the label 'kulak' was applied—to remote areas like the Urals, Siberia and the far North where they were set to work in timbering or on the construction of plants, such as the Magnitogorsk iron and steel complex in the Urals. The vast expansion of the forced labour camp empire dates from this time. To cite Solzhenitsyn, 'in 1929-1930, billowed and gushed the multimillion wave of *dispossessed kulaks*....In sheer size this nonrecurring tidal wave (it was an ocean) swelled beyond the bounds of anything the penal system of even an immense state can permit itself. There was nothing to be compared with it in all Russian history. It was the forced resettlement of a whole people, an ethnic catastrophe.'[33] But while in size there was nothing in Russian history to compare with it, this mass use of deportation and forced labour for industrialization had a definite historical precedent in Petrine Russia. In the Stalinist industrial revolution from above, therefore, just as in the rural revolution from above, there were elements of a revival of the tsarist pattern of revolutionism from above. In this respect, Stalinism showed the influence not simply of the historically recent Witte system of state-sponsored industrialization, but of the much earlier system of direct exploitation of servile labour in the Russian state-building process.[34]

The Russian historical perspective can contribute in still a further important way to our understanding of Stalinism: it helps to make intelligible the relationship between the first and second phases of the Stalinist revolution. Following the phase that took place from 1928/9 to 1933, there was a kind of pause in 1934, after which the revolution from above moved into its second phase. Signalized by the murder of the party leader Sergei Kirov in Leningrad in December '1934—an event conceived and organized from Stalin's centre of power in Moscow as a pretext for what followed—the mass terror of the Great Purge enveloped the party and country in the later 1930s. The Great Purge destroyed not simply the majority of Old Bolshevik veterans of the anti-tsarist struggle but very many of their juniors who had joined the movement after 1917 and served as active implementers of Stalinism in its first phase. It virtually transformed the composition of the Soviet regime and the managerial elite in all fields. This in turn was accompanied by still other manifestations of the revolution from above in its second phase, such as the destruction of the Pokrovsky school of Bolshevik historiography, the concomitant reappropriation of major elements of the Russian past as part of the official Soviet cultural heritage, the restoration of pre-1917 patterns in art, education, law and the family. In these aspects, which extended into the 1940s, there were distinctly reactionary or counter-revolutionary elements in the revolution from above.

It has been said, rightly in my view, that 'Stalin's revolution in agriculture and industry and his assault on the party which consummated this revolution must be seen as integrated parts of one and the same process.'[35] But it remains to explicate the nexus between the two phases. It does not suffice to take the position, as Schapiro does and as Deutscher did after him, that 'it was primarily the need to perpetuate the Great Change in the countryside that perpetuated the terror'.[36] This line of explanation is strained and in the end simply unsatisfactory, if only because—as the postwar Stalinist years in Russia showed—rule by terror can be effective without being massive. It is not a persuasive argument that terror on the scale of the Stalinist holocaust of 1934-9 was necessitated either to perpetuate collectivization or to prevent Stalin from losing power. Yet, the point about the two phases being 'integrated parts of one and the same process' carries conviction.

A partial explanation of this linkage can be derived from the thesis that the Stalinist revolution from above recapitulated in essentials its tsarist predecessor's pattern. The latter involved the binding (*zakreposhchenie*) of all classes of the population, from the lowest serf to the highest noble, in compulsory service to the state. As the Muscovite autocracy grew in power, the hereditary landowning nobility was transformed into a serving class whose title to the land was made conditional upon the rendering of military service to the state. The Petrine revolution from above reinforced this situation by instituting an aristocracy of rank (*chin*) based upon the table of fourteen military and corresponding civilian ranks, under which nobility became a function of rank rather than vice versa. In one of its phases, moreover, the reduction of the boyar ruling class of Kievan and early Muscovite Russia to a serving class during the reign of Ivan IV (better known as Ivan Grozny or Ivan the Terrible) in the sixteenth century, the chief instrument of the process was the anti-boyar terror carried out under Ivan's personal supervision by his private retinue and security police, the *oprichnina*. Ivan himself was the first of the Muscovite rulers to assume the title of tsar. Tsarism as a system of absolute autocracy was itself in part a product of this sixteenth-century purge, which, from evidence at our disposal, we know that Stalin consciously took as a model for emulation during the

Great Purge of the 1930s; he had come to view Ivan Grozny and not alone Peter the Great as a Russian statesman of socialist formation. With very few exceptions, the independent-minded Old Bolsheviks were cast as his boyars.

The pertinence of this to the problem of the nexus between the two phases is clear. The Great Purge was at once the crucible of the restoration of an absolute autocracy in Russia—under Stalin now—and concomitantly a continuation of the process of formation of Stalin's neo-tsarist version of the compulsory-service state, an entity that may properly be called 'totalitarian'. The first phase of the revolution from above had seen the binding of the peasantry and working class in servitude to the ever swelling, ever more centralized, ever more bureaucratized, ever more police-dominated Stalinist state; and this new *zakreposhchenie* grew still tighter in later years. The second phase brought the party itself and the intelligentsia (in that greatly expanded Soviet sense of the term which embraces managers, officials, specialists, technicians and professionals of all sorts) into line with the rest of society. They too became a serving class whose status as such was made tangible and visible with the introduction in the later 1930s and 1940s of a Stalinist table of ranks that bore a distinct resemblance—as did the uniforms and insignia—to the corresponding tsarist set-up. Completing the process ideologically, the Stalinist order developed its own ideology of Soviet Russian statism which was epitomized by Stalin's courtier, Georgi Malenkov, when he said to a party conference in 1941: 'We are all servants of the state.' Stalin had given the cue two years before, when, at the Eighteenth Party Congress, he corrected Engels' (and by implication Marx's) mistaken idea that socialism meant the withering away of the state.

To what extent was the Stalinist revolution 'from below' as well as from above? Not until the social history of the period is written will this question be fully answerable. Undoubtedly, we should avoid two untenable extreme positions: that taken by Stalin in the above-cited passage in the *Short Course* that the revolution from above was 'directly supported from below by the millions...,' and the opposite view that the process had no support from below. But given the still fragmentary state of our knowledge, differences of opinion and emphasis are inevitable when we move beyond this obvious starting point. Perhaps it would be useful, as a setting for analysis and discussion, to observe two distinctions. First, the distinction between the two phases (1929-33 and 1934-9). Second, the distinction between two different possible meanings of 'below': persons in low-level roles in the regime or closely associated with it, notably the membership of the Communist Party and Komsomol; and the population at large. Using Soviet terminology, we may call them respectively the *aktiv* (activists) and the *narod* (the people). Although numerically substantial, the former was no more than a relatively small minority of the latter.

The *aktiv*, or large elements of it, including contingents of Soviet youth, was a vitally important instrumentality of the regime in the first phase of the Stalinist revolution. Many participated in the collectivization and industrialization drives not only actively but enthusiastically and self-sacrificingly. But it is not clear that any considerable portion of the *narod* gave the regime its voluntary support during this phase. As in the time of War Communism, the regime attempted to foment class war in the countryside by making the poor peasants (*bedniaki*) its allies in mass collectivization. To what extent this policy was a success is not entirely plain, as there is evidence, including documentary evidence from the Smolensk party archives, that mass collectivization was not only opposed by the well-off and middle peasants in their greater majority, but unpopular as well among no few of the *bedniaki*.[37] Even a *bedniak* could grasp what 'V.K.P.' meant and not like it. As for worker participation in collectivization, we have the case of the 25,000 industrial workers who were enrolled by the party to go into the villages as collectivizers. But evidence also exists that at least some portion of the 'twenty-five-thousanders' joined this movement under pressure of dire family need combined with material incentives to assist in the collectivizing.

In the second phase, the social picture changed significantly. Now large elements of the first-phase *aktiv* exchanged the role of implementers of the revolution for that of its victims. Very many of these people died or went to camps during the Great Purge. To a far greater extent than the first phase, the second was a police operation, and the supreme collective victim was the Communist Party itself as constituted in the early 1930s. By this very token, however, very many who did not actively participate in the second phase, whether they belonged to the *aktiv* or the *narod*, nevertheless became its beneficiaries. For the decimation of the pre-1934 regime, party and intelligentsia in the Great Purge opened career opportunities on a vast scale to those from below who showed ability combined with the acquiescent, state-oriented and Stalin-centred attitudes that were hallmarks of the *chinovnik* under full Stalinism. This influx was largely an influx of the peasant-born. Citing Boris Pilniak's statement of 1922 that 'The dark waters of muzhik Russia have swept and swallowed the Petrine empire', Nicholas Vakar has argued that the Stalinist revolution, by filling the Soviet hierarchy with persons of peasant stock and infusing age-old peasant *mores* and values into the Soviet way, marked the complete *peasantization* of the Russian Revolution.[38]

VI

This chapter has advanced a culturalist interpretation of Soviet Russia's history under Lenin and Stalin. The revolution of 1917-21, it was held, produced a situation characterized by the uneasy coexistence of two cultures, a new Soviet culture growing out of the revolution and a still surviving old Russian culture with its stronghold in the village. The Soviet culture itself underwent considerable change during the NEP. The Stalinist revolution of 1929-39 yielded an amalgamated Stalinist Soviet culture that, paradoxically, involved at once the full-scale sovietization of Russian society *and* the Russification of the Soviet culture. The Soviet Union was re-Russified in the very revolutionary process that purported to complete Russia's sovietizing, or to transform NEP Russia into a socialist society. In keeping with the tsarist tradition, this Stalinist Soviet Russian culture bore a pronounced official (*kazënnyi*) character. Not surprisingly, one consequence was the rebirth in Stalin's time of an unofficial, underground body of thought, feeling and art which was heretical with reference to the Stalinist culture and which, again not surprisingly in view of Russian tradition, emerged among the educated youth and intelligentsia. In the post-Stalin era, the underground Russia came into semi-public view via *samizdat*.

In addition to interpreting the Stalinist revolution in culturalist terms, this essay has attempted to explain it so. The circumstantial explanation of the revolution from above was rejected in favour of one which stressed, first of all, the way in which the circumstances of 1927-8 were perceived and defined by a political leadership many of whose members including Stalin, had come of age politically in the era of the October Revolution and War Communism and responded to those circumstances in the revolutionary spirit of the earlier time rather than in the evolutionary spirit of NEP culture. Further, the form taken by the Stalinist revolution, the relation between its two major phases, and the nature of the new Stalinist order that it created have been treated as a recapitulation in essentials of the pattern of revolutionism from above that belonged to the political culture of old Russia and was visible in the tsarist state-building process from the fifteenth to the eighteenth centuries and the socio-political order it produced.

But the question inevitably arises, why did history repeat itself so in this instance? Cultural patterns out of a nation's past do not repeat themselves in the present simply because they were there. Nor can we explain the phenomenon by reference to like circumstances, such as NEP Russia's relative international isolation and economic backwardness, for we have argued that circumstances do not carry their own self-evident meaning, that what people and political leaders *act upon* is always the circumstances *as perceived and defined by them*, which in turn is influenced by culture. But also, we must now add, by personality. And so we come at the end to what was mentioned at the start as a third important explanatory factor underlying the revolution from above—the mind and personality of Stalin.

To a certain extent the personal factor is covered by the culturalist explanation itself. In general, there is no conflict between culturalist explanations and those that make reference to the special historical role of a leader-personality. As cultural anthropologists have pointed out, 'culture' and 'personality' are, to a considerable degree, two ways of viewing one and the same phenomenon, culture being something which has its being mainly *within* people.[39] In terms more immediately pertinent to our argument, a leader-personality becomes politically acculturated through his life-experience both in early years and during manhood. Thus, 1917 and the Civil War were a formative acculturating life-experience for Stalin and many others of his party generation, leaving a deep residue of the revolutionary political culture of War Communism within them. On this level of explanation, Stalin's historical role in the late 1920s was to make himself, as effectively as he did, the leader and spokesman of an outlook that he shared with numerous others in the party leadership and not alone the men of his own faction.

The retracing of the tsarist pattern of revolutionism from above presents a more difficult problem of explanation in culturalist *or* personality terms, if only because Russian tsarism, in all its manifestations, was what the Bolshevik revolutionary movement had taken originally as its mortal socio-political enemy. However, the Russian nationalist feeling aroused in a section of the party during the Civil War years was an element in the new culture that *could* predispose a Bolshevik to perceive certain patterns out of the heritage of old Russia as relevant to the circumstances of the present. On the other hand, it did not do so in the generality of instances of which we know. It is true that Bukharin grasped the direction of Stalin's policy thinking in 1928, with special reference to forced collectivization, and alluded to its tsarist inspiration by terming it 'military-feudal exploitation of the peasantry'. But the party resolution of 23 April 1929 against the Bukharinist group stigmatized Bukharin's charge as 'a libellous attack...drawn from the party of Miliukov'.[40] This was hardly an admission that Stalin's neo-tsarist Marxism (the use of such a phrase may sound monstrous to Marxists, but Marxism is capable of many metamorphoses) had found favour with a substantial body of party opinion. In this case, the explanatory emphasis must fall more on 'personality' than on 'culture'.

To put it otherwise, acculturation is not to be viewed simply as a process in which an individual is affected by formative life-experiences and thereby internalizes culture patterns, including patterns out of the past, as dictated by his psychological needs or predispositions. Stalin, the commissar for nationality affairs and as such the presumable protector of the rights of the minority nations in the Soviet federation, was in fact, as Lenin discovered to his horror shortly before his death, one of those

Bolsheviks infected by 'Russian Red patriotism'. Unbeknown to Lenin, Stalin's sense of Russian nationality, if not his true-Russianism, had dated from his youthful conversion to Lenin's leadership and to Bolshevism, which he saw as the 'Russian faction' in the empire's Marxist Party, Menshevism being the 'Jewish faction'. It was on this foundation that Stalin, during the 1920s, went forward in his thinking, as the generality of his Russian-nationalist-oriented party comrades did not, to envisage the tsarist state-building process as a model for the Soviet Russian state in its 'building of socialism'. And it was the great personal power that he acquired by 1929, with the ouster of the oppositions from the party leadership, that made it possible for him to proceed to carry out his design.

If the thesis concerning the reversion to the state-building process places heavy emphasis upon personality even in the context of a culturalist approach, a final explanatory consideration concerning the Stalinist phenomenon narrows the focus on to personality to a still greater degree. Unlike any other Bolshevik to my knowledge, Stalin as we have noted, defined the Soviet situation in 1925 and 1926 in eve-of-October terms, implicitly presaging thereby a revolutionary assault against the existing order, that is, the NEP, in the drive to build socialism. Then, looking back in the *Short Course* of 1938 on the accomplishments of the Stalinist decade, he described them, and collectivization in particular, as equivalent in consequence to the October Revolution of 1917. Underlying both the definition of the situation in the mid-1920s and the retrospective satisfaction expressed in the late 1930s was Stalin's compulsive psychological need, born of neurosis, to prove himself a revolutionary hero of Lenin proportions, to match or surpass what all Bolsheviks considered Lenin's supreme historical exploit, the leadership of the party in the world-historic revolutionary success of October 1917. The great revolutionary drive to change Russia in the early 1930s was intended as Stalin's October.

In practice it achieved certain successes, notably in industrialization, but at a cost of such havoc and misery in Russia that Stalin, as the regime's supreme leader, incurred unpopularity among many. This helps to explain, in psychological terms, the lethal vindictiveness that he visited upon millions of his party comrades, fellow countrymen and others, in the ensuing years. It was his way of trying to come to terms with the repressed fact that he, Djugashvili, had failed to prove himself the charismatically Lenin-like Stalin that it was his lifelong goal to be. If this interpretation is well founded, he was anything but the most impersonal of great historical figures.

VIII

Having sketched here a culturalist interpretation of Stalinism as revolution from above in the 1930s, it remains to conclude with a comment on the historical sequel. I wish to indicate the relevance of the analysis to the Stalinist phenomenon in its subsequent development. We may distinguish two subsequent periods: that of the Soviet-German conflict of 1941-5 and that of postwar Stalinism (1946-53). In this sequence, 1945 forms a sort of historical pause or hiatus, rather as 1934 did between the two phases of the revolution from above of the 1930s.

The Second World War was, in a way, an interim in Stalinism's development. Not that the 'Great Fatherland War', as it was called, had no serious impact on Soviet Communism as a socio-political culture, but that mainly it reinforced tendencies already present before the war began. Thus, the war gave a powerful further impetus to the Great Russian nationalism which had become evident in Stalin's personal political make-up by the beginning of the 1920s and a prominent motif in Stalinist thought and politics in the 1930s. The official glorification of national Russian military heroes of the pre-Soviet past, notably generals Suvorov and Kutuzov and Admiral Nakhimov, and the opening of special Soviet officers' training academies named after them, were among the many manifestations of this trend.[41] Too, the war intensified the militarist strain in Stalinism, which has here been traced back to the time of War Communism. It strengthened and further developed the hierarchical structure of Stalinist Soviet society as reconstituted during the revolution from above of the 1930s, and augmented the already far-reaching Stalinist hypertrophy of the state machine. There were also covert trends at that time toward the official anti-Semitism which became blatant in the postwar Stalinist campaign against 'rootless cosmopolitans', the murder of large numbers of Soviet Jewish intellectuals, and the infamous 'doctors' affair' of Stalin's last months in 1953.

In the postwar period after 1945, we see a situation which appears to conflict with a revolutionary interpretation of the Stalinist phenomenon. The dominant note in Soviet internal policy during those years was the reconsolidating of the Stalinist order. An example was the early postwar action of Stalin's regime in cutting back the private garden plots which—both for purposes of wartime morale and the nation's food supply—the collectivized Soviet peasants had been allowed surreptitiously to increase in size during the war years. This was a conservative or reactionary policy in the special sense of reinstating what had been a revolutionary change at the time of collectivization fifteen years before.

But Stalinism as revolutionism from above did not end with the completion of the state-directed revolutionary processes of the 1930s and the coming of the Second World War. It reappeared in 1939-40 and again in the late war and postwar Stalin years in a new form: the externalization of Stalinist revolution from above.[42] The years 1939-40 are singled out in this connection because they witnessed the Soviet takeover of eastern Poland and the three Baltic countries during the time of Soviet—Nazi collaboration under the Stalin—Hitler pact of August 1939. Under an organized sham pretence of popular demand, the eastern Polish territories were incorporated into the Ukrainian and Belorussian Soviet republics; and Lithuania, Latvia, and Estonia became constituent ('union') republics of the USSR. Meanwhile, under cover of the Red Army occupation of these lands, the Soviet party, police and economic authorities proceeded with the forcible transplantation to them of Soviet political culture in its Stalinized form, complete with deportation of all suspect elements of the population into the Russian interior. The revolutionary transformations from above, interrupted by the German invasion of Russia in June 1941, were resumed and completed upon the Soviet reoccupation, later in the war, of what had been eastern Poland and the independent Baltic states.

Then the Stalinist revolution from above was carried into the Balkans and much of East-central Europe in the wake of the Soviet army's occupation of Bulgaria, Rumania, Hungary, the rest of Poland, and the eastern parts of Germany. Czechoslovakia likewise succumbed to it following the Communist coup of February 1948. Yugoslavia, where a Communist movement had come to power independently through successful partisan warfare during the German occupation, quietly but effectively checked the subsequent efforts of Stalin's emissaries to direct the Yugoslav transformation from above in such a way as to ensure firm Soviet control of the Yugoslav Communist political system; and as a result Yugoslavia was excommunicated by Stalin in 1948.[43]

In its wartime and postwar externalized form, the Stalinist revolution from above comprised both the takeover (or attempted takeover) of a given country, normally via military occupation, and then the use of a Soviet-directed native Communist Party and its subsidiary organizations as agents of the country's transformation into what was called at first a 'people's democracy'. The establishment and consolidation of Muscovite control over the organs of power in the country concerned was, as indicated above, an essential element of the process. There were variations in the methods and timetables, but in essence the East European revolution, in so far as it took place under Soviet auspices in a number of smaller countries, involved the transfer to foreign lands of much of what had taken place in Russia in the 1930s. The same may be said of the postwar revolutionary transformation in North Korea, which had been occupied by the Soviet army at the war's end. China, a potential great power in its own right, presented for that very reason a special problem for Stalin—and for Stalinism. In so far as the Stalinist revolution from above had been aimed at transforming Soviet Russia into a great military-industrial power capable of fully defending its independence and interests in the world, Stalinism was not likely to appeal to the very Russian-nationalist-minded Stalin as a proper prescription for Communism in China, save to the extent that Russia could place and keep China under its control. Very likely it was these considerations, together with the shrewd realization of the impossibility of long-range success in keeping a Communist

China under Russian control, which explain Stalin's ambivalence toward—not to say distaste for—the coming of the Chinese Communists to power. By the same token, we can see in all this a key to the attraction that certain aspects of Stalinism, not including its Russian nationalism, had for Mao zedong.

Finally, despite what has been said above about the generally conservative nature of Stalin's postwar internal policy, it may be suggested that in some paradoxical sense Stalinism as revolution from above returned to Russia during 1946-53 within the setting of the conservative internal policies then being pursued. For Stalin's very effort to turn the Soviet clock back to the 1930s after the war carried with it a shadowy re-run of the developments of that earlier decade. In other words, the postwar reaction was a reaction *to* a period of radical change— from above.

In his major postwar policy address of 9 February 1946, Stalin placed a series of further five-year plans on Russia's agenda as a guarantee against 'all contingencies', that is, to prepare the country for a possible future war. This meant the re-enactment of the prewar policy of giving priority to heavy industry over consumer goods, with all the privation that entailed for the Soviet population. A minor recollectivizing campaign, as already mentioned, was put through following the above-mentioned early postwar decision to cut back the size of the peasants' private garden plots. Furthermore, in the dictator's final period there were increasingly clear indications that he was preparing, if on a lesser scale, a sort of replica of the Great Purge of the 1930s. There would be show trials of the Soviet Jewish doctors, accused of complicity in an imaginary international Anglo-American-Jewish conspiracy to shorten the lives of Soviet leaders; and no doubt other show trials as well. These would provide the dramatic symbolism needed as an accompaniment and justification of the purge, just as the show trials of the Old Bolsheviks of left and right did in the earlier version of the revolution from above.[44]

Before the first of the new trials could begin, however, the dictator suddenly fell ill and died. So providential was the timing of this death for very many whose lives were threatened by the oncoming new Stalinist blood purge, including men in highest places, that it has aroused a persisting suspicion that Stalin's passing was hastened in one way or another.

However that may have been, Stalin in his macabre way remained to the end a revolutionary, albeit from above. Of few if any of those whom he chose as his associates and executors, and who survived him in power, could the same be said. This helps to explain why, in Russia at any rate, Stalinism after Stalin was going to differ very significantly from the Stalinism of his time. Without its progenitor alive and in charge of events, Stalinism lost its very Russified revolutionary soul. Then and there it became what it has remained ever since: extreme Communist conservatism of strong Russian nationalist tendency.

NOTES

1. For Trotsky's thesis on the antithesis between Bolshevism and Stalinism, see his pamphlet, *Stalinism and Bolshevism: Concerning the Historical and Theoretical Roots of the Fourth International* (New York, 1937). The thesis is elaborated further in his book *The Revolution Betrayed* (New York, 1937).
2. Leon Trotsky, *Literature and Revolution* (Ann Arbor, 1960), 94.
3. See Chapter four, 56–7.
4. *History of the Communist Party of the Soviet Union/Bolsheviks/Short Course* (Moscow, 1945), 305.
5. On the disparity between Plan and practice, involving also the 'wild target increases issued in 1930 and 1931', see Holland Hunter, 'The overambitious first Soviet Five-Year Plan', and the comments on Hunter's article by Stephen Cohen and Moshe Lewin, in *The Slavic Review* (June 1973). Hunter's reference to the wild target increases appears on p. 239.
6. For a representative statement of this belief, see E.H. Carr and R.W. Davies, *Foundations of a Planned Economy 1926-29*, vol. One—I (London, 1969), 269–70, where the authors write, *inter alia*, 'if industrialization was a condition of collectivization, collectivization was a condition of industrialization.'
7. James R. Millar, 'Mass collectivization and the contribution of Soviet agriculture to the First Five-Year Plan: a review article', *The Slavic Review* (December 1974), 764, 765.
8. Isaac Deutscher, *Stalin: A Political Biography*, 2nd edn (New York, 1967), 313. The phrase 'a grave social crisis' appears on p. 312.
9. *ibid.*, 318, 322. Deutscher repeats this interpretation in briefer form in *The Prophet Outcast. Trotsky: 1929-1940* (New York, 1965), 67–8.

10. Carr and Davies, *op. cit.*, 264, 268, 269.

11. E.H. Carr, 'Revolution from above: the road to collectivization', in *The October Revolution Before and After* (New York, 1969), 104, 109. The cited essay was first published in 1967.

12. E.H. Carr, 'Reflections on Soviet Industrialization', *ibid.*, 121.

13. Alexander Gerschenkron, *Economic Backwardness in Historical Perspective* (New York, 1965), 144–5. Gerschenkron further states (145) that: 'Viewed as a short-run measure, the purpose of the First Five-Year Plan was to break the disequilibrium through increase in consumer-goods output based on increase in plant capacity', although once the peasants had been forced into the *kolkhozy*, 'The hands of the government were untied. There was no longer any reason to regard the First Five-Year Plan as a self-contained brief period of rapid industrialization, and the purpose of industrialization was no longer to relieve the shortage of consumer goods' (146). It does not appear accurate to say that the main purpose of the first Plan was to increase consumer-goods production; in any event, the thrust of the industrialization drive in 1929-33 was toward the building up of heavy industry, and consumer-goods supply declined in Russia upon the termination of the NEP.

14. *Stalin: A Political Biography*, 273.

15. E.H. Carr, *Socialism in One Country 1924-1926* (New York, 1968), vol. I, 177, 185. The characterization is repeated with only very slight modification in *Foundations of a Planned Economy* (vol. II, 448) where Carr and Davies describe Stalin as 'the representative figure of the period', adding: 'Stalin's personality, combined with the primitive and cruel traditions of the Russian bureaucracy, imparted to the revolution from above a particularly brutal character, which has sometimes obscured the fundamental historical problems involved.' The authors do not say what they mean by 'the fundamental historical problems involved', but invite the inference that they are invoking what we have called the circumstantial explanation of the revolution from above.

16. *Stalin: A Political Biography*, 295.

17. *ibid.*, 319. Stalin, Deutscher observes, at that earlier time dismissed Larin's notion as a 'cranky idea'.

18. *ibid.*, 303.

19. John P. Sontag, 'The Soviet war scare of 1926-7', *The Russian Review* (January 1975), 77. See also Leonard Schapiro, *The Communist Party of the Soviet Union* (New York, 1959), 383, where it is stated: 'There was little prospect of any kind of invasion in 1928.'

20. Dana G. Dalrymple, 'The Soviet famine of 1932-34', *Soviet Studies* (January 1964), 261.

21. Millar, *op. cit.*, 766. One of the sources cited by Millar in this review essay is an article by Karz, who writes that 'the damage done to agriculture within the first three years of the industrialization drive was so severe that it affected adversely its ability to contribute significantly to further economic development'. Karz concludes that 'there is a

significant probability' that the Soviet dilemma in agrarian policy toward the end of NEP 'was not one that *had* to be resolved by collectivization and the associated compulsory procurement of farm products or by the abandonment of a sensible and fruitful industrialization drive'. See Jerzy F. Karz, 'From Stalin to Brezhnev: Soviet agricultural policy in historical perspective', in James R. Millar, ed, *The Soviet Rural Community* (Urbana, 1917), 41, 51.

22. For an argument to this effect, see Moshe Lewin, *Political Undercurrents in Soviet Economic Debates: From Bukharin to the Modern Reformers* (Princeton, 1974), 52—61.

23. *ibid.*, ch. 12.

24. The Bukharin—Kamenev conversation is Document T1897 in the Trotsky Archives at Harvard University. Further historical testimony to the effect that the disastrous consequences of the Stalinist course were foreseen by some well-known Soviet economists in the later 1920s is given by N. Valentinov, 'Iz proshlogo', *Sotsialisticheskii Vestnik* (April 1961), 68—72.

25. For an argument by the young Stalin along these lines, see his essay of 1906, 'Anarchism or socialism?' in Stalin, *Sochineniia* (Moscow, 1954), I, 345—6. He cited as his authority here not Lenin but the passage in *The Communist Manifesto* about the proletariat's becoming the ruling class and using its political power to deprive the bourgeoisie of its capital step by step, etc.

26. *The Lenin Anthology*, 478.

27. For the argument that War Communism brought about a militarization of the revolutionary political culture of Bolshevism, the correlative argument that we must distinguish two Leninisms—that of War Communism and that of the NEP, and the further view that Stalin was a representative of the War Communist strain, see Robert C. Tucker, *Stalin as Revolutionary 1879-1929: A Study in History and Personality* (New York, 1973), 208—9 and 395—420.

28. See *ibid.*, 402—3, 413, 415—6, for documentation on the survival of the War Communist spirit during the NEP. According, for example, to Valentinov, who was a resident of Moscow in the NEP years, 'the party, particularly in its *lower cells*, was instinctively, subconsciouly, antagonistic toward the NEP'. As for the apprehensive awareness of the imminence of a social cataclysm, see the above-cited article by Valentinov, 'Iz proshlogo'.

29. For example, in 'The importance of gold now and after the complete victory of socialism', *The Lenin Anthology*, 517.

30. *Political Undercurrents*, 98—9.

31. See, for example, Leonard E. Hubbard, *The Economics of Soviet Agriculture* (London, 1939), 115—16.

32. *ibid.*, 18—19.

33. Aleksandr I. Solzhenitsyn, *The Gulag Archipelago 1918-1956. An Experiment in Literary Investigation I-II*, trans. Thomas P. Whitney (New York, 1973), 54. Hubbard (*op. cit.*, 117) estimates that during

collectivization 'probably not less than five million peasants, including families, were deported to Siberia and the Far North, and of these it is estimated that 25 per cent perished'. Moshe Lewin has written that 'what is certain is that several million households, to a total of 10 million persons, or more, must have been deported, of whom a great many must have perished'. *Russian Peasants and Soviet Power: A Study of Collectivization* (Evanston, 1968), 508.

34. Sergei Witte was the Russian minister of finance from 1893 until 1903. On the 'Witte system' and its inspiration in Friedrich List's teaching that backward countries could overcome 'the peril of remaining behind' by giving priority to the machine-building industries in industrialization, see Theodore H. Von Laue, *Sergei Witte and the Industrialization of Russia* (New York, 1973), esp. 58–60.

35. Schapiro, *The Communist Party of the Soviet Union*, 430.

36. Isaac Deutscher, *The Prophet Outcast*, 109. Schapiro's argument (loc. cit.,) is the rather more comprehensive one that, having ruled by terror in the first phase of the revolution from above, Stalin was faced with the strong possibility of losing power if the terror came to an end, hence chose terror as the means of his remaining in command. To explain the colossal scope of the terror in the second phase, he refers only to a personal characteristic—Stalin's 'thoroughness'.

37. For collectivization as reflected in the archive, see Merle Fainsod, *Smolensk Under Soviet Rule* (New York, 1958), ch. 12. In *Russian Peasants and Soviet Power* (488), Lewin implies a more active, positive participation of the village poor.

38. Nicholar Vakar, *The Taproot of Soviet Society* (New York, 1961). The statement by Pilniak, cited by Vakar on p. 16, comes from his novel *Goly god*.

39. See, for example, Ralph Linton, *The Cultural Background of Personality* (New York, 1945), chs. 4–5.

40. *Kommunisticheskaia partiia sovetskogo soiuza v rezoiutsiakh i resheniakh s'ezdov, konferentisii i plenumov Tsk* (Moscow, 1954), II, 555.

41. On Stalinism and Russian nationalism after 1939, see in particular the informative account by F. Barghoorn, 'Stalinism and the Russian cultural heritage', *Review of Politics*, vol. 14, no. 2 (April 1952), 178–203, and Barghoorn's *Soviet Russian Nationalism* (New York, 1956).

42. One could argue that the Stalinist externalization of the revolution from above had an ancestry in the forcible sovietization of the three Transcaucasian republics of Georgia, Armenia and Azerbaijan, and some other parts of the former Russian Empire, during the Civil War period. But it has not been the position of this essay that Stalinism had no ancestry in the Lenin period and in Leninism.

43. The classic account remains Vladimir Dedijer, *Tito* (New York, 1953).

44. An interpretation of the show trial as an element of Stalinist political culture has been presented by the present writer in 'Stalin, Bukharin

and history as conspiracy', in *The Soviet Political Mind*, ch. 3. The transplantation of the Stalinist show trial to postwar Eastern Europe, Czechoslovakia in particular, is discussed by H. Gordon Skilling in *Czechoslovakia's Interrupted Revolution* (Princeton, 1976), ch. XIII.

6 Swollen State, Spent Society: Stalin's Legacy to Brezhnev's Russia

Brezhnev's Russia is a mighty world power, with the largest territory of any state, a population of 270 million, great mineral resources in a resource-hungry world, and a geopolitical position that gives it a large role in both European and Asian affairs. It is a military superpower with intercontinental and intermediate-range nuclear missiles in large numbers, supersonic airplanes, a huge standing army based on universal military service, and fleets in all oceans. It controls an East and Central European empire extending deep into Germany and the Balkans. Its power and influence radiate into Asia, the Middle East, the Mediterranean, Africa and Latin America.

This formidable global presence is serviced and maintained by an internal state system centred in Great Russia's capital city, Moscow; the formal autonomy of the outlying, non-Russian Soviet republics is constitutional fiction. Staffed by an army of party, government and other officials (it has been estimated that full-time party officials alone number close to half a million), the party–state edifice comes to a peak in the twenty-three departments of the party's Central Committee, whose Politburo is the focal point of decision-making authority. Under this supreme directorate, about sixty government ministries provide centralized administration of the Soviet realm. Two of these bureaucracies, the police and the military, have roles and prerogatives of special importance. Their chiefs, along with the chairman of the Council of Ministers and his first deputy, the minister for foreign affairs, the principal Central Committee secretaries, the first secretaries of the Moscow, Leningrad and one or two republic party organizations, sit with the general secretary on the Politburo and take part in policy-making. This system lays official claim to the title 'socialism'. A source inside the Soviet establishment, writing under the name of Fedor Zniakov, more aptly called it 'supermonopoly capitalism'. Ownership, he explained, is concentrated in a single centre, the 'supermonopoly', which possesses the plenitude of economic and political power.[1] The economic system may be likened to a single gigantic conglomerate incorporating industries and other state-controlled activity, including state and collective farm agriculture, under unified management at the Politburo level.

The Politburo's control is ensured by a hierarchically organized ruling class that represents and defends the supermonopoly's interests in all spheres of social life. The fundamental aim is the preservation, strengthening and extension of the supermonopoly's power. The ruling class starts at lower levels with plant directors, collective farm chairmen and heads of local party and governmental bodies, and extends to Central Committee secretaries and members of the Soviet government at the top.[2] It is sometimes informally called the 'nomenclature class' because of the system of nomenclature (*nomenklatura*), or lists of posts appointment to which requires the approval of a given higher or lower party body. The nomenclature class comprises those cleared for assignment to responsible positions in the party–state.

Its members and their families live in a relatively closed world of privilege, which so sharply differentiates their life-experience from that of ordinary citizens that they could almost be living in different countries. People of the nomenclature class have comfortable apartments, cars and, in many cases, country houses. They are served by a network of so-called closed distributors, inconspicuous special shops where food and other products, including foreign goods, are available at subsidized prices. They have opportunities for foreign travel, adequate health care, and can enjoy the facilities of desirable Soviet resorts at desirable times of the year. Through informal channels of influence their children can make their way into the restricted number of openings for higher education and thence into careers in the official world.

Perquisites in that world are carefully differentiated

according to gradations of rank. Thus in the Science Settlement at Novosibirsk, according to an ex-Soviet science journalist, 'A full member of the Academy lives in a villa, a corresponding member has half a villa; a senior research officer has an apartment with three-meter ceiling height, while a junior has one with a two and a quarter meter ceiling, on a higher floor with a communal bathroom.'[3]

I

Was this rigid, centralized and highly stratified socio-political structure an inevitable outgrowth of the single-party dictatorship established by Lenin and his fellow Bolsheviks after the October Revolution? Or did it evolve as one possible sequel to the revolution, the result of historical decisions that might have been taken differently and that reflected, in some measure, the unique political personality and outlook of Lenin's successor, Stalin?

I believe the latter is the case. Although Brezhnev's Russia differs from Stalin's in the absence of an all-powerful dictator ruling by terror and in other ways to be discussed below, in the fundamental aspects already mentioned it was indeed an inheritance from the Stalin era. It took shape in the course of what can best be called a state-building process that was launched around 1929 when Stalin finally achieved ascendancy in the Soviet political leadership. Taking advantage of the ability that this gave him to manipulate the regime's policy, Stalin steered a course in internal affairs predicated upon the imperative need to build an industrially and militarily powerful Soviet Russian state within ten years in preparation for what he considered an inevitably oncoming great new war—a war that, with assistance from his own diplomacy, did break out about ten years later, in 1939.

Under Peter the Great in the early eighteenth century, the Russian state had undergone a coercive remodelling from above through a Europeanization that involved the borrowing of advanced technology from the West and the forced development of Russian industry under governmental auspices for military power in the continuing process of external aggrandizement. Thus the primacy of foreign policy and the need for military strength for external defence and expansion were the mainsprings of the internal state-building process. In his summation of this process, the pre-1917 historian V.O. Kliuchevsky wrote that 'the expansion of the state territory, straining beyond measure and exhausting the resources of the people, only bolstered the power of the state without elevating the self-confidence of the people.... The state swelled up; the people grew lean.'[4]

The pressure of external upon internal policy relaxed with tsarist Russia's achievement of its commanding world position by the close of the eighteenth century, making it possible for the government to give more attention to the needs of internal welfare rather than territorial expansion. The earlier binding of all classes in compulsory state service gave way to a partial unbinding of classes with the release of the nobility from its compulsory service obligations in the late eighteenth century.[5]

The 'unbinding' proceeded in slow uneven steps. Not until 1861 was the peasantry released from serfdom by imperial decree. That action inaugurated a time of transforming change (from above) known as the epoch of Great Reforms. Although it witnessed a considerable liberalization of Russian life, the autocratic, authoritarian, centralized, bureaucratic state structure that evolved in the state-building process was too well entrenched, its repressive powers too formidable, and the history-bred submissiveness of the people too enduring, for the processes of change to work their way to fruition peacefully. What had developed as a dynamically active autocratic state authority in the earlier state-building process proved so strong as a static force later on that it could successfully block its own thorough transformation, as shown by its capacity to withstand the nationwide insurrectionary movement of 1905. Only under the unbearable strains of the third year of the World War did the structure finally buckle and collapse in 1917.

II

The Bolshevik party–state that emerged in control of what remained of the Russian Empire after the ensuing time of troubles was not initially oriented toward a renewed state-building process in the Russian national tradition. The Marxist ruling party's programmatic commitment was not to the restoration of a militarily powerful bureaucratic Russian state under a new tsar—autocrat, but to 'socialist construction', meaning the building over time (a generation at least, Lenin said) of a socialist or communist society characterized by co-operative forms of production in a setting of economic and technological advance, by material abundance for the entire populace, and by a steady growth of popular self-administration in place of rule by a governmental bureaucracy. By the seizure and monopolizing of power and the establishment of a party dictatorship, Lenin and the Bolsheviks had, however, created a medium in which a dynamic resurgence of statism could occur. Moreover, by virtue of the losses of territory in the revolutionary period and the new state's isolation in an unfriendly international environment, now called a 'hostile capitalist encirclement', the country's situation in the 1920s showed a certain parallel to that of the early Muscovite period.

Among the leading Bolshevik contenders for power after Lenin died, Stalin alone was disposed by personal politico-ideological orientation to take that historical parallel seriously. His orientation is best described as 'Russian national Bolshevism', an amalgam of Bolshevik revolutionary theory and practice with Great Russian nationalism. When he expressed it in moderate terms in the platform of 'socialism in one country' that he advocated against the party left in the debates of the mid-1920s, it had strong persuasive appeal to large elements of the ruling party, particularly the younger party members. But linked as it was with his special perception of a parallel between Muscovite Russia's situation in earlier times and Soviet Russia's now,[6] Stalin's actual position was far more radical in its political implications than his followers suspected—until he began acting upon it in 1929.

Such basic elements of the Bolshevik programme as the construction of a socialist society in Soviet Russia and the international Communist revolution were preserved but at the same time transformed by Stalin's Russian national Bolshevism. Communist revolution abroad was reconceived as a process spreading out from a base in the USSR to neighbouring countries, hence as, in part, a revived 'gathering of Russian lands', such as those lost to Poland and to the independent Baltic states during the revolutionary period.

In Stalin's Russian national Bolshevism, further growth of the international Communist revolution and Soviet Russian expansion, territorially or in terms of spheres of influence, were fused into one process. Since a focal area for expansion was Eastern Europe and the Balkans, a diplomacy of accord with Germany, looking (among other things) to a new partition of Poland, was a fixture of Stalin's foreign policy conception from early on. While encouraging Foreign Commissar Maxim Litvinov to pursue in the mid-1930s an open diplomacy of collective security and popular fronts against fascism, Stalin made his way by secret diplomacy toward the Nazi-Soviet pact that he concluded in 1939.

Thus Russian national Bolshevism resurrected the historic Russian primacy of foreign policy, and with it the necessity—to Stalin's history-oriented mind—of a renewed, but this time *Soviet* Russian state-building process centring on forced-draft industrialization with emphasis upon heavy industry and military-industrial power. Collectivization was designed to undergird the industrialization drive by organizing the peasantry into collective and state farms. This ensured government control of the great bulk of agricultural produce, including large amounts for export abroad to finance the importation of technology. That aim required lightning collectivization rather than the long-range 'co-operating' of the peasantry by persuasion that Lenin had envisaged. Lightning collectivization was, and could only be, accomplished by terrorist methods, whose utilization on Stalin's orders backfired because the mass of peasants, seeing in the collectives a revived form of Russian serfdom (which they were), slaughtered a huge proportion of their livestock before entering them. Although the state got control of the produce by the draconian means Stalin employed, it did so at the cost of millions of lives lost in the ensuing great famine.

Restoring as it did something comparable to old Russia's serfdom, collectivization was not only a coercive revolution from above but a first phase of a renewed state-building process. Stalin moved to bring every element of society under regimentation and control. He re-enacted the 'binding' of all strata in compulsory service to the state authority. He pursued a policy of direct exploitation of the human resources of the economically backward country for amassing military power through industrialization. Total exploitation of the populace meant totalitarian control. Since a large bureaucratic apparatus of police and other governmental regulation was needed for this, a leviathan of a state resulted. Not only was a powerful, highly centralized, bureaucratic state revived; its control of people's lives extended well beyond the limits reached by tsarist rulers.

Russia's history in Stalin's time retraced, therefore, the course epitomized by Kliuchevsky in his phrase cited earlier: 'The state swelled up; the people grew lean.' The people 'grew lean' in the shrinkage of the unregimented parts of their lives, and in the simple sense of being hungry, living on rations, going without desperately needed housing, and enduring other hardship. Nevertheless, Stalin publicly proclaimed in 1936, when promulgating a new Stalinist version of the Soviet Constitution, that the foundations of a socialist society had now been built. This claim contradicted Leninist assumptions that socialism connoted richer lives rather than poorer, more equitable distribution rather than less, less bureaucratic regimentation rather than more, more meaningful public involvement in administration rather than less. But it was consistent with Stalin's Russian national Bolshevism, in which socialism-building and state-building were fused, so that a mighty Soviet Russian military-national state in which all strata were bound in compulsory service to the state power became the fundamental meaning of 'socialism'.

Much of this was alien to the thinking of the great majority of surviving Old Bolsheviks, as well as to many of their juniors in the new party generation that had matured during the early years of the Soviet regime and was heavily influenced by the Old Bolsheviks in its way of thought. Even many who had been 'Stalinists' in supporting Stalin's platform of building socialism in one country, were unprepared for what his Russian national Bolshevism meant in practice—a replication under Soviet conditions of the patterns of revolution from above that had found earlier expression in the tsarist state-building process. They were appalled by the ghastly tragedy of collectivization by terror and the resulting hushed-up famine of the early 1930s. They were, many of them, repelled by the new, stratified society of privilege that they saw emerging in those years of privation, and by the swelling of a bureaucratic state that, to minds conditioned by Marxism and Leninism, should have been beginning to atrophy if socialism were really being built in Russia.

Their disenchantment with the new statist society over whose construction Stalin was presiding was expressed in negative attitudes, even in opposition, to him. Some Old Bolsheviks made an abortive attempt before the Seventeenth Party Congress in 1934 to carry out, belatedly, Lenin's parting confidential advice to the party elders that Stalin be removed from his position of power. His lethal response was the Great Terror, which began with the assassination of the Leningrad party leader, Sergei Kirov, in December 1934, and is estimated to have cost the lives of about two million Communists and previously expelled party members, plus large numbers of their non-party relatives and associates.[7]

The Terror, by opening careers *en masse* to replacements for the victims, brought into being a new, state-created as well as Stalin-oriented Soviet elite. It lived far better than ordinary citizens but was just as securely bound in service to the state as were the peasants and the workers. Hence, the Great Purge was another revolution from above, or another phase in the larger revolution from above of the 1930s. It recapitulated in a highly magnified twentieth-century way the binding of the landed aristocracy in compulsory state service. Like the boyars of old, the Old Bolshevik ruling elite was exterminated in large part and, for the rest, submerged in a new Soviet service nobility. The purge as a revolution from above was, moreover, the crucible of the re-emergence of Russian absolutism in a Soviet setting, the rule of a new tsar−autocrat in whose dictatorial system the still ostensibly dominant political party was, like all other institutions of Stalin's state, a transmission belt for implementing his policies.

This interpretation of the Stalinist 1930s conflicts with a view that has enjoyed wide credence in the West. That view sees

Stalin's revolution from above as a harsh and cruel way of bringing backward Russia into the modern world, a revolution of
'modernization'.[8] There is no question but that Russia underwent considerable industrialization and urbanization in the
Stalinist 1930s, accompanied by growth in literacy, in the
availability of education, chiefly technical, and in other
indices. Yet all this took place in a state-building process
similar in a fundamental way to one seen earlier in history.

The upshot is that what happened in Russia in the 1930s is not
only superficially described but actually obscured by the use of
a term like 'modernization'. In fact, the nation underwent a
reversion to the Russian past in its developmental mode.
Without a clear comprehension of this it is not possible truly to
understand either the legacy of Stalin and Stalinism to the
Russian present or the depth of the problems confronted by
Stalin's successors.

III

'Russ is where the true belief is', a noted *émigré* interpreter of
Russian thought and society has written.[9] His point was that
Rus' developed in history as a community of right believers,
meaning those of the Russian Orthodox faith. In its sustaining
myth, Russian society was a political community of the
faithful, an Orthodox tsardom. So persistent was this pattern
that as late as the early twentieth century a peasant—and the
vast majority of Russians were peasants then—would speak of
himself not as 'Russian' but as 'Orthodox' (*pravoslavny*).[10]
Russian was his language; Orthodoxy, his identity. Since the
tsar was a centrepiece of the mythos, waning faith in the tsar
was a sign of the coming end of the tsardom. Bloody Sunday in
January 1905 has been mentioned in this context. On that day
a priest-led, icon-bearing procession of common people was
met with murderous gunfire on its walk to the Winter Palace in
Petersburg to ask the tsar for redress of grievances. The priest,
Father Gapon is said to have declared in the midst of the
carnage, 'There is no tsar any more.'

The revolutionary reconstitution of a society always sees the
rise of a new conception of the meaning of membership in that

society. Bolshevism's revolutionary republic, which Lenin called *Rus'* in an article of 1918, soon generated its own sustaining myth in the concept of Soviet *Rus'* as a community of 'builders of socialism'. The Bolsheviks' militant atheism, their unremitting effort through anti-religious propaganda to dislodge Orthodoxy from Russian minds, was the other side of their project of instilling in those same minds a new set of right beliefs, a new transnational orthodoxy. The society was envisioned as a collective of citizens united in believing in future socialism and eventual full communism as a transcendently worthy life goal.

During the remainder of his active life, Lenin tried to formulate guidelines for building what must initially be a socialist rather than a fully communist new society. It would entail the creation of a machine industry based especially on electric power, overcoming persisting class differences, the growth of general prosperity, and the 'co-operating of Russia', that it, the enlistment of the whole population, peasantry included, into co-operative societies and co-operative forms of work. The coming socialist *Rus'* would likewise be to a great extent popularly administered, free of the 'bureaucratism' bequeathed by history. The construction of socialism was not envisaged as a state-building process of the kind that subsequently occurred, although Stalin, in part by selective quotation of earlier Lenin texts, sought to obscure the gulf between Lenin's guidelines and his policies.

Under Stalin, the meaning of Soviet citizenship continued to be defined as belief in socialism and communism, but the contents of the belief-system changed. As of about 1936, a Soviet citizen was supposed to believe that Stalin's Russia of the five-year plans had basically made the transition to socialism and was now on the way to an indefinitely deferred communist future which must serve as the nation's goal. Furthermore, the belief-system was personalized in a new way. It had already been personalized upon Lenin's death because the deceased founder of Bolshevism was made into a cult figure, a venerated supreme authority whose writings figured as sacred texts on, above all, the society's goal and the way to achieve it. Then, in the early and middle 1930s, the Lenin cult became overlaid and overshadowed by official glorification of Stalin as the 'Builder of Socialism'. Soviet citizens were expected to believe not only in socialism as a fait accompli and in communism as the further objective, but also in Stalin as the party's genius–leader to whom credit was due for the society's history-making breakthrough to the socialist stage of development foretold by Marx, Engels and Lenin but not realized in their lifetimes.

The Old Bolsheviks, as already indicated, were mostly Old Believers as well (to borrow another term from Russian history), and so were many of their younger contemporaries who had come into the party during the Civil War and the 1920s. Most of them had been willing followers of Stalin when he spoke in the mid-1920s of socialism in one country. But not being Russian national Bolsheviks of his peculiar stripe, few could accept the unprosperous, deeply stratified, bureaucracy-ridden society of the mid-1930s, with its reimposed state of virtual serfdom and its increasingly bound working class, with its more and more strident Great Russian nationalism, as a 'socialist' society. Nor could they believe in Stalin, the colossal bungler of collectivization, as the leader of genius portrayed in his personality cult. Those generations of Leninist Old Believers were mowed down wholesale in the terrorist purges of the later 1930s.

We should beware, however, of assuming that the people who took their places in leading positions, or in lesser ones with higher status in store, were cynical, opportunistic non-believers. Some, perhaps many, were, to be sure, just that. But Stalin, however vicious, was not stupid in this phase of his state-building policy. He consciously brought along a new generation of state servitors who could be, and in very many cases would be, believers of a new kind. These people accepted the society he was building as the socialist one he proclaimed it to be. They admiringly looked upon him as indeed the Builder of Socialism.

Risen from simple, often peasant origins, these New Believers were culturally disposed to think of Russia as a new Orthodox tsardom of Marxist-Leninist-Stalinist persuasion, naturally with a new tsar, albeit an uncrowned one, at its head. They could accept the equation of a socialist Soviet Russia with an industrially developed and militarily strong one, take satisfaction in their participation in the state-building effort, and be proud of the country's emergence as a great power. They, or many of them, could uncritically accept the results of the devious foreign policy that made a deal with Hitler which turned his aggression westward and meanwhile opened the way for Russia's and Communism's expansion into Eastern Europe.

IV

When, after confounding Stalin's calculation on a long debilitating war in the West, Hitler 'perfidiously' (as the Soviet version goes) hurled the full force of the Wehrmacht against his ally of 1939-41, the New Believers were a rock of support for the defence effort. As for the common people, they were wary as the war began, not knowing what to expect from the Germans, who were European and hence (as Russians had always supposed) a 'cultured' nation. When they discovered that the invaders were behaving like savages rather than liberators, they were ready to respond to the Stalin regime's call to arms. It did not say, 'Rise in defence of Soviet socialism', but, 'Mother Russia calls you.' The symbols invoked, such as General Kutuzov who commanded Russia's defence in the war against Napoleon, were Russian national ones.

Having no one to defend it but the people, whose material conditions of life had to grow worse rather than better in wartime, the regime made the one concession possible: it lifted the terror-tinged atmosphere of the prewar years and allowed the warring nation a relaxed sense of more-freedom-to-come. During those awful years of death and privation, commitments were quietly made to the population. Not by open proclamation but by spreading the word through the grapevine that serves the country's real communication needs, the regime encouraged the people to believe that victory would be a great turning point toward materially better as well as freer conditions, that peasants would be allowed to leave the collectives, that intellectuals would enjoy a respite from cultural regimentation, that there would be opportunities for foreign travel and study in a no longer hostile world, and even that the Americans would be invited to open department stores in Soviet cities.

So, at a cost of twenty million casualties and with critically important aid from the Western allies, Russia prevailed. The war itself became a popular one in the sense that the great bulk of the population was behind it. Stalin himself became, for the first time, a popular hero as beleaguered Russia's rugged war leader. The fact that he had panicked and had a temporary nervous breakdown at the beginning was not known outside a tiny circle at the top. Nor did the people know about his grievous faults as supreme commander of the fighting forces. Many had but a hazy realization, if that, of the fact that his terrorist collectivization and methodical destruction of seasoned cadres in all fields in the fury of the Great Purge had done far more to wreck the war effort in advance than to prepare for it.

It was an article of faith in the Soviet public mind that the end of the war would bring the beginning of a new period in the country's life, a time of peace, liberalization, and growing plenty. I heard a Red Army officer cry, 'Now it is time to live!' during the joyous victory celebration in Red Square on 10 May 1945. But the anticipated and longed-for new period of economic betterment and liberalization did not come with the victory for which the people had paid so dear a price.

Instead, Stalin, now a supremely glorified hero as well as absolute ruler, defined the postwar period as a new prewar period. That was the underlying message of his postwar address of 9 February 1946, in which he spoke of the necessity of three or four more heavy industry-oriented five-year plans in order to prepare the country for 'all contingencies' in a world where the continued existence of imperialism made new wars inevitable. Although Russia was no longer isolated and threatened as before, Stalin was decreeing a new round of the state-building process for what was already then becoming, in his foreign policy, an era of Cold War and near total isolation of the nation from the outside world. That meant a new round of strain, sacrifice and austerity internally. A Russian of the older generation in whose Moscow apartment I sat as Stalin's words were transmitted to the people by radio, placed his head on his folded arms when he heard them. All over Russia people figuratively were doing the same. In a society founded on the presumption of belief, that signified the beginning of a crisis.

Aware of the mass disenchantment, Stalin prescribed as antidote what has been called the *Zhdanovshchina*, the campaign, initiated in 1946 by his party lieutenant Andrei Zhdanov and others, to revitalize political consciousness and belief. They castigated what was called 'apoliticality' and 'non-ideologism.' The phenomena so designated were real, whereas the means employed to counteract them, including propaganda of Russian chauvinism and, increasingly, anti-Semitism, were impotent to reinstil active commitment in a generally dispirited people that had lost hope for a better life in their time. Fear became the main stimulus, and the security police lorded it over all other organs of power, including the theoretically ruling party. By Stalin's death in 1953, the society was in the grip of something close to paralysis.

V

Stalin's successors were bound to pursue a politics of change although they were divided over how far and fast it should proceed, in what directions, and who should preside over it. Some staunch Stalinist conservatives, such as Lazar Kaganovich and Vyacheslav Molotov, appear to have wanted only limited change hypercautiously administered, whereas younger leaders like Georgi Malenkov and Nikita Khrushchev stood for substantial reform but differed over the course it should take and who should implement it. Having achieved a sort of supremacy in a two-year struggle, Khrushchev embarked in 1955 upon a reform course and made the Twentieth Party Congress in February 1956 his forum for it. His reform course was aimed at making the Soviet system work by restoring it to a condition of economic and socio-political health.

A peculiar blend of Old and New Believer in his make-up, Khrushchev was a tirelessly itinerant politician who went around Russia and the world preaching the superiority of the Soviet way. But his faith in the Soviet system did not stand in the way of a realistic appreciation of its failings. This believing Communist could be astonishingly frank in exposing the actualities, whether it was the grim state of Soviet agriculture in

1953, or the ills of the Moscow-centred bureaucratic management of the economy, or Stalin's criminality in the terrorist purge of the party. It took a deep believer in the fundamental underlying rightness of the Soviet order to be such a scourge of past tragedies and present malfunctioning.

The watchword of Khrushchev's special brand of reformism was 'Back to the path of Lenin', connoting, above all, revival of the system of single-party rule that had been eclipsed for twenty years by Stalin's police-based personal depotism. Accordingly, the grand theme of his secret report to the Twentieth Congress in 1956 was Stalin's violation of the 'Leninist norms' of rule by the Communist Party as a collectivity. His chilling *exposé* of tyranny was not published in Russia, but its contents soon became known through the grapevine after the speech was read at closed meetings of party cells all over the country. Hence the whole of politically literate Russia became aware, if it had not been before, of the Stalinist heritage of anti-party terror, and millions of its still surviving victims began returning to Soviet society from concentration camps.

Khrushchev was acutely aware that a widespread failure of belief was both a part of and a cause of the crisis bequeathed by Stalin to Soviet society, and hence that the system could not be made to work well, even under reformed party auspices, unless belief was rekindled in the minds of Soviet citizens. He realized that this would not be possible unless people could anticipate concrete benefits in the not far-off future. After decades of privation accompanied by promises of future bliss, the people must be shown that the system, meaning first of all the economic system, could be made to work for their welfare, and soon. In a literal sense, it was time to deliver the goods. Khrushchev made plain his awareness of this by sponsoring the slogan: 'The present generation of Soviet people will live under communism!' It appeared on signboards everywhere, along with a still more concrete message that a visitor could see even along dusty Siberian roads in the summer of 1958, 'We shall overtake and outstrip the USA, in per capita production of meat, milk and butter!'

This was to be accomplished in a few short years. The new programme adopted by the Twenty-Second Party Congress in 1961 formalized the theme: during the 1960s, the USSR would outstrip the United States in per capita output, make agriculture flourish, provide a sufficiency of material goods, basically meet the country's housing needs, and become the land with the shortest working day. In the 1970s, it would establish the material base for full communism, secure material and cultural abundance, make a start on distribution according to need (e.g., rent-free housing and free public transit). *'Fundamentally a communist society will be constructed in the USSR,'* the program declared in italics, leaving the construction to be 'fully completed' in 1981-90.

Many new departures in domestic policy were aimed, if not at achieving communism by 1980, then at raising depressed Soviet living standards very sharply in the near future. They included the large-scale cultivation of virgin lands in southern Siberia and northern Kazakhstan for grain production, the effort to solve the fodder problem by the cultivation of corn, the sale of the farm machinery of the state-owned machine-tractor stations to the collectives, and various changes in the structure of economic administration. The great Stalinist ministerial bureaucracies were dissolved and their officials scattered across the country into regional economic councils in an effort to decentralize the economy.

When this failed to produce the desired results, Khrushchev resorted to another organizational panacea: the party apparatus was split into industrial and agricultural divisions locally so as to compel party officialdom to concentrate upon problems of production. Under the banner of democratization, certain reforms were adopted that chipped away somewhat at the privileged status of higher officials. Ministerial salaries were reduced from extremely high Stalinist levels. The new Party Rules adopted in 1961 mandated rotation of membership in party committees, the Central Committee included. A reform affecting children of persons from the privileged class, along with others, made vocational experience mandatory between school and higher education.

Inherent in Khrushchev's reform orientation was a shift in the relationship between domestic and foreign policy that had been fundamental to the Stalinist state-building process. Stalin had harnessed the nation's energies to war preparation before 1941, war-making during the Second World War, and the Cold War after 1945. Now, under Khrushchev, the Cold War gave way to competitive coexistence in Soviet foreign policy, and domestic needs, including consumer needs, took high priority as part of the effort to make the system work. To divert resources from the military to the civilian economy, as Khrushchev tried with some success to do (for instance, by restricting the growth of the Soviet navy), it was imperative to seek relief from the relentless demands of the arms race; for this, a changed relationship with Russia's chief adversary, the United States, was essential. Hence the theme of coexistence as a complex process of competition *and* co-operation appeared in Soviet official thinking, and détente with the West became an intermittently pursued goal.

Ironically, the effort to economize on war preparation did not always lead to reduced tensions. Thus Khrushchev's missiles gamble in Cuba in 1962—a move to offset US strategic superiority cheaply, so as to allocate to civilian needs resources that would otherwise have to be invested (and were later invested) in a costly programme of intercontinental ballistic missiles—temporarily halted the search for a modus vivendi with the United States. But the nuclear test ban agreement of the following year found Khrushchev back on the road to an understanding with Washington.

Impetuous in style, given to organizational solutions, Khrushchev lacked a coherent, longer-range reform programme that would have liberated middle- and low-level management and people at large to unleash initiative untrammelled by party overseers. His economic decentralization only transferred power over the economy to regional party bosses, and the party as such could not serve as the reform instrument that he thought it could be. So, his optimistic faith in the capacity of reforms within the frame of the restored single-party system to make the economy perform productively for the benefit of the populace proved largely misplaced.

There were some successes, especially in housing construction, and the virgin lands scheme paid off temporarily. But the promises of overtaking America in per capita food production and of giant strides toward full communism in the near future were not borne out. Sino-Soviet relations deteriorated drastically during Khrushchev's tenure, while relations with the West showed no corresponding improvement. The Cuban missiles gambit backfired in a manner that was politically damaging to him at home. The military leadership undoubtedly chafed at his effort to hold back on military expenditures. Conservative hackles were raised by the liberalizing ferment that the de-Stalinization campaign aroused in the creative intelligentsia. Meanwhile, his shake-up of the party and state bureaucracy intensified the opposition in high places to his leadership and prepared the ground for the palace revolution that swept him out of power in 1964.

Before this final defeat, however, he made a last-ditch attempt to mobilize support against the conservative pro-Stalinist opposition by bringing his anti-Stalin campaign into the open at the Twenty-Second Party Congress in 1961. Here he and his party lieutenants repeated in public many of the sensational revelations that had been made behind closed doors in 1956, and the congress ended with a dramatic decision to remove Stalin's remains from the mausoleum on Red Square and erect a monument to the victims of his bloody crimes.

It is not clear whether this bluff man, not given to psychological subtleties, realized what impact the revelations about Stalin would have upon the minds and spirit of very many people in Russia. We have noted above how, with the rise of Stalin's personality cult in the 1930s, the entire official Soviet belief system became personalized in a special way: to believe in socialism and communism as the goals of Soviet society meant believing in Stalin as the Builder of Socialism and the inspired leader who was guiding Russia on its path to the ultimate goal. Now this leader stood condemned before the people as a man guilty of criminal abuse of power on an appalling scale. Many in the generation of New Believers who had come up during the heyday of Stalin's rule in the 1930s and the war years were deeply shocked and disoriented. Some resisted the blow to their beliefs; other ceased to believe in anything. To still others, the revelations about Stalin meant a welcome break with the Stalinist past and a promise of more far-reaching reforms pointing the way to a humane socialism in Russia. That point of view found expression in Roy A. Medvedev's *samizdat* work, *Let History Judge: The Origin and Consequences of Stalinism*. On the whole, however, Khrushchev's politics of de-Stalinization worked against his effort to revitalize the Communist faith in Soviet minds. By the time of his removal from power, the crisis of belief was in some ways more serious than it had been when he assumed the leadership and embarked upon his reform course.

VI

Taking over from the wilful, erratic, yet believing and reform-minded Khrushchev, Brezhnev and his associates changed the course and pace of policy. To them Khrushchev's administrative reorganizations were (to use their words) 'harebrained scheming' and fraught with a potential to destabilize the system. Taken together his reform efforts had been worse than a failure. Not only was the slowed growth of the Soviet state's military machine undesirable. Not only was the promised high economic performance not forthcoming. Unreal hopes had been aroused among the people for early economic betterment, and among intellectuals for more liberalization. This too was potentially a source of trouble. So, the new group's coming to power spelled conservative and in some ways reactionary government. To be sure, a modest managerial reform was promulgated in 1965 under Premier Alexei Kosygin's auspices, but its effect was negligible. If Khrushchev had the reform impulse without a coherent overall design, his successors lacked the impulse. Their central concern was to keep the great centralized state system that Soviet built in being. They gave Russia a regime of stabilization.

Structurally, they restored the system to something close to the form it possessed in Stalin's time, minus the autocracy at the top and police supremacy over the party hierarchy. They undid Khrushchev's organizational innovations and re-established the centralized economic ministries, enabling the ministries' official families to return from the provinces to Moscow. Khrushchev's emphasis upon vocational education for the younger generation was discarded. The nomenclature class was given to understand that it could, finally, breathe easily in the knowledge that the new masters of the state would be protective of its interests. Such was the deeper meaning of the slogan,

'Trust in cadres', which Brezhnev introduced early in his period in power.

Higher officialdom was released not simply from the perpetual fear endured under Stalin's terroristic despotism—Khrushchev had seen to that—but also from the career uncertainties, the insecurity of tenure and privilege that Khrushchev's zigzag reform course had entailed. But only the privileged section of society was so emancipated. This development bears some comparison with the 'unbinding of the nobility' in the Russia of the late eighteenth century. It affected particularly the men at top levels of political life. In place of the strong personal leadership that Khrushchev sought to furnish with the aim of change, Brezhnev offered consensual leadership for order and stability. He has been content with, and may owe his longevity in power to, his willingness to be first among equals in a truly oligarchical regime in which the various power blocs, including the military and the police, wield a heavy influence on policy.

This shift in character and orientation of the regime led to a resumption of the steady build-up of military power. The Soviet military-industrial complex was accorded resources that it had, for a time, been denied. The unsuccessful effort to overtake America in per capita production of meat, milk and butter gave way to an eventually successful one to rival her in missiles and other components of strategic military power. The formidable Soviet blue-water navy of today is largely a product of this change in policy, and an intensified search for bases in distant places has been one of the accompaniments. The focus on military strength that characterized Stalinist policy was restored in Brezhnev's time.

This meant less effort to redirect resources into expanding the civilian economy and less hope of improved conditions for the mass of non-privileged Soviet citizens. True, in the aftermath of Poland's food-price riots of late 1970 and amid portents of unrest at home, Brezhnev came before the Twenty-Fourth Party Congress in March 1971 with a programme for raising depressed Soviet living standards. But it was not made meaningful by a concomitant decision to hold back on military outlays. One possible way out was the vigorous attempt made by the Soviet government in the early 1970s to obtain Western and Japanese economic aid on a large scale through technology transfer, enlistment of Western firms in developmental work for the Soviet civilian economy, and farm imports. This called for a policy of limited détente which was formalized in the US-Soviet Moscow summit meeting of 1972.

If Khrushchev intermittently sought accommodation with the West in order to economize on military expenditures, Brezhnev seems to have done so for the opposite reason: to enable the Soviet government to provide more for the population *without* skimping on military expenditures and without making fundamental changes in the Soviet system. Above all, he needs a relationship with the United States that would ensure the regular flow of American grain to a Russia whose agricultural economy is chronically ill because of the regime's refusal to relinquish those hopelessly failed institutions, the state and collective farm.

The regime of stabilization very quickly put an end to Khrushchev's periodic *exposés* of Stalin's tyranny and imposed restraints on efforts by writers and scholars to testify in writing what Stalinism meant. Stalin himself was restored to posthumous official respectability, especially in his role as Russia's war leader in 1941-5, and further attempts to excavate the political history of his time and lay bare the facts about it were driven underground. While no real revival of the cult of Stalin occurred, a regime determined to preserve so much of his institutional and political legacy had to enforce a fictional history of his reign. For Khrushchev the raking over of the Stalinist past appears to have served as personal penance as well as a political expedient. His successors, on the contrary, seem to reason the way the character of Glebov does in the play based on the late Yuri Trifonov's novel *House on the Embankment*: 'The past is what we remember. If we stop remembering, the past will have ceased to exist, and we'll be all right.'

A post-Khrushchev crackdown on the creative intelligentsia began in earnest in 1966 with the political trial of two prominent writers, Andrei Sinyavsky and Juli Daniel, and the campaign of protest against their conviction by numbers of intellectuals inaugurated the official Russian human rights movement whose leadership was subsequently assumed by Academician Andrei Sakharov. Speaking more broadly, the dissident movement in Russia can be traced in large measure to the abandonment of regime-initiated reform under Brezhnev. So long as Russians could pin their hopes for change on the party−state's leadership, many were willing to try to work within the system and to envisage change in the system's own terms. The disappointment of those hopes after the passing of the Khrushchev era encouraged a further quest for new directions in national life.

As the dissident movement grew, especially after the Soviet military suppression of Czechoslovak Communism's reform movement in 1968, the Soviet leaders pursued an increasingly repressive policy toward people of unorthodox views. Its forms ranged from exile and imprisonment to punishment by psychiatric confinement to the hounding of individuals of talent and spirit into emigration.

The military takeover of Czechoslovakia made manifest a determination to preserve one other large part of Stalin's legacy: imperial rule in the Communist sphere, and, in particular, single-party rule on the Soviet model in Eastern and Central Europe. Unlike 1956, when the Hungarian uprising confronted Moscow with a direct prospect of the departure of a Communist-ruled nation from the Soviet sphere, the Czech reform movement presented a case of a Communist regime's internal transformation through democratization. As the Czech reformers saw it, socialism was not being abandoned; it was being realized. When the Czechoslovak and Soviet leadership groups met at the border town of Cierna not long before the Soviet invasion, Alexander Dubček offered assurances to Brezhnev that socialism was not going to be given up in Czechoslovakia. Brezhnev made his regime's philosophy brutally plain by replying, 'Don't talk to me about "socialism". What we have we hold.'[11]

Is the Brezhnev period to be described, then, as one of Stalinism's revival? Despite its reactionary tendencies, such a characterization would be wide of the mark. The renewed military build-up and associated economic priorities were far from resurrecting the Stalinist state-building process in its pattern of revolution from above. Intense Soviet competition for political influence in the Third World is a different phenomenon from the Cold War as waged by Stalin. Severe as it is, the Brezhnev regime's repressiveness is not a replica of what went on in Stalin's terror state. The country is not isolated from the world as under Stalin. There is no freedom of emigration, yet many thousands of Jews and others have been allowed to leave. There are no freedoms of speech, press and assembly, yet an unpublished and unpublishable literature of *samizdat* has its shadowy existence and there is freedom of table talk among friends in their homes. The nation is not reduced, as in Stalin's time, to communicating in frightened whispers. This list of differences could be extended.

'Not Stalin's heirs but his heritage', Josip Broz Tito of Yugoslavia is said to have remarked about the men who succeeded Stalin in power. Just so, their regime is not one of Stalinism resurgent, but of attempted custodianship of much of its legacy: the swollen centralized state with superpower status in the world enforced by military might, the hierarchical system of power, the economic supermonopoly, the state and collective farm set-up in the countryside, the foreign Communist empire, the closed world of privilege for the nomenclature class. There is, however, another great part of Stalinism's legacy that the custodians would have liked to eliminate or alleviate but cannot: the crisis of Soviet society.

VII

Economically as well as politically, the state swelled up during the Stalin era and continued doing so in the recent past so far as basic industries and military production are concerned. Second only to the United States in gross national product, Russia is first in the world in steel, pig iron and cement, second in aluminum and gold. Its aerospace establishment is America's sole competitor. It produces ample arms for its own and subject states' needs and for export far and wide. It is self-sufficient in oil production and exports oil and gas to countries of its empire and beyond.

Yet, the people in their great majority remain 'lean'. This great industrial power does not, and within the frame of the system of supermonopolistic capitalism inherited from the Stalin period cannot, provide the bulk of its population with a decent standard of living. The transfusions of foreign technology during the Brezhnev détente only somewhat eased the situation without seriously altering it. Above all, agriculture is in bad shape. It does not feed the country adequately, and the food situation grew worse during the later 1970s and start of the 1980s, save for the privileged minority. Bread alone remains cheap and plentiful, at least in urban centres.

Moscow food stores have been closed on Sundays to stem the flow of people who travel for considerable distances from the surrounding countryside on their day off in search of locally unobtainable produce that can be bought in the country's best supplied city—its capital. A resident of Russia's second city, Leningrad, when asked in the 1970s when the food situation there had been worse than it was then, answered: 'During the [World War II] blockade.' The food shortage seems to be worst in small provincial towns in central areas of the country, and even on some of the state-run farms themselves. Thus, children living on a large state farm whose produce is taken for Moscow have been observed with stomachs distended from malnutrition. There is no one cause of the deteriorated food situation, but the fundamental fact is that Soviet state-run agriculture, a legacy of Stalin's re-enserfment of the peasantry by brute terror, is an unmitigated disaster.

The shortage of factory-produced goods is not comparably acute, but neither are they, with few exceptions, in plentiful supply. Many goods are of shoddy quality, and some construction projects go for years uncompleted. An entire 'second economy' has come into being to provide goods and services not obtainable from the first. Moreover, graft and corruption abound in the official economy itself, for example, in the common practices of bribery and the temporary hiring under flimsy arrangements of so-called *shabashniki* (people who work privately for cash payment) by state managers who cannot get a job done properly by their unmotivated state-employed workers. In sum the Soviet people, in its great majority, is underfed, under-housed and under-almost-everything except under-ruled, under-policed and under-propagandized.

Since the limited targets for higher living standards, adopted by the Twenty-Fourth Party Congress in 1971, not to mention

Khrushchev's glowing promises in 1961 of communism by the 1980s, had not been fulfilled, the leadership had to radically revise (downward) its timetable for the society's advance toward communism. Brezhnev went before the Twenty-Sixth Party Congress in February 1981 and declared that it was necessary to rewrite the party programme adopted in 1961, eliminating its vision of the complete construction of a communist society during the 1980s. It was inappropriate, he explained, for the programme to stipulate specifics. Yet, the idea of the party's and society's commitment to the goal of full communism is indispensable to the regime. Upon it rested and rests the Communist Party's claim to a rightful monopoly of all power and an authoritative guiding role in all governmental and non-governmental organizations in Russia. The legitimacy of the system turns on the concept of the one party as the possessor of a true teaching, Marxism-Leninism, which holds the key to the society's (and every society's) ultimate goal of communism. If there were no such goal and no authoritative knowledge of the way to it, the party could not present itself to the people as their 'conscious vanguard' in the long march to what its propaganda has called the 'glittering heights' of communism.

Here is the context for understanding the crisis of society in contemporary Russia. Every society has its real existence in the minds of its members, their sense of constituting together an association with historical significance, of common participation in a worthwhile collective enterprise. This is what the society's sustaining myth signifies. In the Soviet case, as a consequence of all the shocks that the history reviewed here has administered, the myth no longer sustains more than a small minority, if that. People *en masse* have stopped believing in the transcendent importance of a future collective condition called 'communism'. They have stopped believing in the likelihood of the society arriving at that condition and the desirability of trying to achieve it through the leading role of the Communist Party, or through themselves as 'builders of communism', which is how the official party programme defines Soviet citizens. In a society with an official culture founded on just those beliefs, this spells a deep crisis.

The evidence for this comes in many forms, first of all the testimony of knowledgeable people. Andrei Sakharov has said:

'There are few people who react seriously anymore to slogans about building communism, although there was a time when, perhaps as a result of a certain misunderstanding, Communist slogans reflected a wish for a justice and happiness for all in the world.'[12] A Moscow intellectual, himself a party member, estimated recently that no more than one or two per cent of party members are true believers, and said: 'Most of them would not belong if they could get away with it. But they are afraid.'[13] The popular mind, as expressed in anecdotes, suspects that the leaders themselves no longer believe the slogans they repeat. According to an anecdote I heard in Russia in 1977, the country is a train headed for a destination called 'Communism', with Stalin, Khrushchev and Brezhnev in charge. When, after a time, the train grinds to a halt, Stalin orders the engineer shot and the fireman sent to a concentration camp. The train moves on and then stops again. Now it is Khrushchev's turn to give orders. He posthumously rehabilitates the executed engineer and frees the fireman from camp to drive the train. When that happens, the train moves on, then comes to a halt again. Now it is Brezhnev's turn to solve the problem, and he says: 'Let us draw the curtain and pretend the train is moving.'

The widespread failure of belief is at least one of the main causes of a variety of other, more overt phenomena indicative of a profoundly troubled society: the desire of many people, and not just Jews, to start new lives elsewhere, despite the risks and difficulties entailed; the defections of prominent cultural figures who enjoyed every advantage that high position in Soviet society could bring, such as the orchestra conductors Kirill Kondrashin and Maksim Shostakovich; the veritable epidemic of chronic alcoholism that afflicts Russia; the already mentioned shoddy work that so many perform on the job; and the near universal indifference toward what is written in the official press. These facts must be balanced, however, against the realization that Russians still have patriotic feelings and that many doubtless take a certain pride in, and are defensive about, the military might of their state and its superpower status in the world. But even this pride is intermixed with a haunting fear of another great destructive war in a society where the memory of the horrors of World War II is still alive and the authorities consciously play upon war fears in order to solidify popular support.

The failure of belief in the official myth of Soviet Communism among the many has been accompanied by a recovery of belief in new forms among some—those known in the West as the 'dissidents'. Indeed, the dissident movement might more accurately be described as *a belief movement*. For those who have joined it, whatever the divisions between them in the content of their beliefs, are united in the discovery, one way or another, of a *Rus'* that they *can* believe in as distinct from the official Russia of their daily lives. As one of them, Lev Kopelev, said on his departure from Moscow airport in December 1980, in parting words to his friends: 'I believe in Russia.' If the movement had a motto, that could be it.

The *Rus'* that Aleksandr Solzhenitsyn and his followers believe in is a resurrected pre-Bolshevik Orthodox Russia. Andrei Sakharov and some others believe in a *Rus'* convergent with open societies, one in which human rights are secured and whose government co-operates with others in addressing the great problems of conflict, population growth, resource depletion, pollution and the like on the darkening globe of the late twentieth century. Roy A. Medvedev and his fellow reformers envisage a movement from the closed Soviet system to a democratized Marxist Russia. Many people have reverted to some form of religious belief, and many in the non-Russian republics have found meaning in their own forms of nationalism.

The belief movement should not be written off as of little significance because of the relatively small numbers actively involved and the fact that most of the activists have been imprisoned or intimidated into silence or expelled from the country. Its roots lie in the very failure of belief that characterizes contemporary Soviet society. The recovery and profession of belief in new forms is a response by those individuals for whom the frequently found combination of inner unbelief and outer conformism is not a tolerable way of living. If this is so, the movement can be temporarily repressed but not stamped out.

We have credible indications that there are in the middle rungs of the Soviet establishment itself some people who have come to feel that the supermonopolistic economy has reached an impasse and that fundamental changes are essential. They are linked with the regime by the circumstances of their lives and careers—most are members of the Communist Party. They are not visionaries with recipes for Russia's salvation, but simply patriotic functionaries with training and experience in the management of an industrial society and concern over the critical condition of their society. Fedor Zniakov in the already cited memorandum describes them as an emergent 'middle class' of factory directors and others who desire liberation from 'supermonopolistic totalitarianism' so that their production units may function autonomously according to economic criteria.[14]

Alexander Yanov, writing from his extensive experience as a journalist who interviewed industrial executives before his emigration from the USSR, cites as typical the views of one important Leningrad industrialist. He and other managers, engineers, economists and the like who have learned to think independently would like, the industrialist said, to be able to *work* independently. He went on: 'They are ashamed of Soviet backwardness, its dependence on foreign technology, its humiliation. They believe that one reason for this backwardness is that their hands are tied—and tied tightly. Give them free rein, and tomorrow they will fire half the workers in their shops and pay the rest two, three, or five times more, depending on their skills (this assures them of sympathy and support from the skilled segment of the working class); they will introduce innovative, fundamentally new modes of work organization; they will be ready to experiment day and night.' The only obstacle, he added, is 'the party administration's total domination of the economy.'[15]

How widespread such views and feelings are in the ranks of middle and higher management is a matter on which we can only speculate. What can be said for certain is that those views and feelings exist. The people who harbour them have the mental freedom to think critically because, despite their linkages with the supermonopoly, their personal futures are not necessarily bound up with its perpetuation or its continuation in the present form; their talents and energies would be as needed in a post-supermonopolistic Russia as in the present one and would, indeed, have far more useful outlet. They are a potential constituency for change. The kind of change they envisage, however, is peaceful, evolutionary change, not an upheaval. Given the country's historical traditions and political culture, the *sine qua non* of liberalizing change of the sort envisaged would be strong political leadership from above.

A fact that must be faced is that the one part of the Soviet system that truly works efficiently is the police and the military establishment, which cannot make the system perform well but can keep it from being changed. As in tsarist Russia, what developed as a dynamic autocratic state authority in the state-building process remains so strong now as a force for the preservation of the system that the state can successfully block its own thorough transformation—unless leadership for change appears from above. Such leadership is out of the question so long as the Brezhnev-era aging oligarchy remains in control. Whether it will emerge when new leaders take over in the not distant future is hardly likely, but we should not rule it out as unthinkable.

VIII

Writing in European exile in the second half of the nineteenth century, the expatriate Russian, Alexander Herzen, said of the contemporary tsarist state that 'It wields power in order to wield power.' It had lost whatever spiritual *raison d'être* it had earlier possessed. By force of the whole circular movement of Russia's history in the twentieth century, that judgement once again came to apply. As a system of power expressed in military and police institutions, Soviet Communism remains strong, very strong. But as a culture it is in deep trouble, because the belief-system on which it was founded has lost vitality.

This, despite everything, puts change on Russia's agenda, although no one can say how and when it will start and what direction it will take. The great problem is how to overcome the legacy of the past, to bring about a Russian renewal peaceably and evolutionarily. That would mean a change in the relationship between state and society—not something unprecedented in the country's history. The tsar-initiated reforms of the 1860s inaugurated the gradual emancipation of Russian society from the all-encompassing tutelage of the bureaucratic state. Official Russia contracted somewhat, under its own leadership, and Russia's society emerged into the open from behind the 'shroud' with which, as Herzen put it, the state had covered it up previously. Social forces acquired some scope for self-expression. As noted earlier, this process stopped short of its natural culmination in the transformation of the state system itself.

Can such a process of society's emancipation develop in the Soviet Russia of our time? There is reason for pessimism when one considers the weight of the legacy, its deleterious effects on the popular consciousness and ethos, the strength of the repressive agencies, and the material interest of a dominant minority as a group in the system's preservation more or less as is. On the other hand, there is ground for hope when we consider the critical condition of the country as described above, and the fact that there are people among the intelligentsia, among the working classes and in the bureaucracy itself who are conscious of and troubled by the situation and see the urgent need for some kind of change in the state—society relationship. They have no better spokesman that the exiled Soviet writer, Vladimir Voinovich, who says: 'Democracy is the natural state of society, as a live organism that can stumble, be mistaken, get burned. But society has its nerve endings that register pain and force the whole organism to learn its lesson from those mistakes....No problems in the Soviet Union, economic, political, national, or religious, can be decided without democratization of the whole society. Is that possible? I don't know.'[16] The matter had best be left on that sensible note of uncertainty.

The rest of the world has a vital stake in the Russian renewal in question here. But does the West, the United States in particular, have any meaningful part to play in facilitating it? Only in an indirect way, it seems, but this indirect way is an important one. The West can, first, continue, as it has done in the recent time of détente, to accord Soviet Russia the status that it claims as a great power with worldwide interests and responsibilities. But, beyond this, it can seek incessantly to engage the Soviet Union in co-operative efforts toward constructive solutions for increasingly menacing world problems. At the same time, it can and should do everything possible to create a less tense international atmosphere in which it will be easier for Russian minds to concentrate attention, as they need to do, upon their difficult internal and imperial situation and find a way out of it.

NOTES

1. Fedor Zniakov, 'Pamiatnaia zapiska' ('Memorandum'), *Arkhiv samizdata*, document no. 374, 3. Fedor Zniakov is believed to be a pseudonym. The memorandum is dated May 1966.
2. *ibid.*
3. Mark Popovsky, *Manipulated Science: The Crisis of Science and Scientists in the Soviet Union Today*, trans. Paul S. Falla (Garden City, 1979), 179.
4. V.O. Kliuchevsky, *Kurs russkoi istorii (Course in Russian History)*, vol. III (Moscow, 1937), 11. First published in 1911.
5. Alexander Kornilov, *Modern Russian History from the Age of Catherine the Great to the End of the 19th Century*, trans. Alexander S. Kaun (New York, 1943), 18–19. First published in 1917.
6. See, for example, his speech of 4 February 1931, 'The tasks of business executives', J.V. Stalin, *Works*, vol. 13 (Moscow, 1955), 40–1.
7. Roy A. Medvedev, *On Stalin and Stalinism* (New York, 1979), 214. Based on evidence now available, Stalin's responsibility for arranging the Kirov murder as a pretext for the Great Purge is beyond reasonable doubt.
8. Thus Isaac Detscher writes that Stalin undertook 'to drive barbarism out of Russia by barbarous means', and Deutscher adds, 'The nation has, nevertheless, advanced far in most fields of its existence. Its material apparatus of production, which about 1930 was that of any medium-sized European nation, has so greatly and so rapidly expanded that Russia is now the first industrial power in Europe and the second in the world. Within little more than one decade the number of her cities and towns doubled; and her urban population grew by thirty millions. The number of schools of all grades has very impressively multiplied. The whole nation has been sent to school.' *Stalin: A Political Biography*, 2nd edn (New York, 1967), 568.
9. Nicholas Berdyaev, *The Russian Idea* (London, 1947), 9. 'Russ' (*Rus'*) is the ancient Russian word for Russia.
10. Leonard E. Hubbard, *Soviet Labour and Industry* (London, 1942), 10.
11. I have this on the authority of a person who was present and overheard Brezhnev's words.
12. 'Sakharov: a letter from exile', *The New York Times Magazine*, 8 June 1980.

13. Craig R. Whitney, 'Crisis in ideology in Soviet turns rulers to old values', *The New York Times*, 12 October 1980.
14. Zniakov, *op. cit.*, 9.
15. *Détente After Brezhnev: The Domestic Roots of Soviet Foreign Policy* (Berkeley, 1977), 29.
16. Vladimir Voinovich, 'I am not a dissident', trans. Elizabeth Tucker, *The New York Times*, 23 May 1981.

7 To Change a Political Culture: Gorbachev and the Fight for Soviet Reform

> The society is ripe for change. If we step away, the society will not agree to a return. The process must be made irreversible. If not us, then who? If not now, then when?
>
> Gorbachev in a closed meeting with a group of Soviet writers,
> June 19, 1986.

I

When Gorbachev became the party's general secretary on 11 March 1985, at the age of fifty-four, Soviet Russia acquired as its foremost leader a reform-minded man of the younger political generation that came of age after Stalin died. Soon he was speaking of the need for 'new thinking', for 'acceleration of social-economic development' and for deepseated changes amounting to a 'reformation' of the country's political culture.

So opened—as before in Russia's history, from above—the second era of attempted reform of the statist system handed down from Stalin. In some ways the new would-be reformer was better equipped to succeed than was Khrushchev in the early aftermath of Stalin's death; in others, his task was still more daunting. Better educated than Khrushchev and not personally involved in Stalin's crimes, Gorbachev also had the advantage of the lessons to be learned from Khrushchev's ultimate failure. He lacked, however, one large advantage that Khrushchev had: the ready receptivity of the great majority of the Soviet ruling elite, especially the provincial party chiefs, to the dismantling of the police-based Stalin autocracy that had plagued the elite as well as others in the despot's last years.

Khrushchev made clear by his indictment of Stalin in the unpublished Twentieth-Congress speech that he was committed to reconstituting the oligarchical rule established under Lenin and would respect the 'sacred Leninist norms' of collective leadership, which meant that he would govern by consultation with the higher political bodies. This reform was not undone after Khrushchev's fall.

Although he never became a dictator, the rough-hewn Khrushchev proved a willful and domineering leader in power. He set out to revitalize the Soviet system and make it productive for national needs, first of all the elementary need for enough food. His measures ranged from corn-growing and cultivation of virgin lands to sweeping organizational changes. One was abolition of the state-owned machine-tractor stations and sale of their machinery to the collective farms, which were over-burdened by the obligations thus placed on them.[1]

Shaped as he was by the political culture whose workings he wanted to improve, Khrushchev realized too late that his earlier reforms were not radical enough to make the Soviet economy the shining example for the world that he proudly proclaimed it could and would be. His authority sagged as his economic-amelioration schemes failed to pay off. Many influential Communists were disgruntled by reorganizations of the apparatus that upset their lives. The military establishment had its own weighty reasons, including Khrushchev's announced reduction of the armed forces by 1,200,000 men, for supporting opposition to him. The outcome was his removal from power in 1964.

Before that happened, a noteworthy new trend developed in agriculture: the appearance of the 'link' (*zveno*) or 'team' (*otriad*), a work unit consisting of several peasants, often family members, who would work a plot of land on the collective or state farm with borrowed seed and equipment, be in full charge of all operations, and be paid for their produce. Having a direct material incentive, they were far more productive than the typical large (often composed of a village population) field brigades that carry out a single farm operation like ploughing on a piece-work basis that puts a premium on fulfilling quantitative norms at the expense of quality. Khrushchev showed approval of the link movement when he told a Central

Committee session in 1961 that it was time to end 'the facelessness of the earth'. The pro-link campaign reached its highpoint in the Soviet press in 1965. Even afterwards some liberal establishment economists and pro-link journalists published books and articles advocating the link on account of the 're-personalization' of labour and 'mastery of the land' that it represented, while orthodox opponents' articles showed concern that links would develop 'as a quiet and relatively painless return to a form of functional private farming without the reconversion of land into a private market commodity.'[2] By the end of the 1960s the link movement was petering out under the conservative post-Khrushchev regime.

From an émigré scholar who covered rural affairs as a Soviet journalist in the 1960s and was an advocate of the link we have a firsthand account of the movement's rise and fall. He argues that a cleavage in the political culture, expressed in a rift between reformist and anti-reformist elements of the Soviet establishment, was involved.[3] The movement found leaders in men like Ivan Khudenko, who developed in the link a functional alternative to the bloatedly bureaucratic, hopelessly non-productive, mechanized serf system of farming practised on the huge collective and state farms. Support for the link movement came from enterprising peasants, members of the rural middle managerial stratum, and liberal intellectuals in the circle that grew up around the literary monthly *Novy Mir*, edited by Alexander Tvardovsky, a Central Committee member.[4]

Opposition to it came from a legion of rural party functionaries from whose standpoint the spread of the link was a threat to them as the existing system's guardians and supervisors. In 1962 Khrushchev moved against this powerful interest group by abolishing the rural district party committees and demoting their heads to be secretaries of party organizations in new production directorates set up in the districts. That probably hastened his day of reckoning.

In 1969, with help from D. Kunaev, party chief of the Kazakhstan Republic, Khudenko obtained permission to use a piece of wild Kazakh desert soil, Akchi, to organize an experimental farm for the growing of lucerne with the use of well-paid labour to do the work. The experiment's huge economic success was its political undoing. The experimental farm was shut down, Khudenko was arrested in 1973, fought back at his trial by accusing his accusers, and died in prison in 1974.[5] His fate wrote a temporary epitaph for the efforts of free-thinking, concerned citizens to change the politico-economic culture of the deeply ailing Soviet countryside.

In Khrushchev's successor Leonid Brezhnev, the party-state acquired a quintessential *apparatchik* at its head, one who kept faith with his motto of 'trust in cadres'. The bureaucratic elite now acquired, along with the security of person that Khrushchev brought to it, the security of tenure that his restlessly reforming ways denied it. Brezhnev was a consensus leader, and helped ensure by his promotion of mediocrities to high position that the consensus would be a conservative one. Most of Khrushchev's reorganizations were quickly undone. 'Developed socialism', an ideological formula that Brezhnev introduced in 1971 to describe where the USSR supposedly now was on the road to complete communism, came into prominence as a rationale for complacency, suggesting that nothing but minor tinkering was needed to perfect the system. Meanwhile, Brezhnev's administration tolerated all manner of shady dealings that ran the gamut from the barely legal to the outright illegal in the underground second economy.[6]

Under Brezhnev, Stalin's one-time cowed service nobility became a master class, freed not only from the ministrations of the secret police but also from worry that some new 'harebrained scheme' would disrupt their comfortable lives. No matter that the bulk of the people lived poorly, that open expression of noncomformist thought was impossible, that the economy had growing problems, that the external situation was in some respects getting worse. The men of the political elite and their families finally had a good life, with their network of closed special shops and clinics, ample opportunity to place their children in higher educational institutions and desirable careers, little or no danger that anyone would raise a critical voice against them in the workplace, and little or no risk of punishment for machinations that ranged from bribetaking to smuggling of goods from abroad and large-scale embezzling. Their consolidation in power under Brezhnev was going to make the work of a new reform leader extremely difficult.

II

Mikhail Sergeevich Gorbachev was born of peasant stock in Privol'noye, a village in the agriculturally rich North Caucasian territory of Stavropol. In the year of his birth, 1931, Stavropol, like most rural regions of the country, was gripped by the great famine caused by Stalin's terroristic collectivization. Undoubtedly he heard about the famine's horrors while growing up. He studied law in 1950-55 at Moscow University, where he met a philosophy student, Raisa Titorenko, whom he later married. After graduating, he returned to Stavropol where for twenty years he worked his way up the political ladder, meanwhile earning a second degree as an agronomist-economist from the Stavropol Agricultural Institute.[7]

By 1968 Gorbachev had moved up from work in the territory's Komsomol organization to become second secretary of its party committee, responsible for agriculture. Two years later he was its first secretary and, as the top-ranking leader of an important province, in line for membership in the all-union party Central Committee, to which he was elected at the Twenty-Fourth Party Congress in 1971. His tr nsfer to Moscow to take the post of Central Committee secretary responsible for agriculture came in 1978. In the following year he became a candidate member of Brezhnev's Politburo and in 1980, at forty-nine, a full member, and by far the youngest one.

The post-Brezhnev struggle over Soviet change was shaping up before Brezhnev, increasingly infirm in his final years, died in November 1982. His regime of stabilization had succeeded at a steep price: overall economic performance slowed; agriculture's failure grew more manifest; all manner of graft and corruption grew unprecedentedly rampant, involving even members of Brezhnev's family; public listlessness deepened; still more people turned to the bottle; and new external danger loomed with the threatened emplacement of US Pershing 2 and cruise missiles in Europe. Some senior Politburo members became very worried about the situation. Among them were Foreign Minister Andrei Gromyko, Defense Minister Dmitri Ustinov, and a career party official, Yuri Andropov, whose long stint as KGB chief under Brezhnev had made him probably the Soviet official best informed about the factual state of things in the USSR.

In the contest for power Andropov bested Brezhnev's long-time aide and choice for the succession, Konstantin Chernenko. This happened, it seems, primarily because Chernenko, a man of limited ability and already in poor health, was so sorely lacking in the capacity to provide effective leadership in the country's difficult situation, whereas Andropov's qualifications were strong. Although his own health unexpectedly gave out in 1983, Andropov managed in his short period as leader to get the country started on a new course. The policies he pursued were largely disciplinary, with a drive against venality in high places and absenteeism in the workplace.

But there were other steps too. Andropov approved an economic experiment whose aim was to decentralize planning in plants of five industrial ministries, giving their managers power to make many decisions normally made by the higher economic bureaucracy. He sponsored a new law on work collectives that sought to give industrial workers some say in management decisions affecting them by obliging plant managements to consult them on such matters as dismissals, housing allocation, and shop-floor managers' appointments. In keeping with this move, Andropov reintroduced into Soviet discourse the Russian term *glasnost*, meaning public openness, which was a reformist watchword in the 1850s and 1860s and was used by Lenin in the early Soviet period. Andropov told a Central Committee session that more *glasnost'* in the work of party and state organs would bring them closer to popular needs.[8]

Unlike his predecessors Brezhnev and Khrushchev, Andropov was something of an intellectual with a capacity for analysis that, combined with his desire for change, worked to the advantage of reform-minded intellectuals in the Soviet establishment. The Novosibirsk Institute of Economics and Industrial Organization, then headed by Abel Aganbegyan, is one of their centres. In April 1983, a section head in that institute, the sociologist Tatyana Zaslavskaya, gave a report on the economy to a closed seminar held under high auspices: the party Central Committee's economic departments, Gosplan, and the Academy of Science. Andropov's interest in openness did not extend to having the report published, but one of seventy numbered copies circulated among insiders was leaked to the foreign press in Moscow and found its way West.[9]

In it Zaslavaskaya traced the deteriorating economic situation to the basic fact that the now greatly expanded and complex Soviet economy was still operating within the politico-economic culture forged in the 1930s for a relatively primitive country: centralized state management of the economy, with predominance of administrative over economic methods, absence of a market for production, limits on enterprises' economic rights, hence also on their economic responsibility for results, and restrictions on people's informal economic activities. Under this system in its formative stage, she wrote, workers were coerced—for example by the late-1930s laws making it a criminal offence to miss or be late for work—into functioning as 'cogs' in the economic mechanism (Zaslavskaya used Stalin's term without giving him as its source). But in the different situation of today, the system fails to motivate the workers. Results are 'an indifferent attitude to the work performed and its low quality, social passivity, a low value attached to labour as a means of self-realization, an intense consumer orientation, and a rather low level of moral discipline.' Likewise, the centralized system penalizes the more talented, bold and energetic managers while rewarding the more obedient ones who mechanically follow orders from above.

The report offered no design for the needed new economic mechanism beyond saying that so complex an economy can no longer be regulated from a single centre and that working people must be given 'a sufficiently wide margin of freedom of individual behaviour'. But its diagnosis of the system as severely sick ('this mechanism is "tuned" not to stimulate but to thwart the population's useful economic activity') carried an implicit prescription for radical economic reform. This conclusion is supported by its further argument—ideologically heterodox in affirming the existence of conflicting group or class interests in Soviet society—that changes of the sort needed were sure to be opposed by groups whose interests would be adversely affected. These included the multitude of officials in economic ministries, trusts and the like 'who at present occupy numerous "cosy niches" with ill-defined responsibilities but thoroughly agreeable salaries'; some officials at higher levels who would fear the greater demands made upon them by economic as distinguished from administrative methods of management; and those more apathetic, passive and less qualified workers and technicians who would shun the enhanced responsibilities inherent in expanded rights. Given this warning of the difficulty of altering cultural patterns in the economy, together with the absence of a clearcut design for the needed new economic mechanism and of a strategy for bringing it into being, the Novosibirsk report was far from a plea to Andropov for hasty action on the economic-reform front. He confined himself to the modest reform experiment mentioned above.

His main contribution to coming reform was in political appointments. According to the independent minded Soviet historian Roy A. Medvedev, Andropov deliberately sought out able officials dissatisfied with the situation under Brezhnev for promotion to high office.[10] Among those whom he advanced were Yegor Ligachev and Nikolai Ryzhkov, who joined him on the Central Committee Secretariat, Vitaly Vorotnikov, who became head of the Russian Republic's government, Viktor Chebrikov, who became chief of the KGB, and Lev Zaikov, who would become a Central Committee secretary later on. But his most consequential act was the choice of Gorbachev as his protégé and successor-to-be.

What probably impressed Andropov about Gorbachev, apart from the younger man's commitment to change, was his unusual capacity for fulfilling two cardinal policy-making functions of an effective leader: incisive analysis of problem-situations and devising creative ways of dealing with them. In his March 1985 Central Committee speech nominating Gorbachev for the post of general secretary, Gromyko said:

if a scientific session were taking place in this room now, everybody would probably say: this man is able to approach problems analytically. That's the honest truth. He can take a question apart into elements before drawing a conclusion. Not only is he good at analyzing problems; he also draws generalizations and conclusions. Politics sometimes requires not just that questions be broken into components—that way they'll lie motionless—but that conclusions be drawn for incorporation into our policy. More than once he's shown this in meetings of the Politburo and the Central Committee Secretariat.[11]

Gromyko gave no examples of Gorbachev's ability to size up problems and devise solutions. But later events suggest that in Gorbachev's mind at that earlier time was a diagnosis of the general Soviet situation as critically unsatisfactory, and various ideas on what might be done about it.

Andropov's unexpectedly early fatal illness and his death in February 1984 gave the Brezhnevites on high a breather. A deal was apparently struck whereby the already ailing Chernenko would become a short-term general secretary on the understanding that Gorbachev, as chosen leader-to-be, would gain more experience, including foreign experience (he visited Great Britain in late 1984) in preparation for becoming general secretary in the near future.[12] The reform impulse slackened in the following months. But the emphysemic Chernenko was the conservative faction's last gasp. Had he held on through the scheduled new party congress, a conservative stamp could have been placed on policy for the coming five-year period. But he died on March 10, 1985. Even then the Brezhnevite Politburo old guard reportedly made a last-ditch attempt to cling to power by nominating one of their number, the Moscow party chief Viktor Grishin, for the top position. The move failed, and Gorbachev got the job.[13]

He lost no time in coming out as a leader for change. Addressing a Central Committee session a few weeks after becoming the general secretary, he called for 'a qualitatively new state of society, and that in the broadest sense of the word'. The first order of business, he made clear, was economic reform, and the Novosibirsk report's influence was obvious in what he had to say about desirable changes from administrative to economic methods of management.[14] Following up on his assertion that the administrative apparatus must be reduced, the Soviet government formed an agricultural super-ministry, the State Committee for the Agro-Industrial Complex (*Gosagroprom*) in place of five ministries that it abolished: agriculture, fruit and vegetable farming, rural construction, meat and dairy industry, and food industry.[15] This structural reform, forerunner of others to come, freed some thousands of ministry officials to take jobs closer to production. Vsevelod Murakhovsky, who had succeeded Gorbachev in 1978 as party chief in Stavropol, was shifted to Moscow to head

Gosagroprom and appointed a first deputy prime minister.

Gorbachev linked his economic reform plans with a drive to combat the mass scourge of alcohol abuse. Going far beyond the modest beginning in this direction under Andropov, his administration introduced a set of measures short of outright prohibition.[16] They raised the legal drinking age from 18 to 21, ordered reductions over three years in alcoholic beverage production (Gorbachev reported in September 1986 that vodka sales had dropped by 38 per cent since August 1985), curtailed the number of liquor outlets and restricted their working hours, set up an all-union temperance society to foster non-drinking habits (it had 35 million members nationwide by summer of 1986), commanded party and other officials, much to the chagrin of many, to be exemplars of sobriety, and mandated efforts for leisure-time enrichment by creating art, music, literature, chess and physical fitness groups in plants, farms and other institutions. Although these measures deprived the state of billions of rubles in annual profit from the liquor trade, they promised far greater benefits in work efficiency, reduced fatalities from liquor-caused injuries, a lowering of the high divorce rate, and reduced public health costs. No initiative taken by Gorbachev in his early period in power so clearly cast him in the role of a leader for change of one of the country's most widespread real cultural patterns.

While developing his economic reform plans with advice from Abel Aganbegyan, who was moved from Novosibirsk to Moscow to head a new Commission to Study Productive Forces, Gorbachev presided over a renovation of the higher elite. A new political cohort, led by men of Andropov's choosing, came to high power. By mid-1986 only four of the fourteen full members of Brezhnev's 1981 Politburo—Gorbachev, Gromyko, Kunaev and V. Shcherbitsky, the party chief of the Ukraine, remained members; Ustinov, who would have remained, had died in 1984. New full members included Ryzhkov, now head of the Soviet government, Ligachev, Vorotnikov, Chebrikov, and Eduard Shevardnadze, the new Soviet foreign minister in place of Gromyko, who was now titular head of state as chairman of the Supreme Soviet presidium. Five of seven Politburo candidate members and six of seven Central Committee secretaries—one of them, for a change, a woman—

had joined these bodies under Gorbachev. Lower down, the turnover was far less sweeping but heavy. As reconstituted by the Twenty-Seventh Party Congress in early 1986, the 307-person party Central Committee had 135 new members. Nearly a third of the 157 regional party chiefs had received their appointments during Gorbachev's first year as general secretary.[17] New people had also appeared among the deputy chairmen of the USSR Council of Ministers and at the head of various ministries and corresponding republic agencies.

The turnover was not merely generational although not a few of those displaced were older persons. Nor was it solely motivated by Gorbachev's undoubtedly strong need to solidify his power base. His desire to foster change also figured in it. When a leader sets out to change a long established political culture, he must (if he is to succeed) advance people who in their modes of thinking and working already are, like himself, exponents of the kinds of change intended—in this case persons of drive and ability who will not take bribes, who are not alcoholics and lovers of easy living, who will not surround themselves with obsequious mediocrities, who see the imperative need to change old Soviet ways, to root out official corruption and inertia, to set aside reform-blocking ideological formulae like the description of the USSR as a land of already 'developed socialism', and to give a hearing to criticism from below. By the influence they exert from high position, by the force of example and persuasion, they can serve as agents of cultural change.

The renovated political hierarchy of late 1986 was no phalanx of reliable Gorbachev supporters. He was at most *primus inter pares* in a Politburo that decides contentious issues by majority vote and not always according to the general secretary's desires.[18] At lower levels, including the Central Committee and its departments, the military and police establishments, the ministerial economic bureaucracies, the foreign-affairs and foreign-trade ministries, the cultural, educational, scholarly, trade-union and Komsomol bureaucracies, there were no few Brezhnev-era holdovers and unregenerate neo-Stalinist devotees of statism along with older or newly advanced reform-minded people. All these sectors of the bureaucratic party-state were still, in varying degree, strongholds of the old political culture.

What Gorbachev's advent to power betokened, then, was struggle for reform. He himself was well aware of this. 'All our cadres have been given the chance to understand the demand of the moment and reform themselves', he said extemporaneously in Leningrad in May 1985. 'He who can't or doesn't want to do this—let him go away.'[19] One can imagine many of those to whom the message was addressed saying among themselves: 'Not if we can help it! Better that you and your kind go away!'

III

When the Twenty-Seventh Soviet Party Congress opened in Moscow on February 25, 1986, it was Gorbachev who gave the keynote address and set his reformer's mark upon it. He did so, first, by defining the state of the Soviet Union as unsatisfactory. For some years, he said, the country had been in a 'turning-point situation' about which nothing was done, mainly because of 'subjective' factors (i.e., lack of requisite leadership—R.T.). Signs of stagnation occurred owing to inertia, bureaucracy, and paralysis of administrative procedures. Although changes were called for, the central and local organs showed a peculiar psychology of 'seeking improvement without changing anything'.[20]

On the economy Gorbachev said that particular improvements would not do; a 'radical reform' was needed. He cautioned, however, that the necessary revamping of the economic mechanism was just getting started, that it would take time and effort, that difficulties might arise, and that there was no guarantee against mistakes along the way. Directions in which change should proceed were: an overdue shift from extensive economic growth to intensive, i.e., technological modernization of existing plant; ending the practice of interference by the centre in the day-to-day operations of lower-level economic units; making enterprises financially self-sustaining, their income becoming directly dependent on the effectiveness of their work; giving them the right independently to sell surplus output and unused equipment and supplies; making prices into an active instrument of economic and social policy; shifting from administrative to economic methods of management throughout the economy; having Gosplan focus on long-range planning; and adopting a new financial policy under which losses by unprofitable enterprises, ministries and regions would no longer be covered by profits of well functioning ones. In justification of the call to adopt economic methods of management, Gorbachev said it was time to 'overcome the prejudice against *commodity-monetary relations*'. How deviant such a position seemed to Soviet conservatives quite recently, and must still seem, is shown by a 1984 statement in which the then editor of the party's theoretical journal *Kommunist*, Richard Kosolapov, assailed unnamed proponents of market-oriented reforms for 'commodity-monetary romanticism'.[21]

New methods were needed in the agrarian sector, said Gorbachev, and the key to success was giving people incentive to work actively, with professional skill and urge to innovate. The contract system, under which plots of collective- or state-farm land are allotted to work teams (brigades, links, or families) for the contractual period, was going to become widespread. In effect, Gorbachev here endorsed a first step toward revival of the link reform whose hopeful beginning and unhappy previous ending have been recounted above. Second, he said that a *prodnalog* or tax in kind (this cornerstone of Lenin's NEP in 1921 freed the peasants to market their produce after paying a state tax in food products) would be applied under 'contemporary conditions' by setting for collective and state farms fixed five-year procurement targets not subject to annual upward shifts, with freedom to sell all surpluses as well as some part of the planned amounts of potatoes, fruit and vegetables. To resurrect the idea and practice of *prodnalog*, even in so limited a form, is to extend food sale at market-determined prices beyond what has long been allowed.[22]

In another departure from orthodoxy, Gorbachev came out strongly for encouraging cooperatives, which should become widespread, he said, in the production and processing of goods, in housing, orchard and garden construction, and in trade and services. He also called for 'full clarity in the question of cooperative property'. Wherein such clarity was lacking he did not say. But ideologically sophisticated people could see that he was challenging the tenet of Stalinist statism that ranks cooperative below state property in a socialist society and holds that progress toward full communism dictates transformation of what remains of the former into the latter. Had Gorbachev wanted and been ready to confront the doctrinal issue head on, he could have shown that for Marx and Engels the state as such, hence also state property, has *no place* in a fully socialist society, not to mention a communist one, and that this is a position which Lenin upheld and to which he gave considered expression when he wrote late in life that 'the system of civilized cooperators is the system of socialism'.[23] In a further dig at Stalinist statism, Gorbachev said that 'Ministries, departments and territorial organs are not proprietors of the means of production, but merely institutions of state administration responsible to society for effective use of what belongs to the people.' In Stalin's time he could have been sent away for making a statement like that.

Attacking 'technocratic approaches' to economic problems, Gorbachev linked his call for economic reforms with the need for a new social policy of observing the 'principle of social justice' and using welfare measures to provide people with work incentives. They could not be expected to work well if their welfare needs continued to go unattended, as by the central and local authorities' practice of following the 'residual principle' in allocating resources to living conditions and facilities for leisure-time pursuits. Minimum pensions for pensioners and invalids should be raised. Every family must be assured a separate apartment or house by the year 2000. Public participation in decision making must be made meaningful.

Gorbachev spelled out this last theme in numerous ways. The three-year-old law on work collectives not yet having produced the expected results, the basic mechanism for making its norms a reality must be improved by broadening the range of problems on which work collectives' decisions are final and enhancing the role of general meetings of workers and employees, in part by setting up 'councils of worker collectives' in the enterprises to function in the intervals between general meetings. Women's councils should be revived in work collectives. The range of questions resolvable by state organs only with participation or prior consent of trade union, youth and women's organizations must be widened. Workers must not be kept ignorant of their plant's plans as they may be now, or see their suggestions go unconsidered. A law must be drawn up to provide for nation-wide discussions and referendums on major issues and the same on draft decisions of local Soviets. Governing must not be a privilege of a narrow circle of professionals.

With the aim of making public participation in political life meaningful, Gorbachev went on in the congress speech to issue a resounding call for expanding *glasnost*'. Otherwise, he said, there was no way for people to become actively involved in administration. To fears being expressed—he did not say by whom—that airing of flaws and difficulties was unwise, he answered that the need was for truth and that openness works against those who do shoddy work and cover it up, hence was 'a point of departure for the psychological reorientation of our cadres'.

In no sphere was new thinking so evident in Gorbachev's congress speech as international affairs, superpower relations in particular. Not long before the congress he extended the unilateral Soviet nuclear test moratorium started on the Hiroshima anniversary, 6 August 1985, and issued a programme of arms-control measures including a fifty per cent cut of Soviet and US strategic nuclear weapons in the next five to eight years on condition that both states renounced space-strike weapons; total elimination of medium-range Soviet and US missiles in Europe; agreement, initially by the USSR and USA, to end all nuclear test explosions, with provision for on-site verification as needed; and reduction and eventual freezing of both sides' conventional forces in central Europe.[24]

Gorbachev's congress speech set forth the main tenets of the 'new thinking' in international affairs. Innovatively for a Soviet leader, he spoke of 'global problems', such as conservation of resources, and of the 'interdependence of the states of the world community'. In both contexts the implication was transcendence of the old pattern of Soviet official thinking which stressed a 'class' approach to world problems. For global problems in an interdependent world of class—diverse nation—states, an internationally cooperative and in that sense supra-class approach is dictated. Not surprisingly, then, Gorbachev spoke of 'the aim being not confrontation, but dialogue and mutual understanding'.

He grounded the possibility of improving US-Soviet relations on the novel view that, even though the United States remains 'the locomotive of militarism', it has 'genuine national interests' not identical with those of its military—industrial complex. That distinction is of crucial importance for Gorbachev's thesis—a centrepiece of the speech—that the time has come when Soviet and American security 'can only be mutual'. Elaborating, he said:

The supreme wisdom does not lie in being concerned exclusively about yourself, much less to the other side's disadvantage. The need is for all to feel equally secure, for fears and alarms of the nuclear age can give rise to unpredictability in policy and concrete acts. It's very important to take account of the time factor's critical importance. The appearance of new mass-destruction weapon systems reduces the time, restricts the possibilities of taking political decisions affecting war and peace in times of crisis.

Such thinking in mutual-security terms seems to underlie some of Moscow's subsequent actions, including its effort to make far-reaching arms-control progress with Washington at the Iceland summit meeting in October 1986, and its signing of an accord at the 35-nation Stockholm conference on confidence-building measures by which it agreed to on-site inspections by foreign observers in areas of military manoeuvres and to six-week advance notice of manoeuvres involving as many as 13,000 men or 300 tanks.

In the congress speech Gorbachev repeatedly spoke of *perestroika*. What does this talismanic term of his mean? Foreign observers normally translate it 'restructuring' or 'reconstruction' and it does mean that—but also more. According to the Soviet Academy of Sciences' Russian-language dictionary (1983 edition), *perestroika* takes its meaning from the corresponding verb, which signifies: 'To change the procedure of one's work, the direction of one's activity, of one's views'. Gorbachev's usage has this larger sense of a reordering, reorientation, or reformation.

Thus we find him referring in the congress speech to the need for a '*perestroika* of thinking', one which demands 'constant review and renewal of established stereotypes of administration'. In other passages he called for a '*perestroika* of the economic mechanism', a '*perestroika* of higher and secondary special education', a '*perestroika* of party work', a 'radical *perestroika* of the management mechanism', and, as already noted, a 'psychological *perestroika* of our cadres'. His *perestroika* is best translated 'reformation'. His Politburo colleague, Ligachev, gave it this larger meaning when he declared in a later speech in the Soviet Academy of Sciences that science, too, is in need of a *perestroika*, meaning 'not minor, partial improvements, but a radical change in the way of acting, a radical change in all spheres of activity'.[25]

In so far as the envisioned Soviet reformation includes a drive to root out official corruption in the party-state, an appeal to original sources of doctrinal authority, and a stress on the individual's own responsibility for self-reform in work and private life, comparison with the Reformation in early modern Europe, while distant, is not altogether far-fetched. In event of success, Gorbachev's reformation would mean a pervasive within-system reform of what, in this book, have been called real culture patterns, and to some extent of ideal patterns as well; in other words, a deep change of customary ways of thinking and acting in institutions and common situations in Soviet society and in the government's way of thinking and acting in internal and external policy.

Many citizens, not being versed in culture theory, have been puzzled by Gorbachev's persistent demands for a *perestroika* of one thing and another. Speaking in Khabarovsk during a swing through the Soviet Far East in July 1986, he admitted this: 'Sometimes people ask, just what is this abstruse thing *perestroika*, how is one to understand it, "what do you eat it with". We're all really "in favour", but we don't know how to go about it'. That's what many are saying, Gorbachev went on. Responding, he gave it as the Central Committee's and Politburo's view that everyone should start with *perestroika* of himself, 'by determining his position as a citizen, by activizing his political and work activity, taking on more responsibility for the work and its end results'. He said that the reformative process should go on simultaneously 'from above and from below', that it should take place at all echelons of administration and policy, and should be geared in with reformation in work collectives. And after referring to the transition to NEP in Lenin's time, he said:

Today we are speaking of transformations on no less a scale. The present *perestroika* covers not only the economy but also all other aspects of social life: social relations, the political system, the spiritual–ideological sphere, the style and methods of party work, of all our cadres' work. *Perestroika* is a big word. I would equate it with the word revolution.[26]

A cultural revolution, in the sense of a fundamental transformation of a great many customary Soviet ways of acting and thinking, is what he apparently had in mind in drawing this equation.

He had acknowledged this project's immense difficulty when, in June 1986, four months after the party congress, he addressed a plenary session of the party Central Committee. The reformation was just beginning, he said then, and was so far proceeding slowly and 'with stoppages'. In too many enterprises the old custom of end-of-the-month storming on the motto, 'The plan at any price', was still in force. Redistribution of rights and responsibilities between ministries and plants was going very painfully. People were still influenced by old approaches in offices, plants, scientific institutes and political organs. Executives who talked about openness and participation but allowed no real changes to take place were creating an 'illusion' of reformation. Some heads of central departments were desperately clinging to their old rights of command despite the fact that under present-day conditions it was inadmissible to decide all questions from the centre.

In this same speech Gorbachev singled out for discussion a revealing example of a real culture pattern that resists change: the *val* or gross-output measure of a unit's performance under the planning system. As the 'gross' is measured in rubles, and bonuses are paid for overfulfillment, it is in every plant's or ministry's interest to maximize its monthly gross, even by such means as boosting prices or making poor-quality or useless goods or, in the case of a transport organization, running up a monthly mileage far higher than needed to deliver all loads:

in order to increase the 'gross', use is often made of expensive materials, heavier machines are produced, more ton-kilometers are run up, etc. We're fighting for efficiency, but look what a truly stupid situation executives wind up in: if they've made something more economically, they are rebuked for producing too little in ruble terms; if they've innovated and thereby economized on resources, they've thereby put the plant or even the branch of industry at a disadvantage.

By way of experiment, Gorbachev went on, some ministries' transport agencies received plan incentives to deliver loads at minimal cost rather than to increase ton-kilometers, and results were excellent. But instead of adopting the new work method, higher Gosplan officials fought tooth and nail to preserve the 'gross' system. The time has come, he said, to chop through this 'gross knot'.[27]

Another serious obstacle to the reformation, Gorbachev said, was the persistent addiction to bureaucratic paperwork that causes local party and other officials to thwart initiatives from below and innovative people with new ideas. For example, the head of a scientific-research institute in Cherkassy in the Ukraine designed new machine tools and then, when appointed acting director in 1985 of a local plant in need of such tools, organized their production without awaiting formal authorization. Officials complained that he had acted without instructions. He was removed and the case referred for prosecution. The Central Committee and Procurator General found no case against him. But the local party bureau expelled him from the party; and when some party members sent a letter to the Twenty-Seventh Party Congress protesting this, it didn't reach Moscow because 'local organs' removed it from the letter box.[28]

Time and again Gorbachev hammered in his speeches on the necessity of a new social policy to give people work incentive by improving their living conditions and making it worth their while to work well. To 'activize the human factor' was his very Soviet way of expressing this. It pitted him against the many managers who still operate according to the old culture pattern of subordinating all else to plan fulfillment on the plan-at-any price principle. For this cultural innovator the price of wretched conditions for the working man was too high—too high, indeed, for the economy itself. 'On the whole, comrades', he said in his Khabarovsk speech after observing that in the nearby big industrial center of Komsomolsk-on-the-Amur the waiting time for housing space is ten to fifteen years, 'it must be said that the old tradition remains in force: fulfill the production plan, build, expand, and how the working man lives—that's for some managers a secondary question'. They should help solve that question by allocating factory resources to housing construction.

Speaking back home in Stavropol a full seven months after the party congress, Gorbachev acknowledged that the reformation was still not going as swiftly as desired. It must take place first of all through each person himself, through his mind and conscience, and without fail through his personal interest. To arouse creative innovation and achieve an intensive economy, not just a new system of management would be needed but also a wide and effective democracy in public life. The right way was not to drive people on by heavy-handed pressure, not to club them into fulfilling obligations, but to give each an incentive to do his best and an understanding that his work is important not just for himself and his family but for the farm, the factory, the region, the country. That wouldn't come without a struggle against everything routine and outworn. 'For the *perestroika* we will have to fight. Resolutely, without compromise. All together and each individually.'[29]

In the pre-congress public discussion of the draft new party programme that was to be adopted by the Twenty-Seventh Congress, some citizens' letters to editors showed that the fight would be a very hard one. *Pravda* published extracts from letters in an article called 'A Cleansing'. One came from a worker in Tula region named Ivanov, who said that 'between the Central Committee and the working class there still sways a slow-moving, inert and swampy "party-administrative stratum" that isn't very keen on radical changes. They only carry party cards, but have long ago stopped being Communists. They only expect privileges from the party and are in no hurry to give back to the people their energies or their knowledge.' Another came from a party member in Kazan, N. Nikolaev, who wrote:

Speaking of social justice, one cannot close one's eyes to the fact that party, Soviet, trade union, economic and even Komsomol leaders sometimes objectively deepen social inequality by using all kinds of special buffets, special shops, special hospitals and the like. Sure we have socialism, and everybody should receive according to his labour. Let leaders have higher money wages, without levelling. But the other privileges ought not to be. Let the boss go with everybody else to an ordinary shop and stand in the same line—maybe then they will soon get rid of the lines, which make everyone sick. Only it's doubtful that those who profit from special benefits will give up their privileges. For this, a law and a thorough purge of the apparatus is necessary.

To the demand for a thorough purge the article's writer responded that mass purges are a thing of the past for the party, and: 'This is not a purge, but precisely a cleansing'.[30] Nevertheless, the article's appearance must have aroused some consternation in the inert and swampy stratum, and reassurance was needed. At the party congress two weeks later, Central Committee Secretary Ligachev alluded to the piece by saying in his speech that some papers, not excluding the *Pravda* editors, 'got ahead of themselves' in the pre-congress discussion.[31]

Pravda's chief editor, Viktor Afanasiev, reportedly received a reprimand for 'Cleansing'. While in Moscow in May 1986 this writer heard that afterwards he phoned Gorbachev and asked whether he should resign his post. 'Why do that?', Gorbachev was said to have answered: 'I liked the article'.

IV

For all the impact that top leaders have had in Russia's times of change, support from high and low, or the lack of it, has been decisive in the end. Gorbachev, it was suggested above, has sought support especially from persons who, like himself, already are, or want to be, exponents of change. The state being a party-state, he must first seek out supporters of reformation among party officials, and has done so.

An exemplary success was the choice of Boris Yeltsin, a man from Sverdlovsk in the Urals, to replace the ousted Grishin as first secretary of the Moscow Party Committee, in which capacity Yeltsin also became a candidate member of the Politburo. His speech at the party congress in February 1986 stirred intense public interest. Speaking the day before Ligachev did, and not unlike the Ivanov and Nikolaev of 'Cleansing', he said:

Why has the obviously alien word 'stagnation' appeared in our party lexicon? Why for so many years have we failed to extirpate bureaucratism, social injustice and abuses from our life. *Why even now does the demand for radical changes sink in an inert stratum of time-servers with party cards?* In my view, a main reason is that some party leaders lack the courage to assess the situation and their own roles objectively and in good time, to speak the truth, even if bitter but the truth, to view each issue or action, their own, a work colleague's or higher leaders', not in terms of one's interest at the moment but politically.

He called for changes in the structure of the Central Committee Secretariat, some of whose departments duplicated ministries, Gosplan or the Council of Ministers, causing, he said, years of delay in coordinating. Why had nobody in the Central Committee seen the degeneration of leaders in Uzbekistan (whose deceased Brezhnev-era leader, Rashidov, has been posthumously exposed for corruption—R.T.), Kirgizia and various towns and provinces? No posts and no office-holders should be above criticism. If the delegates wanted to ask why he hadn't said these things at the previous party congress in 1981, his frank answer was that he didn't then have the courage and the political experience.[32]

As Moscow's party leader, Yeltsin acted in ways reflecting his new orientation. On 11 April 1986, some three months after taking over the new post, he met with Moscow party propaganda workers. He revealed that the capital, with a population now of 8.7 million, had 2.5 million in need of housing. The historical face of the city had been disfigured by the demolition of 2,200 historical monuments since 1935. Others were in pitiful shape or being misused. The Energy Ministry, which was using the church where Pushkin was married as office space, had agreed to move the offices after he went there with the minister. The city was short of 5,000 taxi or bus drivers while 200,000 people sat around jobless. Drunkenness had been chased off the streets into the home, where household crimes had gone up. Prices were way too high in the peasant food markets; cooperative shops should be set up in them to compete by selling better-grade food at reasonable prices. The city fathers were engaged in window-dressing: all is fine, we're the best in the world; there's no need to expose Moscow's problems. Whoever continued to think that way should leave his job and get out.

Yeltsin responded to many of 300 written questions, most unsigned, after the talk, revealing—in response to one about whether Moscow party officials were giving up any privileges—that their special store had been closed down and that they were no longer being allowed to use official cars for personal needs. Did he see ordinary citizens, one questioner asked. Yes, he recently saw a young woman shop clerk who explained to him the system of kickbacks operating in the trade network, where in recent months 800 store managers have been arrested. 'We dig and dig, and the bottom of this filthy well is still not visible. We're trying to uncover criminal links, to isolate the ringleaders and put honest and gifted party people in their jobs and then gradually probe from there. It's going to be a long and hard job, but we are resolved to dig out this filth.' And there were unsigned messages illuminating resentful resistance to reformation. One said: 'Khrushchev already tried to make ordinary labourers out of us. He didn't succeed and you won't either. We've stolen in the past and we'll steal in the future,' to which Yeltsin answered: 'Comrades, we can only break this circle by our common efforts.' Another said: 'You have Napoleonic plans; what do you think you're up to? Gorbachev simply needed his own man. Go back to Sverdlovsk before it's too late,' to which some in the audience cried 'shame' and Yeltsin replied, 'Don't worry comrades. I don't think this question comes from someone in the audience. It is written by a sick person.'[33]

How many Yeltsin party types there are to think and act anew in their posts and press vigorously for change against resistant representatives of the old cultural ways, and how many younger party people advanced to responsible positions will emulate him and with what results, is for the future to show. Meanwhile, Gorbachev has turned to another stratum of society for active support in the reformation: the professional and creative intelligentsia. He has gone much farther in this direction than Khrushchev did when he encouraged Tvardovsky to use the literary journal *Novy Mir* in the early 1960s as a forum for reformist writings. He is the first Soviet leader since Anatoly Lunacharsky, the commissar of education in the 1920s, to look to the intelligentsia as a key support group in the politics of cultural change. His policy of openness may be seen in part as a mandate for its expression of ideas that can help move Soviet Russia along new pathways.

True, the intelligentsia, many of whose influential members carry party cards, is inwardly divided, as is party officialdom, between proponents and opponents of change. Still, large elements of the professional and creative intelligentsia are for reform. For the talented ones reform means greater freedom in their work and more opportunity for their work to make a difference. Also, like their forbears in Russia's nineteenth-century intelligentsia, many present-day intellectuals are intensely concerned with questions of right and wrong and the search for true belief. This can make reformers of them in so far as prevailing practices diverge from what they consider the rightful ways. Indeed, it can make reform leaders of them, especially since Russia remains, far more than most others, a country of avid readers and theatre-goers, where, as a Moscow intellectual put it to me in 1986, 'The theatre is our parliament'.

A new play shows, as others do, the theatre-parliament in action. Called *Speak* and based on themes from the late writer Valentin Ovechkin, it is set in a country district shortly before and then after Stalin's death. Before, the Stalinist district party first secretary habitually employs shouted threats to drive local collective-farm heads to ensure fulfillment of their delivery targets. When a district party committee member, Martynov, says in a committee meeting, 'The land does not belong to the party committees' (anticipating Gorbachev's comment to the Twenty-Seventh Congress that ministries are not proprietors of the means of production), a fellow member says that for such a remark he can be punished under the Criminal Code's Article 58, dealing with counter-revolutionary crimes. After Stalin's death, Martynov becomes the district first secretary. He invites local peasants to talk to him about farm problems, but matters do not improve much. The peasants do not voice their views on these problems openly; they only discuss them in low tones among themselves. A visiting writer-observer (Ovechkin) implores Martynov to stop trying to solve the problems by himself, and to encourage the peasants to speak up, which at the end—to their amazement—he does. The play's message is that officials will not find good solutions unless ordinary people join them in addressing the problems. On the back of the play programme one received on entering Moscow's Yermolova Theater to see *Speak* was a facsimile of Lenin's 1917 decree declaring the land the possession of the people (not of party committees).

Another new play with a similar message is M. Shatrov's *The Dictatorship of Conscience*. Its action is inspired by a *Pravda* article of 22 April 1920 which told how some Soviet railway workers had staged, in honour of Lenin's fiftieth birthday then, a propaganda 'trial of Lenin' in which his defenders were a worker and a soldier, his accusers a bourgeois man and an idler. In Shatrov's new Lenin trial, the witnesses speak their minds openly according to the dictates of their consciences. They voice opinions on issues of both present and past, including Stalin's Great Purge, in which one witness espies a parallel with Pol Pot's huge massacre in the Cambodia of the 1970s. 'Without a real past, there is no real future', a Soviet critic comments. He adds that this play awakens in spectators' minds and hearts a need for independent thinking and action by showing that artificial creation of 'forbidden zones' for thought leads in the end to 'double-think' *(dvoemyslie)*.[34] As 'speeches' in Russia's theatre-parliament, *Speak* and *The Dictatorship of Conscience* may be seen as an invitation to the receptive members of the intelligentsia and other citizens to join with reform-minded elements of the political leadership and help the reformation to succeed by speaking their minds freely.

A positive response came in the May 1986 Fifth Congress of the Cinema Workers' Union, at which speaker after speaker criticized the state body for oversight of the film industry, the USSR State Cinematography Committee *(Goskino)* and then, at the end, carried out an upheaval against its own long-time Union leadership, which was subservient to *Goskino*. E. Shengelaia, first secretary of the Georgian Republic's branch of the Union, called *Goskino* 'a bureaucratic carousel built around a living thing'. V. Vashuk, a Belorussian film director, demanded 'full artistic and economic independence' for film studios. N. Mikhalkov, a Moscow film director, said it had become easier to speak but not to work because 'The bureaucrat engages in mimicry. In the fight to survive he is taking on a new coloration, camouflaging himself to blend in with the surroundings and chattering about the party congress's decisions; he is taking on a new form but his content remains unchanged.'[35] When it came time to reelect the Union's leadership at the end, a group of delegates proclaimed the need for a change to a secretariat composed of younger persons, and they won the day. Two-thirds of the Cinema Union's previous leadership failed of reelection. The man elected to replace its head was Elem Klimov, a talented film director whose films were given a hard time by *Goskino* until recently.

Klimov's new-wave film *Go and See* is a chilling document about the stark savagery of war as experienced in occupied Belorussia during World War II. It is not pleasing to those Soviet military chiefs who like war films that spare the gore in glorifying the dashing valour and victory of Soviet forces. Following the congress, the Union, now under new leadership, formed a disputes commission to look into the validity of bans imposed by *Goskino* in the past two decades on films that seemed too daring and unorthodox to its conservative functionaries. An example of the long-banned ones is the now showing *Testing on the Roads*, a film about a wartime Soviet deserter to the Germans who comes back in disgust to join Soviet partisans in fighting the Germans, only to remain ever suspect in the eyes of the Stalinist commissar of the partisan detachment although, in the end, he proves his loyalty by sacrificing himself in a partisan action to seize a locomotive in the railway yards.

The Eighth Congress of the Soviet Writers' Union, which met in Moscow in the following month, was another significant reformative event. Just beforehand Gorbachev invited thirty writers, both liberals and conservatives, for a four-hour conversation in which he conveyed to them his desire to enlist writers' support in the drive for reform. He wanted to change things, he said, but couldn't do it all by himself. When a writer commented that not all theatre directors were in favour of proposals for theatre reform that would give them more initiative, Gorbachev saw an analogy with problems his economic reforms were encountering. 'Mediocrity does not always welcome freedom', he said. 'It's easier for mediocre people to live within the framework of controls.' He made it clear to those present that he hoped the impending congress would be a free-spoken one.[36] It proved to be just that. Stage-management in the pattern of Stalinist Soviet political culture was out. Reformist speeches mingled with those reflecting conservative outlooks.

The boldest call for change came from the poet Andrei Voznesensky. He began by insinuating that the Moscow writers' organization falsified the results of the election of congress delegates by excluding fourteen well known writers, including Bella Akhmadulina and Bulat Okudzhava. Readers, he said, turn away from books that conceal the truth about 'the monstrous force of evil' (an evident reference to the Stalinist past), and about lawlessness, corruption, extortion, humbug and duplicity. They oppose those things in real life and then receive editorially dolled-up timid books, 'not *Dead Souls* but vaudeville.' Only a few writers have sounded alarms about the 'monstrosity of the crimes'. Nowadays the main enemy in society is the bureaucratism that resists reformation and the old thinking that hasn't given up the fight. The writings of E. Zamiatin (author of the early 1920s dystopian novel *We*) and Vladislav Khodasevich, Voznesensky went on, should be published, as should Anna Akhmatova's complete works. So should the complete works of Boris Pasternak, whose holy house in Peredelkino should become a museum. Even well known writers spend ten per cent of their time writing books and ninety per cent getting them into print. Now a self-management experiment is taking place in which theatres themselves will decide what plays to produce. Why not a writers' commission to expedite publication of long-held-up manuscripts, and a cooperative publishing house for the same purpose? In conclusion: 'Our fatherland may be in danger now if there is no full-scale democratization, no reformation, if the new thinking doesn't win out.'[37]

The theatre reform mentioned by Voznesensky was formally announced after an August 1986 conference in the party Central Committee on reformation of theatrical life. Under it, 69 theatres in eight Soviet republics are adopting new forms of organization, planning and financing, and those that prove justified will be extended to all theatres in 1989. Until now the political culture of theatrical life has been modelled on the system set up in 1946, the heyday of Stalin's postwar regimentation of high culture. Then an Artistic Council of the State Arts Committee was given responsibility for theatre repertoires. A play approved by the Chief Administration for Safeguarding State Secrets in the Press (better known as *Glavlit*) must then be approved by the USSR Ministry of Culture's Chief Administration for Repertoire Control as well as by the local party committee's culture department. Under the experiment, the directors and artistic councils of the 69 experimental theatres will themselves decide what plays to put on, and the councils will be elective although the theatre directors will still be appointed from above.[38] In a country where the stage and screen are a parliament for characters' discussion of vital issues of past and present, the reform potential of this experiment is obvious.

In the heady atmosphere of unprogrammed expression at the writers' meeting in June there was talk of reducing *Glavlit*'s powers to questions involving military and national-security matters, and of editors and publishers obtaining more autonomy in judging manuscripts' publishability. A favourable omen for a publishing reformation was the attack on 'book-publishing conservatism' by M.F. Nenashev, a reform-minded man recently promoted from editorship of the newspaper *Soviet Russia* to head the USSR State Committee for Publishing Houses, Printing Plants and the Book Trade. He spoke of changing the publication planning system by 'expanding information and openness at all levels of decision-making', a reform under which, he said, the State Committee would work closely with the Writers' Union and rely on libraries, the Book-Lovers' Society and the media for relevant information.[39] Although the writers' congress in June saw no such leadership upheaval as the one that took place at the cinema workers' congress in May, four of the fourteen nondelegates whose names were given by Voznesensky, including Akhmadulina and Okudzhava, were elected to the new Writers' Union board, and the Union's long-time head, the literary bureaucrat Georgi Markov, was replaced by his deputy Vladimir Karpov, a relatively respected man of letters.

Finally, the writers' congress became a platform on which several prominent 'ruralist writers' took advantage of the openness policy to mount a severe attack *as citizens* on an ecologically dangerous project that under Brezhnev and after was moving forward, over intellectuals' opposition, through the ministerial bureaucracy: the plan for diverting part of the northern and Siberian rivers' northward flow to Soviet Central Asia in the south. The elder writer, Sergei Zalygin, a non-Communist who after the congress replaced Vladimir Karpov as editor of *Novy Mir*, compared the earth and its five billion inhabitants to a 'communal apartment with one sewage pipe for all', then assailed the Ministry of Melioration and Water

Economy (*Minvodkhoz*) for stubbornly proceeding with the diversion project's development so as to get new credits in order to pay off the billion rubles it owes to the state. The Siberian ruralist Valentin Rasputin, author of the moving novelette *Saying Farewell to Matyora*, which sees a symbolic farewell to Mother Russia in the flooding of an island and its peasant village in the Angara River because of a power station project, ripped into various Academy of Sciences institutes, *Minvodkhoz* and other ministries for stealthily pushing the diversion project. He attacked Gosplan for holding up urgently-needed steps to protect Siberia's deep-water Lake Baikal from ecological destruction by cellulose plants, and appealed to Gorbachev to get to the bottom of the situation regarding Baikal and the northern rivers 'and take a decision in favour of our people, not of the interested agencies'. The ruralist Vasily Belov, from Vologda in European Russia's north, told of writers having waged a ten-year struggle against 'diverters' so as to save the northern lands from ruination, all to no avail. 'Departmental demagogy' had carried the day. Preparatory work was still in progress. Whole divisions of the Academy of Sciences were opposed to it, but in vain. And why? 'Because the diverters have the support of Academician Aleksandrov himself' (the Academy's president—R.T.). And Voznesensky, though no ruralist himself, denounced the diversion plan's 'criminality', adding that his father, a hydraulic engineer, had charged him to oppose 'this senseless project'.

The most eloquent plea for conservation came from the writer Yuri Bondarev, who said in his congress speech:

If we do not stop the destruction of architectural monuments, if we don't stop violating the earth and rivers, if there is no ethical explosion in science and criticism, then one fine day, which will be the last, the funeral day, we with our endless optimism will wake up and see that immense Russia's national culture, her spirit, her love for the parental land, her beauty, her great literature, painting and philosophy, have been wiped out, crushed forever, put to death, and then, naked and beggarly, we'll sit on the ruins trying to recall our dear native alphabet and won't remember, for thought, feeling, joy and historical memory will have disappeared.

Bondarev's speech was equally notable for its withering portrait of bearers of the bureaucratic political culture passed down from Stalin's time. 'Terrible is the careerism that claims to be guided by social needs', he said, 'the careerism peculiar to *chinovnik*-type protectors not of man but of statistics, who actually compromise the planning idea and make it a brake on the economy.' Science, he went on, which in our century should preserve a rational equilibrium between man and the environment, can murder both. When it turns up in the hands of 'slippery characters who deceive us with promises, ingratiating men of ambition lusting after glory, the next higher rung on the official ladder, science destroys, does to death, turns nature into a sewage ditch, and so commits murder of nature and mankind.'[40]

After the public outcry at the writers' congress came political action on high. The Politburo decided on 15 August 1986 to stop all work on the river-diversion project in view of the need for further study of ecological and economic consequences. The public announcement of the decision said that halting the project was something 'which wide circles of the public advocate'. October 1986 saw a related action: the foremost scientific 'diverter', Academy president Anatoly Aleksandrov, was retired at age 83 and replaced in his influential job by reform-minded G.I. Marchuk, a mathematician and ethnic Ukrainian who founded and directed the computer center at the Siberian Division of the Academy in Novosibirsk.

We cannot conclude that open public opposition halted the river-diversion project. Gorbachev may have subtly solicited the expressed opposition by mentioning the word 'rivers' in a passage of his February party-congress speech touching on environmental problems, and later by encouraging the writers to speak up freely in their own impending congress. He may have done this to help along a decision he intended to advocate in the Politburo. Still, the openly voiced opposition was useful for quashing the controversial project, which had support from interested ministries, Central Asian political authorities, and other agencies capable of exerting influence at high levels.

Something of historic import is involved: the appearance of a no-longer-wholly-regimented society in Soviet Russia, one still closely connected with the state but no longer, as under Stalin, its mere tool. Something of the sort took place in tsarist Russia starting in the late eighteenth century when the nation's energies were no longer strained by the government's incessant efforts to expand the state territory and internal needs claimed priority attention. The earlier state-building process gave way to an incipient state-reform process with the unbinding of classes—initially the nobility—from compulsory state service. A civil society began to emerge, albeit against obstacles; at the end of the nineteenth century it was still in process of formation.[41]

So now, following the revived state-building process under Stalin and the gradual shift of political priorities after his death to Soviet Russia's internal needs, a society has begun to emerge from under the shroud of an all-encompassing state. This phenomenon's early beginnings may be discerned in Khrushchev's time and its quiet continuation in Brezhnev's. In 1978 one of Russia's perceptive minds and fine human beings, the late Evgeni Gnedin, had the following to say in an essay that has so far been published only abroad:

> The state or state apparatus, on the one hand, and society, on the other, are evolving in opposite directions. The party-state apparatus, relying on the 1977 edition of the Constitution, grows more and more sclerotic as society gradually comes to life and grows pluralistic. One can observe the beginnings of a not-yet-mature political pluralism. I mainly have in mind a diversity of outlooks on the world. This ferment in society, proceeding without *glasnost*, does not mean that there is no philistine inertia, no inertia of obedience to the powers-that-be. Yet, this intellectual and spiritual diversity, albeit in concealed forms, is the sign of a search for a way out of the labyrinth. In these conditions, the decisive thing is for individuals to stand up against arbitrary rule and injustice.[42]

But only under the new dispensation of openness, only as the public began (and one must underline *began*) to acquire an untrammelled voice, has the appearance of a society as something more than a mouthpiece of the state become fully apparent. The process is of no less significance for the fact that it was encouraged by a new leader's need for intelligentsia support in a reformation of Soviet life that faces bureaucratic resistance throughout the state apparatus. What we see now is no longer the Stalin-period's 'monologue of the state with itself' (as the historian Kliuchevsky described public life in statist seventeenth-century Muscovite Russia), but the emergence of a dialogue between state and society.

In so far as society has managed to raise its voices—for they are diverse—what kinds of concern does it express? One is the desire to expand the opportunity to speak out openly on public issues, and for what is openly said to bear fruit in real changes rather than being compromised, as an artist puts it, 'by an indifferent hearing and self-interested inaction'. This artist wants the Soviet arts establishment to stop trying to regiment the pictorial arts by, for example, issuing a book whose author prescribes, *inter alia*, what should be the length of an exemplary industrial worker's arm in a picture.[43] Other society concerns are to put what happened in the Stalinist past on the public record; to publish previously banned emigré Russian writers like Vladimir Nabokov and the poet Nikolai Gumilev, who was shot by the Bolsheviks in 1921 (such publication is beginning now); to stop environmental spoliation by plan-obsessed state monopoly organizations called ministries of this or that; to expose and curb the influence of the careerist bureaucratic types spawned by Stalinist statification and kept in place by Brezhnevian conservatism; and to reduce special privilege.

A further concern in society's mind is moral decline. It is expressed, for example, in Viktor Astafiev's best-selling novel *The Sad Detective Story*, about a town somewhere in Russia whose people in the majority have lost moral bearings in life; in Andrei Voznesensky's poem 'The Ditch', about present-day Soviet scavengers of a ditch in the Crimea containing remains (including jewelry and gold dental crowns) of a mass of mostly Jewish citizens slain in a German World-War II atrocity; and in the Kirghiz writer Chingiz Aitmatov's new novel *The Executioner's Block*, which breaks a Brezhnev-era taboo by publicizing drug abuse in the Soviet Union and introduces in its hero a young man who feels the need for a saving new sense of the divine among a mankind in danger of a nuclear Armegeddon. A related concern, voiced in the writings of cultural nationalists, is fear of the Russian past's disappearance through industrialization-driven effacement of old folkways, traditional village life, old churches and other national monuments, and through the many-decades-old practice of renaming historic cities and streets after deceased Soviet personages, e.g., the city and province of Tver' as 'Kalinin'.[44]

Still another social concern are the countless bureaucratic

prohibitions which make it difficult or dangerous for individuals to earn extra money on the side by their private efforts, or by taking a second job if they already have a professional one, even if they have to do these things to make ends meet. From a town in West Siberia a mother of five, who is on maternity leave as a teacher due to the recent birth of the fifth, writes about her family's sad situation. As an engineer her husband is prohibited from taking a second job. At this late point in her maternity leave she receives no pay from her main job. To make it possible to feed the family of seven she must work privately at home doing knitting, but this is illegal unless one has a permit. Bureaucrats in the town financial organs, citing regulations, deny the permit that would legalize her private work. In conclusion she despairingly asks the minister of finance whether it is worthwhile to forbid an engineer under such conditions to take on a second job or the mother of several children to work two or three hours at home for pay without resigning her main job. 'What's the sense of such a prohibition?'[45]

Seeing that it is senseless, society has in mind a solution for the problem; introduce a neo-NEP by repealing stultifying state regulations that make law-breakers out of citizens in this way. Such is the plain message of an article called 'A Horrible Type'. It shows that because of the delays and difficulties they experience with state-operated service shops, citizens regularly resort to the private services of this 'horrible type' who, in off-hours, will fix one's phone or TV set, repair one's furniture, sharpen one's knives, etc., for pay, but quickly and well—and illicitly. Prosecutors, policemen, Young Pioneers and pensioners hunt down the horrible type, yet he lives and he does so because he is in demand. 'There's no place for him in the system. But the system and life, it would seem time to realize, are not one and the same.' What then is to be done? Conclude a peace treaty with him, bring him within the great state power's law, and let him pay 'an honest just tax' on his private earnings. Then one could say to him: 'Thou hast conquered, oh Galilean. Here's your permit, here's your contract, the game of hide-and-seek is over'.[46]

How many 'horrible types' there are is not known, but their numbers run into the millions according to another article, which estimates that services performed privately by those who work 'on the left' (i.e., illicitly) net 5 to 6 billion rubles annually, an amount comparable to the total wages of the 17 to 20 million people employed by the state-managed system of service trades. The article's authors describe an experiment under way in the Baltic republic of Estonia. A state radio and television repair association has rented out one of its shops to a brigade of technicians. They are free to earn as much money as they can after paying the association a monthly premium for each technician plus rent for the premises, equipment, electricity, etc. Results have been impressive. Repairs that the association takes two weeks to make are performed by the experimental brigade in a day or two, its repair work is of top quality, and it seeks ways of expanding its business. The article's message on behalf of society is the need to liberate the service trades from the wasteful, sluggish, uneconomical state management system whose restrictions on individual enterprise are costly to the state, which receives no recompense in taxes from the privateers, and to the population, which either patronizes those privateers or suffers from long delays, inability to have needed services performed, or low quality of services that are performed.[47] A neo-NEP in the service trades is the clearly implied solution.

That is what Gorbachev's economic adviser from Novosibirsk, Aganbegyan, favours. While attending the party congress in early March 1986, he told foreign correspondents that a commission was at work devising measures to permit limited private enterprise in the service trades, and he spoke approvingly of the experience in this regard of East Germany, Bulgaria and Hungary.[48] Not long afterwards, new measures were introduced to combat 'non-labour income'. Their prime targets were crimes for which corrupt officials have been and are being convicted: embezzlement, extortion, bribe-taking and the like. In a press interview about these new measures, USSR Prosecutor General A. Rekunkov explained that 'no one is forbidden to earn good money—not to extort it or pocket it but to make an honest ruble'. He added that a law was being drafted on individual work activity, the purpose of which is not to prohibit such activity but to develop it.[49]

As promulgated on November 19, 1986, this new law

authorized individuals or families to engage, as from 1 May 1987, in 29 different kinds of private enterprise, albeit without the use of hired labour. They include the production of shoes, clothing and furniture, private repair of cars and home appliances, painting of apartments, use of privately-owned cars as taxis, and tutoring in languages and music. The law is a serious step toward legalizing 'horrible types'. An earlier governmental decision authorized voluntary formation of small-scale cooperatives, employing five to fifty members, for preparation and processing of secondary raw materials, initially in selected peripheral republics and two regions of the Russian Republic. They would be self-financed after initial state financing, and subject to closure if unable to operate profitably.[50]

Such moves toward a neo-NEP accentuate the need for systemic economic change, and that has yet to come. Tatyana Zaslavskaya acknowledged this in a press interview during which she took advantage of openness to summarize main points of her Novosibirsk report. The great problem, she said, is to devise a system relying on economic methods of management in place of the one inherited from the 1930s which runs on 'directives and orders'. This requires abolition of much of the middle layer of the three-level economic system: the branch economic ministries and their territorial affiliates, which intervene between the higher central organs like Gosplan and the Finance Ministry, on the one hand, and the enterprises at the bottom level on the other. Eliminating the 'obvious hypertrophy' of the middle layer would lessen the relative weakness of the lower one and, to some extent, of the higher one as well. Asked by her interviewer where would be the best place to start the needed reform, Zaslavskaya answered that agriculture would be, and in justification she cited the experience of 'other socialist countries that have carried out economic reforms'.[51] This was to suggest some form of East-Europeanization of the Soviet economy as Moscow's way of responding to the need to change the statist command economy that Stalin and his men fashioned with Petrine Russia as a model. More concretely, it was to suggest that the swollen state be cut down in size, and that spontaneous social forces be accorded a legitimate role that Stalinism and the earlier post-Stalin system denied them.

At the interview's end Zaslavskaya confessed that such systemic economic reform would be no easy thing to achieve: 'The conception exists, the strategy has to be worked out'. She forebore to add that the strategy problem is not only economic-administrative, but political and ideological as well.

V

Reform leaders, it was said in an earlier chapter, typically object to certain prevailing practices and seek to change them on the ground that they are at variance with the society's professed beliefs. In a party – state claiming to be guided in its policies by an ideological doctrine (even though in fact the doctrine is reshaped from time to time to bring it into accord with new policies), a would-be reformer, no matter how pragmatic his concerns, must be careful to find doctrinal support for the policy changes he would make and to remove doctrinal obstacles to them. Thus Khrushchev—a pragmatist as Communist leaders go—denounced the autocratic rule that Stalin practised after 1934 on the ground that it violated Lenin's collective-leadership principles, and he condemned Stalin's attempted justification for his anti-Communist terror of 1934-39—that 'class struggle' must intensify with the USSR's progress toward communism—as without warrant.

On the other hand, not intending to undo the first phase of Stalin's revolution from above (1928-33), Khrushchev had no criticism in his unpublished Twentieth-Congress speech of the terror used to force the peasants into collectives during those years. In fact, he opened the speech with a reference to Stalin's 'merits' not only in the Revolution and Civil War but also 'in the fight for the construction of socialism in our country'. He thereby implied that Stalin and the party were indeed 'building socialism' when agriculture was collectivized and the command economy developed in the early 1930s.

The question is politically sensitive because Stalin's claim that socialism was being built then has ever since been accepted in official party annals, in the minds of those who tend those annals, and in the minds of political figures educated in the Stalin era, for whom the Stalinist equation of socialism and statism—including collectivized agriculture and the command economy—is politically sound because ideologically valid. This places in relief the doctrinal and political problem that Gorbachev and his supporters face as reformers desiring to make deep changes in both agriculture and the command economy. They cannot avoid addressing the issue of whether, and if so how, Stalin violated the Leninist legacy in his supposed 'building of socialism'.

In addition to being politically sensitive, the issue is historically complex. For as we have noted in this book, there were two Lenins in the Soviet period: the War Communist Lenin who pursued harsh policies to extract grain from the peasantry and prescribed terror against 'class enemies', and the NEP Lenin who went back to his pre-revolutionary politics of party pedagogy and advocated persuasion in a generation-long reformist 'cultural revolution' (a *perestroika*, he could have called it) to create a socialism of cooperatives. Stalin invoked the War-Communist Lenin's pronouncements for doctrinal support when, in 1928-29, he stigmatized the Rykov-Bukharin moderates as 'right deviationists' and launched his coercive, terror-filled revolution from above as a supposedly proper means of constructing socialism.

By the same token, a reform leader seeking to undo some or much of Stalin's statist legacy will invoke the authority of the NEP Lenin and find a part of his politico-ideological platform in the cooperative version of socialism which that Lenin designed in his last articles. In a gingerly way Gorbachev began doing this when he mentioned the *prodnalog* in his party-congress speech and proposed a rethinking of the status of cooperative as against state property under socialism. But generally he has relied on intelligentsia supporters to discover that Lenin's NEP, which Stalin abolished, was the right path to follow all the way to socialism.

A leading figure in this project is a scholarly journalist, Fedor Burlatsky. He shows us the reality of the 'two Lenins' issue in an imaginary 'polemical dialogue on the *perestroika*' between a typical old-style regional party first secretary who is about to be replaced, Streshnev, and the man of the reformation who is about to replace him, Shirokov. The two figures embody different strains in Soviet political culture, the long-established one and the new one struggling to be born. The fierceness of the fight comes out in a comment by Shirokov, who says that 'What I've seen here is a wall. And we can't go around that wall, we'll have to smash it'.

Streshnev is bogged down in day-to-day activity of pressuring collectives to fulfill their plans for grain, cement, meat, refrigerators, etc. He represents the political culture of 'directives and orders' (in Zaslavskaya's phrase). Shirokov stands for economic management methods that will permit enterprise autonomy, and argues that a regional party committee's proper function is to think about long-range prospects, the strategy of the region's development. That, says Streshnev, would be 'a step back from our principles'. Where did you get those principles, Shirokov asks, and Streshnev says they are 'elementary truths of Marxism'. To this Shirokov replies that he wants to know just where those elementary truths are to be found on the pages of Marx and Lenin.

Then it turns out that these two men were students together in the early post-World War II years and studied political economy under a dry little teacher named Baroptalo, who taught them that 'everything pertaining to the state is good, and whatever is social is bad'. Streshnev recalls that Baraptalo gave him a five (the highest mark) on their course examination and censured Shirokov for 'an unscientific formulation of the question'. Yes, Shirokov replies, 'I already then suspected he was misinterpreting Lenin'. How so, Streshnev inquires. Baraptalo, says Shirokov, concealed from the students that Lenin underwent change; he gave them only citations from the Lenin of War Communism—'rations, outright requisitions, prohibitions, enthusiasm without material incentives. And commodities, money, cost—all those things were some sort of capitalist miscarriages.' So, says Streshnev, 'You've uncovered a new Lenin?' It was the Twenty-Seventh Party Congress that did it, Shirokov says, 'And the time of command economy is gone, long gone'. Streshnev doesn't quite understand what he means by 'command economy'. Shirokov explains with an historical example: 'How did Peter I develop the economy? By decrees. He issued a decree: cast pig iron, produce cannon. And they did. For that time, maybe, it's fully explicable. But in our time it's shameful to work that way. And ineffective.'

Shirokov proceeds to lecture Streshnev on what reformation must mean. The most important things, he says, are social justice and democracy, the purposes for which the people made the revolution. Democracy has to be made real in the decision-making of every party organization and working collective. Nothing will come of it, Streshnev says, and he explains: 'That's not our path. It contradicts the whole system'. Earlier post-Stalin reform attempts, responds Shirokov, failed because boldness or political will was lacking. Now the will exists. 'And don't you try to frighten us, Ivan, don't frighten. The time of fears has passed. The time of action has arrived.'[52] The collision between the statist outlook of Stalin's time, which has remained dominant up to now, and the different Leninism that Shirokov-Burlatsky stands for, and certainly Gorbachev as well, could hardly be more sharply drawn.

In an earlier article, speaking in his own name, Burlatsky found Lenin's transition to the NEP relevant to the transition from extensive to intensive economic development now. Then and now, he argues, the country stood at a sharp turning-point. In Lenin's last writings, such as 'On Cooperation', answers may be found to fundamental questions of the Soviet present. Burlatsky recalls that his own father, who served in a detachment that requisitioned grain from a village under War Communism, went back to that village during the NEP to recover from tuberculosis and was astonished at the abundance of milk, eggs, bread and meat that he found there. Everyone was amazed then by the NEP reform's swift economic effect and by the way in which peasants, of their own volition, were forming cooperative ties. Nowadays, the idea of moving to cooperative enterprise, as has happened in some other socialist countries, encounters a doctrinal obstacle in the belief that cooperatives represent a 'backward step' from state stores, cafeterias or repair shops. But nothing in Marx or Lenin supports such a view. As for the objection that cooperative enterprise will lead to social differentiation and unearned gain, experience shows that there's no salvation from that in the 'state form'.[53]

Russia's literature, no less than its theatre, is a parliament where political ideas are expressed through words and deeds of fictional characters. In today's literary parliament there is no stronger voice for the NEP than Zalygin's. His new novel *After the Storm* is about the Civil War (the 'storm') and NEP as what came after. Its first part was published in 1982. Part two, banned under Chernenko in 1984, came out under Gorbachev.[54] It presents the reader with the NEP not as the 'retreat' that Lenin at first called it, but as a programmatic idea, a strategy for constructing a socialist society in a non-violent way. It wasn't simply a set of economic policies but also the setting for a huge outburst of creative energy and, as the author puts it in an interview, 'a stupendous experiment, unique in all world history'.[55]

Gone, by implication, is the Stalinist picture of a NEP Russia in retreat from socialism and happily eclipsed by the socialism-building Five-Year Plan that followed. Zalygin's image of the NEP is personified in his novel's character Lazarev, who embodies the dynamism of Russia's 1920s and sees it as the mission to prove that the storm's horrendous events were worthwhile: 'We fought, we shed blood, and now we've got to show that it wasn't in vain'. This, it seems, is the novel's symbolic message to the country about the mission now: to liberate Russia's creative energies in a new period of peaceful progress after the terrible second storm of Stalin's time and overcome its legacy of a society in crisis.

Some Soviet social scientists, too, have undertaken to review the Stalinist picture of the NEP and stress its positive features that can serve as guidance for economic reformation. But Gorbachev and his colleagues have tried to mobilize them to do more along this line. Addressing an all-union conference of chairmen of social-science departments, Gorbachev said that theory was needed 'for literally our every step forward' and that a qualitatively new state of society could not be achieved without the social sciences' help in devising ways of improving social relations under 'developing' (not, be it noted, 'developed') socialism. He stressed the need for boldness and initiative in advancing new ideas, a process that must go on through 'dialogue and not monologue', in an atmosphere of 'juxtaposing different viewpoints, discussion, breaking down previous stereotypes'. He recognized the serious intellectual resistance to the needed advance in the social sciences, saying that renovation of Soviet life goes along with 'a sharp, not always open but uncompromising struggle of ideas, of psychological approaches, of styles of thought and conduct. The old doesn't surrender without a fight....' The ways of teaching social science are still fostering dogmatism and scholasticism, he added. The social sciences are in need of their own *perestroika*, which would make it easier for people with creative and questing minds to breathe and to work.[56] At the same conference Ligachev spoke of the need for new social-science textbooks, the old ones having outlived their time, and of the 'enormous importance' that the teaching of history takes on now.

We must ask: whence this importance? A political reason is that the Stalin period, which began with the forcible abolition of the NEP at the end of the 1920s, still remains enshrined in Soviet historiography and textbooks as the time of true 'socialist construction' that Stalin claimed the 1930s to be. So long as this is so, the undoing of their heritage in institutions and practices—in political culture—faces a paralyzing ideological obstacle. As the 86-year-old writer Oleg Volkov, a rehabilitated victim of the Stalin period who spent twenty-seven years in penal servitude and is now a member of the Soviet Writers' Union, put it in 'Notes on Openness' that the Soviet press was not yet open enough in mid-1986 to print, 'let's face it that what we most of all need now is to extract the Stalinist splinter from the nation's body, the splinter that still continues to poison our consciousness'.[57]

Many in the intelligentsia are eager to do just that. Some long ago began the work by producing the manuscripts of history books and novels that tell of Stalinist terror and tyranny. In his novel *White Gowns*, parts of which have been published in 1986, the writer Vladimir Dudintsev tells of the suppression of genetics in the Stalinist post-war 1940s. Publication of *Children of Arbat*, a powerful, heavily autobiographical novel by the 76-year-old writer Anatoly Rybakov, has been announced for 1987. Set chiefly in the Moscow of gathering terror in 1934, it offers a literary portrait of Stalin in the midst of machinations that culminated on 1 December 1934 in the assassination of his party rival, the Leningrad party chief Sergei Kirov. Publication of this work called for a decision at the highest political level. Pressure from a large group of prominent literary figures helped the decision along. For a younger Soviet generation that knows very little about the Stalin era, exposure of Stalin's villainy in using the planned murder of Kirov to detonate terror on a huge scale and establish a personal despotism will be a salutary educational event. Anna Akhmatova's *Requiem*, a poetic indictment of Stalin's terror that ranks among the masterpieces of Russian literature, is due to be published in Russia for the first time in 1987. Meanwhile, a new film *Repentance*, made in Georgia in 1984, has begun showing. Its principal character, in whom traits of Stalin's police chief Lavrenti Beria, and of Stalin, are visible, appears as the dictator of a terrorized city who comments at one point that four out of every three persons are 'enemies of the people'. He explains his odd arithmetic by saying that enemies are quantitatively weightier than friends are.

Crucial among Stalin-period events awaiting the searchlight of factual history is the brutal collectivization and resulting hushed-up famine. Thus far it is the parliament of literature that has led the way here. Foremost among the 'speakers' is the writer of war fiction, Vasil Bykov. Himself a war veteran, born in 1924 in Belorussia, Bykov as a small boy watched collectivization happening around him, with its punitive dispossession and deportation to distant camps or construction projects of peasants most often arbitrarily classified as exploitative 'kulaks' subject to—in Stalin's jargon of the time—'liquidation as a class'. They were victimized in this manner so as to terrorize the rest of the villagers into signing up for membership in a collective farm that few except village idlers and malingerers desired to enter.

Bykov's war novel *Omen of Disaster*, which found its way into print under Andropov, uses flashbacks to draw on his personal early memories. As he explained in an interview, there were no kulaks (i.e., farmers employing hired labour) in his poor Belorussian village. But as 'dekulakization' demanded that some be identified and singled out for victimizing, the village activists chose three people to be 'dekulakized', one because he owned not only a cow but her calf, the second because his mare had a foal, and the third because a distant woman relative would come to help him gather the harvest. The result was bitter village discord which, when the Germans occupied Belorussia in 1941, led some villagers to offer their services to the *polizei* so as to avenge themselves on others. The novel reflects these things, showing that Stalin's collectivization was part of the prologue to wartime disaster when very many *kolkhoz*-hating peasants welcomed the invading Germans and only later learned that they were there not to liberate but to enslave.[58]

There are no few pro-Stalin people in today's Soviet society, not all of them aged career beneficiaries of Stalin's rule. The new openness gives them, along with anti-Stalinists, opportunity to air their views. So we find them standing up for Stalin, for example by denying that there was a collectivization-caused famine or praising Stalin's 1938 *Short Course* of party history or picturing him as a great war leader. Thus a General Kovalyov recalls Stalin as a wise chairman of the State Defence Committee, which directed the war effort in 1941-45.[59] The literary parliament also has its Stalin admirers. One is Ivan Stadniuk, whose latest war novel *Moscow 1941-42*, published in 1985 by the Military Publishing House (which would not have issued *Omen of Disaster*) gives the reader no hint of the Stalin who, according to Khrushchev's eyewitness testimony in the unpublished Twentieth-Congress speech, went into a panic and virtual nervous breakdown for a period of weeks when the Germans invaded in June 1941 and he thought Russia's cause was lost.

So, contemporary Russia's right-wing conservatives, militarists, pro-statists, Great Russian chauvinists—in a word, Stalinists of all kinds—rally to uphold the legacy that reformers seek to change. Truly 'the old doesn't surrender without a fight'.

VI

On the evidence adduced in these pages, it is chiefly the need for a fundamental reform of the statist Soviet economy, with attendant deep reduction of the huge bureaucracy, that has actuated the new administration's call to the creative intelligentsia for help, its encouragement of society to speak its mind, its expressed concern for social justice, and its invitation to ordinary people to take part in their institutions' decision-making processes. Nevertheless, these developments have political implications.

The new openness is a controlled one with limits that are definite although subject to change as official policy evolves. This can be illustrated by examples. No few Soviet citizens, including young potential servicemen, oppose the protracted war of pacification that resulted from the Brezhnev administration's decision in 1979 to invade traditionally non-aligned Afghanistan so as to keep in being a Communist-led government that had taken power on its own and was threatened with overthrow. But public misgivings about that war only began to surface in the Soviet press after the government seemingly reached a decision in late 1986 to seek a political settlement permitting Soviet forces to be withdrawn from Afghanistan over a period of time. This suggests that growing *glasnost'* involves an instrumental use of the press to support decisions that the Soviet regime has decided to take or is willing seriously to consider.

Another example relates to Andrei Sakharov. Prior to his release and return to Moscow in December 1986, no fellow member of the Academy of Sciences could publicly object to his detention in Gorky and have that objection reported in the Soviet press. Nor did that press report (although, as we shall see presently, the leadership took careful cognizance of and decided to take some action on) a respectfully worded letter that Sakharov sent to Gorbachev in February 1986 proposing the release from camps and exile of all prisoners of conscience convicted under articles 190-1, 70 and 142 of the Russian Republic's criminal code (and analogous articles in the other republics' codes), as well as prisoners of conscience held in special psychiatric hospitals on account of ideological and political motives, i.e. for beliefs and associated non-violent actions, and prisoners of conscience convicted under articles of the criminal codes on non-political charges.[63] Article 70 prohibits 'Agitation or propaganda carried out with intent to subvert or weaken the Soviet regime'; Article 190-1, the dissemination of 'consciously false fabrications defaming the Soviet social and state order'; and Article 142, which deals with separation of church and state, has often been used to prosecute citizens for non-violent forms of expressing their religious convictions.

Severely-enforced limits on public expression of politically deviant views remain a fact of Soviet life. Yet, the broadening of the range of permissible public discourse under the new dispensation of openness is important, especially so if we are examining Soviet change from the political-culture angle. For it involves a measured departure from the public conformism that has long been a real Soviet cultural pattern, enforced with ferocity under Stalin, partially and briefly relaxed under Khrushchev, and reestablished by means short of terror under Brezhnev. What this conformism has meant is best explained by a Soviet journalist, Vasinsky, in an *Izvestia* article subtitled 'openly on openness'.

He recalls a story by the much admired late Soviet writer Vasily Shukshin, in which a teacher addresses a passionate protest to a man in authority named Shurygin, who is directing three tractor drivers to raze a half-ruined seventeenth-century church in Podolsk, southwest of Moscow. 'Stop immediately', he cries as he stands in front of the church. 'Who gave the order? That's seventeenth century! You have no right! Even the enemies didn't touch it! I'll write about it!' The burly Shurygin picks up the puny teacher and moves him out of the bulldozers' way. Vasinsky imagines Shurygin as an erudite man who suffers from 'bifurcation'. At home he's a lover of Russian antiquity; at work he's committed to fulfilling the plan, which is often at odds with love for cultural monuments. This inconsistency and duality, Vasinsky says, give rise to 'a kind of thinking that I would call cross-thinking (rather like having a cross-eyed mind), in which one part of the head pronounces correct words while another part guides actions quite incompatible with those words.' Concluding, he says 'We talk a lot about openness, but we all still have to learn how to live in conditions of openness.... And among the public doesn't openness presuppose what lies at the root of that idea—having a firm opinion, a bold and fully dignified voice which is not so easy to disregard?'[64]

Such 'cross-thinking' is customary in Soviet life. In Russia it is a very pronounced pattern for reasons that especially go back to the Stalin period, when non-conformist speech in public—or even in private at times—was terribly dangerous. Subsequently, it has been futile, career-costly, or dangerous in so far as persons have been convicted under one or another statute for speaking their minds in public or disseminating dissident views in *samizdat*. Vasinsky is saying that the pattern of thinking one thing in private and being conformist in public will not vanish or radically change simply because *glasnost'* has come into currency as a watchword of policy. Changing the pattern will take time and effort and, above all, some risk-taking openness in action by citizens who speak up as the puny teacher did in Shukshin's story.

How the controlled new openness relates to the phenomenon of dissidence in Soviet society may now be indicated. The Russian word for dissent or dissidence is *inakomyslie*, literally 'thinking otherwise' or being heterodox. The dissidents are those who have transgressed the boundaries of permissible public discourse, violated the code of conformism. In their own ways they have done just what Vasinsky's *Izvestia* article urges all citizens to do: say in public what they may have been thinking or saying only in private, forsake the pattern of pretence which for so long has governed public life in their country.

Now dissidence (as a state of mind) is no more disappearing as yet in Russia than full-scale freedom of speech and press is appearing. For the openness being encouraged is a controlled one. It offers scope for discussing publicly such earlier undiscussible topics as 'cross-thinking', or memories of collectivization's victims, or corruption among officialdom, or the existence of a huge, illicit, private service sector to meet a public demand going unmet by the slothful, uneconomic state sector, or the censorship of creative work, but not for forthright protests against the Afghan war or for publishing Sakharov's above-mentioned letter to Gorbachev. Even so, the change makes a most meaningful difference by transforming, to some extent, what has been *inakomyslie* into possible public discourse. As the range of publicly expressed thoughts expands, that of similar thoughts which have been considered dissident tends to contract.

Confirmation of this analysis comes from the expatriate writer, Viktor Nekrasov, famous for his war novel *In the Stalingrad Trenches* and now living in Paris. 'Soviet newspapers have become interesting to read', he commented, adding that more and more often one finds in them 'materials that in the recent past might have been christened "dissident dirt" and the authors of which might have been sent away somewhere for "slander and the blackening of reality"'. Being today, as he was in the Soviet Union, one who 'thinks otherwise', he closed his article by protesting against the USSR's 'disgraceful colonial war' in Afghanistan.[65]

As the range of publicly unexpressible thoughts contracts, the need to deal punitively with those who have publicized them, say in *samizdat*, should likewise diminish. A Soviet society that is becoming rather more open should, by that token, be growing rather less repressive. Signs of such a trend have in fact been forthcoming, especially since Sakharov's release from exile. This action signalized the Gorbachev leadership's intention to proceed at least some distance down the road that his letter from Gorky had urged it to take.

A governmental decree of February 1987 amnestied about 150 prisoners of conscience, ranging from human rights and peace activists to religious offenders, organizers of an independent trade union and Ukrainian nationalists. Many had been convicted under Article 70. According to information of foreign monitoring groups, there were at the outset of 1987 about 750 prisoners of conscience in the USSR known by name and perhaps as many as 2,000 more on whom detailed information is lacking.

In what ways might the reformation alter Soviet legal institutions? By 1986 there was some open advocacy of incremental changes. A. Yakovlev, of the Academy of Sciences' Institute of State and Law, proposed reforms in the judicial system. He referred to the common practice of local political chieftains requesting judges and prosecutors by telephone to let corrupt officials go free and imprison those who exposed their criminal conduct. So as better to ensure the independence of the courts proclaimed in Article 155 of the Soviet Constitution, but clearly not observed in many past cases, Yakovlev proposed to change the composition of the people's courts (which consist of a judge and two non-professional 'people's assessors') by increasing the number of the latter to five or seven.[66] In February 1987 a 100-member commission was reported from

Moscow to be at work on revisions of the criminal code that might repeal Article 190-1 and modify Article 70 by restricting its application. Some local party and police officials have been publicly reprimanded and, in several cases, dismissed for harassment of local reporters who seek to publicize cases of official misconduct. The widely read weekly magazine *Ogonyok* has reported that in the Soviet Republic of Karelia a number of police officials have been dismissed, and one police officer jailed, on charges of brutally mistreating prisoners by coercing confessions from them.

Such developments are initial moves toward a less repressive Soviet legal, judicial and penal order. Sakharov's assessment of the general trend of events is significant. 'Objectively, something real is happening', he said in an interview in Moscow. 'How far it's going to go is a complicated question, but I myself have decided that the situation has changed.'[67]

VII

As the second anniversary of his rise to top leadership approached, Gorbachev went before a plenary session of the party Central Committee to report on what had been accomplished so far in the *perestroika*, what problems it still faced, and what remained to be done. He said that it had proved harder, and the causes of accumulated problems deeper, than the leaders had earlier realized. The further they went in their efforts, the more new problems inherited from the past came to the fore. Society and the party itself were not sufficiently aware of the complexity of the situation. That was why a 'number of comrades' were asking about measures adopted by the Politburo and government: Are we not taking too sharp a turn?[68]

Gorbachev's answer was a resounding 'no' to those comrades and a stronger message on the urgency of change than the one he gave to the party congress nearly a year earlier. Without mentioning Stalin by name, he explained his diagnosis of the present state of affairs by referring to the Stalinist legacy and the consequences of Brezhnevian conservatism with respect to it. Theoretical notions about socialism, he declared, were even now in many ways still on the level of the 1930s and 1940s, when live discussion and creative thought ceased, authoritarian tenets took over as unquestionable truths, forms of social organization were absolutized, and society was portrayed as devoid of contradictions and diverging group interests. What prevailed later on were inertia, disregard of all that failed to fit into accepted canons, and disinclination to address pressing socio-economic problems.

Gorbachev's withering summation of the consequences of all this history was nothing less than a frank admission of the crisis of society that has been described in the foregoing chapter. These consequences were 'social corrosion', a decline of citizen interest in public affairs, the growth of a social stratum, including some of the youth, for whom material things and consumerism are the whole goal of life, drunkenness, drug abuse and a rise in the crime rate, official law-breaking, bribe-taking, fakery and sychophancy, the regime's past practice of lavishly distributing honours and prizes instead of doing something about people's living and working conditions, cultural stagnation—all of this creating a growing rift between 'the world of daily realities and the world of surface wellbeing'. The party's leaders did not take cognizance of this situation in good time and adopt appropriate measures. The collegial principle lost out as the role of party meetings and elective organs diminished. Many high party officials became immune to control, and ordinary people grew indignant over their abuse of power, suppression of criticism and, in some cases, complicity in criminal actions or organizing of them.

Such was the setting, Gorbachev continued, in which sober assessment of the situation gave rise to the project of changes aimed at effecting 'a deep renewal of all aspects of the country's life, the imparting of the most modern forms of social organization to socialism, the fullest uncovering of the humanistic character of our order in all its decisive manifestations—economic, socio-political, and moral'. The transformative process was still in its early stage. But already it had stirred the society's healthy forces and started to create a new moral atmosphere. Its first steps in the spiritual sphere were especially important because it could not succeed without bringing about a profound shift in the public mind, in the psychology, thinking and attitudes of people.

Turning to economic changes in progress, Gorbachev said that in 1987 all plants and economic associations would adopt new management methods based on full self-financing. A new system of state-quality inspection was now in force for 1,500 leading plants. Soviet plants and associations were being given the right to participate with foreign organizations in joint enterprises. A new law on the status and rights of the Soviet enterprise had been drafted (it was shortly afterwards made public for nation-wide discussion). Entire groups of interconnected branches of the economy were being placed under new governmental organs. Pay differentials were being increased. Unjustified restrictions on individual enterprise had been lifted. The organization of cooperatives was being encouraged.

The report was far from an inventory of successes only. It said that progress in the social sphere was making its way slowly against the formidable obstacle of old habit, although accidents and loss of working time because of drunkenness were on the decline. Many people were slow to outgrow old ways and simply waiting things out; some were actively obstructing change. Many expected changes to come from up above, from organizations other than their own, or from people other than themselves. Naturally it was no simple, painless process to overcome established patterns of thought and conduct; a whole set of steps was needed, including new theoretical ideas based on contemporary realities and 'educating the political culture of the masses'.

All this was prologue to an appeal to go forward in the reformation by infusing elements of democracy, of meaningful public participation, into the workings of the economic and political system. Taking as his text the 'Leninist thought about a live inner link between socialism and democracy', Gorbachev argued that without this no advances could take place in production, technology, science, literature and culture. Lest his prescriptions seem too radical, he assured the Central Committee that no 'breakup of our political system' (i.e. no ending of one-party rule) was intended. Rather, it was a matter of fully utilizing the existing system's potentialities, of 'breathing new life into all cells of the social organism'. Here spoke with full clarity what has been described in this book as the reform mentality, connoting a call to a political community to make its professed principles meaningful in practice by altering customary modes of acting that contravene them.

From early on in Soviet history, let us note, a sham pretence of democratic participation has coexisted with the practice of manipulated elections and decisions from above on appointments to executive office. Elections to local and regional soviets and the Supreme Soviet have been plebiscitary single-candidate affairs. For very many Soviet citizens the act of voting in them has been a silly ritual, concerning which anecdote has it that God, after creating Adam and Eve, said to Adam, 'And now choose a wife'. In 1986 a Soviet jurist proposed multiple candidacies in local soviet elections as a way of encouraging citizens to speak up on local problems and take an interest in them in public discussions with competing candidates.[69] In his January 1987 report to the Central Committee, Gorbachev supported and expanded on this idea as a matter of high policy.

Certain democratizing steps were already being taken, he said. *Glasnost'* was developing further. A council of women was being created. The new law on the enterprise would grant certain power of decision in production matters and in social and personnel policy to plant meetings and the councils of worker collectives. Yet, much remained to be done. The still strong predilection for bureaucratic-administrative methods of management hindered the development of cooperatives. Some comrades were finding it hard to grasp that democratism was not just a slogan but the crux of the *perestroika*. These doubters and slow-coaches had better change their views and habits, or life would leave them behind.

Then, speaking in the Politburo's name, Gorbachev made some concrete recommendations. Multiple candidacies should be the rule in workplace elections and pre-election meetings, and the prevailing practice of nominating candidates for elections to local soviets should be reexamined [the practice has been for party bodies to pre-select the candidates—R.T.]. A draft legislative act on changes in the Soviet electoral system should be made public for nation-wide discussion. Then Gorbachev proposed changes in the ruling party's own internal political culture. All party members should have a voice in the elections of secretaries of party bureaux and committees. The secretaries of district, town, regional and republic party committees, including first secretaries, should be elected by secret ballot at plenary sessions of those party committees, with provision for any number of candidates for the secretarial posts. The procedure for forming the central leading party organs (i.e. the Central Committee, its Politburo, and others) should be democratized, as should be done also in the cases of other public organizations. New criminal legislation should be worked out, with effective protection of citizens' interests and rights; and steps should be taken to increase the role and authority of the courts and ensure observance of the principle of the independence of judges. In Soviet society *glasnost'* should be protected, and there should be no zones closed for criticism. Legislation should be enacted guaranteeing people 'the real opportunity to express their opinions on any question of public life'.

Gorbachev concluded his report with a discussion of policy on personnel. In effect it was an appeal to foster success of the reformation by advancement of the kinds of people needed for that. They would not be representatives of the technocratic and 'administrative-pressuring' style of work, or party officials who couldn't mend their old ways of taking on dispatcher functions and deciding all questions for everybody under their jurisdiction, nor should they be plant managers still under the influence of the long years when they were not expected to concern themselves with social problems so long as they saw that the plan was fulfilled. The crucial qualities for promotion were not specialized knowledge in a field of production, technology or science, important as that was, but breadth of horizon, moral strength, and the capacity to be persuasive as a leader. Thinking people of energy and initiative, able and willing to proceed boldly and achieve success, were needed for posts of authority in higher echelons of adminstration and all walks of public life. And more women should be promoted to leading positions.

In concluding, Gorbachev said he wanted to take counsel with the Central Committee on the thought of convening an all-union party conference in 1988 to consider progress by then in fulfilling the policies approved by the 1986 party congress and discuss 'further democratizing' of the life of the party and whole society. We may note that although the Party Rules provide for the possibility of convening such conferences between the party congresses that take place at regular five-year intervals, the most recent one was held in 1941. And further, that such an all-union conference, if held in 1988, could provide Gorbachev and his supporters with a possibility of replacing a considerable portion of the membership of the present Central Committee, a majority of whose 307 voting members entered it in Brezhnev's time.[70]

That many of these people have been worried about the direction of Gorbachev's reforms and how far they may go in the future is indicated by the plenary session's resolution on his report. It was silent on his thought of convening an all-union party conference in 1988. Although it made his protégé Aleksandr Yakovlev a candidate member of the Politburo, it elected no one in the place of Brezhnev's old associate from Kazakhstan, Kunaev, who was retired from his position as a voting member. And although it echoed many of the general themes of Gorbachev's report and thus gave him a mandate to proceed with his policies, it confined its approval of changes in electoral practice to endorsing the idea that voters should be able to express their attitudes toward a large number of candidates in elections of deputies to the soviets—whether in advance of elections or by choosing between competing candidates it did not say.

Gorbachev had evidently decided that the *perestroika* must take on fresh impetus and become something of a reform movement in Soviet society or else it would face the prospect of slowdown and eventual reversal, and he made the January 1987 Central Committee plenary session a test of the ruling elite's willingness to allow the reform process to go further. Afterwards, he made no secret of the fact that the Central Committee had been reluctant to give him unqualified support. In a meeting with representatives of the Soviet media, he said that criticism is bitter medicine which illness renders it necessary to take. 'You make a wry face, but you swallow it. And those comrades who think it can be administered in doses over time are wrong, as are those who incline to think that phenomena of stagnation have disappeared and now the time has come, as it were, to "draw back".' He also indicated to those present that had the plenary session not agreed that the reformation should go forward, he would have resigned his high office.[71]

Then, armed with the general mandate, he hit the political trail. Mid-February found him on a tour of Latvia and Estonia where he presented his position and plans in meetings reported in the Soviet press. In Riga he stressed the importance of the Central Committee's plenary session in the previous month. Often in the past it had happened that large decisions were adopted without ever being carried out in actual practice. The January plenary session's task had been to propose to the party, the people and the country measures whose realization would really carry out the policies charted by the party congress in 1986. After long thought, it had been decided that to prevent this cause from going the way others had earlier, to keep the effort from foundering after two or three years, it would be necessary to focus on the main task of enlisting the people into this cause 'as the main *dramatis personae* of the reformation'. In effect, Gorbachev characterized the stress on democratization as a way of seeking to mobilize popular support from below in moving the country along the pathways of change in its political culture. The *perestroika*, he said in this connection, was not a one-time act, not a cavalry charge, but a long-term policy aimed at 'deep, really revolutionary changes in our society'.

Documents were in preparation, Gorbachev declared, which would give the policy of democratization a juridical foundation. Experiments with new approaches would be carried out in elections to local soviets in 1987. Boris Pugo, the first secretary of the Latvian Communist Party's Central Committee, had suggested that the forthcoming elections of local soviets in Latvia be used for experimenting with such new approaches, which could subsequently be embodied in new legislation on the Soviet electoral system, and such an idea was well worth considering. A decision on convening an all-union party conference in 1988 would be taken at another plenary session of the Central Committee in the near future. By saying that the conference would consider the character of intra-party elections and the ways of forming elective party organs, Gorbachev made plain that the agenda in his mind was a *perestroika* of the ruling party itself. In another public speech in Riga, he said that new forms of elections in party cells, local soviets and factory managements would be tried out in 1987, and that on the whole much would depend on events of the coming two or three years, which would be the 'most difficult' ones.[72]

Such was the situation as the first two years of Gorbachev's administration came to an end. The reader of these pages will not underestimate the immensity of the challenge that he and those who share his new thinking face. These reformers in power are a minority of a dominant class whose majority is still used to the administrative authoritarianism of Soviet political culture as it has existed, whose members normally act in their own self-interest and put off decisions until a piece of paper comes down from higher authority to relieve them of personal responsibility for the outcome, whence the glacial pace at which the bureaucracy has tended to move. Very many of these people oppose deep-seated change and will resist it by every means available to them. The intelligentsia, or those of its members who are so disposed, can only assist a reform programme pressed by political leadership from above. Many in the worker and peasant population, thrust back as it was during the long night of Stalinist despotism into its centuries-old passivity under the tsars, are demoralized and simply awaiting what happens.

The hopeful fact is that representatives of a younger political generation have come to power as exponents of change in the political culture. Although economic change is the centrepiece of their programme, they abjure merely technocratic approaches to achieving it. They are reaching out to elements of the society that for decades were treated as mere mouthpieces and instruments of the powers-that-be. They see the need for people at all levels to become actively involved as at least workplace citizens in policy-making processes that affect their daily lives.

The crucial evidence that a society is in the throes of cultural change is the emergence of conflict between exponents of new ways and defenders of the old ones. That is what we see now in Russia. Whatever else may be said, it is clear that an effort has begun to cut down the swollen state and re-invigorate the spent society, and that it is encountering heavy resistance. 'A struggle is taking place', said Ligachev in his address on behalf of the new leadership on the 69th anniversary of the Revolution. 'A struggle of the forces of renewal with those that would like to disrupt the *perestroika*, to push us back into the swamp of economic stagnation and public apathy.'[73]

Considering the strength of the inertial resistance, reinforced as it is by 'the furies of private self-interest' (to quote what Marx wrote in another connection), it may seem—as it does to some observers—that the new leadership will never succeed in the fight for reform. All that this scholar can say in reply is that four decades of being a Russia-watcher have taught him the motto: where Russia is concerned, one must never say never.

NOTES

1. Roy A. and Zhores A. Medvedev, *Khrushchev: The Years in Power*, trans. Andrew R. Durkin (New York, 1976), 87–93.
2. Dimitry Pospielovsky, 'The "Link System" in Soviet agriculture', *Soviet Studies*, vol. 21, no. 4 (April 1970), 433 and *passim*.
3. Alexander Yanov, *The Drama of the Soviet 1960s: A Lost Reform*, trans. Stephen P. Dunn (Berkeley, 1984), 109 and *passim*.
4. On this journal's political role in Khrushchev's time see Dina R. Spechler, *Permitted Dissent in the USSR: Novy Mir and the Soviet Regime* (New York, 1982).
5. Yanov, *op. cit.*, 36–9, 120–1.
6. For details see James R. Millar, 'The Little Deal: Brezhnev's contribution to acquisitive socialism', *Slavic Review*, vol. 44, no. 4 (Winter 1985), 694–706.
7. Zhores A. Medvedev, *Gorbachev* (New York and London, 1986), 62–3.
8. *Pravda*, June 16, 1983. Lenin spoke of getting rid of red tape by bringing it before 'the court of *glasnost*'. This was quoted in *Pravda*, 24 May 1986.
9. 'The Novosibirsk Report', *Survey*, vol. 28, no. 1 (120) (Spring 1984), 83–108. The report was leaked to a Moscow journalist, Dusko Doder, whose book *Shadows and Whispers': Power Politics Inside the Kremlin from Brezhnev to Gorbachev* (New York 1986) is a well informed and insightful account of the time of transition.
10. Personal conversation with Mr Medvedev, Moscow, May 1986.
11. *Materialy vneocherednogo plenuma tsentral'nogo komiteta KPSS, 11 marta 1985 goda* (Moscow, 1985), p. 7.
12. This hypothesis finds support in Gromyko's statement in his nominating speech for Gorbachev that he 'ran the Secretariat' while

Chernenko was general secretary and chaired Politburo meetings in Chernenko's absence.

13. On the abortive move to install Grishin, see Medvedev, *Gorbachev*.
14. *Pravda*, 24 April 1985.
15. *Pravda*, 23 November 1985. Also abolished was the State Committee for Supply of Production Equipment to Agriculture.
16. *Pravda*, 17 May 1985.
17. Elizabeth Teague, 'Turnover in the Soviet Elite Under Gorbachev', paper presented to the Washington, D.C. chapter of the American Association for the Advancement of Slavic Studies, May 1986; and Archie Brown, 'Change in the Soviet Union', *Foreign Affairs*, vol. 64, no. 5 (Summer 1986), 1048–52.
18. Credible reports that reached this writer in Moscow in May 1986 said that Gorbachev failed to persuade the Politburo that it would be best to make an undelayed announcement of the nuclear accident that occurred at Chernobyl in the Ukraine at the end of April, winding up in a minority of three, supported only by Vorotnikov and Chebrikov.
19. *Pravda*, 13 February 1986. These words are here attributed to an unnamed Leningrader who heard them spoken.
20. *Pravda*, 26 February 1986. All further references to the speech come from this source.
21. *Literaturnaia gazeta*, 1 February 1984. After the congress, at which he was not reelected to the Central Committee, Kosolapov was replaced as editor of *Kommunist* by a reform-minded intellectual, Ivan Frolov.
22. Murakhovsky made the marketeering implication clear by saying in his own congress speech (*Pravda*, 3 March 1986): 'The socialist market must play a major role.... There is nothing to fear in this.'
23. See chapter 3 above, p. 47.
24. *Pravda*, 16 January 1986. A full English translation of the document appears in *The New York Times* for 5 February 1986, A13.
25. *Pravda*, 17 October 1986.
26. *Pravda*, 3 August 1986.
27. *Pravda*, 17 June 1986.
28. *ibid*.
29. *Pravda*, 21 September 1986.
30. *Pravda*, 13 February 1986. The article was signed 'T. Samolis'.
31. *Pravda*, 28 February 1986.
32. *Pravda*, 27 February 1986. Italics added.
33. A short report on this meeting appeared in the Moscow paper *Vechernaia Moskva* on 12 April 1986. A transcript of the talk and ensuing discussion was leaked to the foreign press and has appeared in Russian-language papers abroad. A full English translation appears in the British journal *Detente*, no. 7 (Autumn 1986), 2–5.
34. 'Bez etogo istina ne rozhdaetsia', *Moskovskaia Pravda*, May 20, 1986. An editorial note appended to this article praises the play's appeal for openness, but finds objectionable the comparison of Stalin's purges of the 1930s and Pol Pot's of the 1970s.

35. *Sovetskaia kul'tura*, 15 May 1986.
36. Paul Quinn-Judge, *The Christian Science Monitor*, 18 July 1986. This article is based on the journalist's interview with two writers who took part in the discussion with Gorbachev and spoke on condition that their names not be used.
37. *Literaturnaia gazeta*, 2 July 1986.
38. *Izvestia*, 18 August 1986, and Yu. Vishnevskaya, 'Teatr i Pravda', *Novoye Russkoye Slovo*, 14 October 1986.
39. *Literaturnaia gazeta*, 2 July 1986.
40. *ibid*.
41. Marc Raeff, *Understanding Imperial Russia: State and Society in the Old Regime*, trans. Arthur Goldhammer (New York, 1984), 182−84.
42. Evgeni Gnedin, *Vykhod iz labirinta* (New York, 1982), p. 117. Gnedin headed the Foreign Commissariat's press section under Maxim Litvinov in the later 1930s. After Litvinov's dismissal in 1939, he was arrested and spent the bulk of two decades in prison, camp and exile before being cleared in Khrushchev's time and returning to live in Moscow.
43. V. Manin, 'Perestroika ili Perekraska?', *Izvestia*, 15 August 1986.
44. On the cultural nationalists see John B. Dunlop, *The faces of Contemporary Russian Nationalism* (Princeton, 1983).
45. Tatyana Kiseleva, 'V sem'e rodilos' piatero detei. Kak byt'?', *Literaturnaia gazeta*, 1 October 1986.
46. Leonid Likhodeev, 'Uzhasnyi tip', *Pravda*, 30 March 1986.
47. G. Gukasov and V. Tolstov, 'I drugie zainteresovannye litsa', *Izvestia*, 19 August 1985.
48. Serge Schmemann, 'Reporter's Notebook', *The New York Times*, 8 March 1986.
49. *Izvestia*, 2 June 1986. For the new measures, see *Pravda*, 28 May 1986.
50. *Literaturnaia gazeta*, 22 October 1986.
51. *Izvestia*, 1 June 1986.
52. Fedor Burlatsky, 'Razgovor nachistotu: Polemicheskii dialog o perestroike', *Literaturnaia gazeta*, 1 October 1986.
53. Fedor Burlatsky, 'Lenin i strategiia krutogo pereloma', *Literaturnaia gazeta*, 16 April 1986.
54. In the literary journal *Druzhba narodov* for July, August and September of 1985.
55. *Voprosy filosofii*, no. 4, 1986, 116.
56. *Literaturnaia gazeta*, 8 October 1986.
57. *Novoye Russkoye Slovo* (New York), 8 October 1986. The cited article is one of a series of two written in May-June 1986. The same point was made in more publishable form by the writer Yevtushenko, who told fellow writers: 'Only fearlessness in the face of the past can help to produce a fearless solution to the present's problems'. *Literaturnaia gazeta*, 18 December 1985.
58. Vasil Bykov, *Znak bedy* (Moscow, 1984), and interview, 'Na vysote sovesti', in *Literaturnaia gazeta*, 14 May 1986.

59. *Pravda*, 30 June 1986. The official reason given for publishing this article is that 30 June 1986 was the 45th anniversary of the Committee's formation.

60. Aleksandr Vasinsky, 'Ni sebe, ne potomkam: glasno o glasnosti', *Izvestia*, 29 June 1986.

61. Viktor Nekrasov, 'Sovetskaia pressa i ee prizyvy k pravde', *Novoye Russkoye Slovo*, 5 October 1986.

62. *Izvestia*, 30 May 1986.

63. *Russkaia mysl'* (Paris), 12 September 1986.

64. Aleksandr Vasinsky, 'Ni Sebe, ni potomkam: glasno o glasnost', *Izvestia*, 29 June 1986.

65. Viktor Nekrasov, 'Sovetskaia pressa i ee prizyvy k pravde', *Novoye Russkoye Slovo*, 5 October 1986.

66. *Literaturnaia gazeta*, 24 September 1986.

67. Philip Taubman, 'Soviet Turns a Big Corner', *The New York Times*, 12 February 1987.

68. *Pravda*, 28 January 1987. Further references to Gorbachev's report are from this source.

69. V. Vasiliev, 'Vlast', otkrytaia dlia vsekh', *Literaturnaia gazeta*, 17 September 1986.

70. I am indebted to Professor Darrell Hammer for bringing this point to my attention.

71. *Izvestia*, 15 February 1987, *Moscow News*, 19 February 1987, for the indication that he would have resigned.

72. *Izvestia*, 18 February 1987 and 20 February 1987.

73. *Izvestia*, 7 November 1986.

Conclusion

We come, finally, to the question of future change in the Leninist single-party political order forged in the years of revolution from 1917 to 1921. According to the argument of chapter three above, this order was not a fortuitous outgrowth of adversities that the Bolsheviks encountered in those early years. It was, rather, an institutionalizing of Lenin's prospectus in *What Is To Be Done?* for a popular movement under the legitimate leadership of a single party—legitimate because of that party's presumed possession of truth revealed by Marxism about past, present and future history.

Some thoughtful Soviet minds believe that the time has come to introduce political pluralism into the system as it exists in our time. They set forth their thinking in a manifesto addressed 'To the Citizens of the USSR', signed 'Movement for Socialist Renewal', and dated Leningrad, 21 November 1985. It was apparently drafted as a contribution to the then ongoing discussion of the draft new Party Programme in preparation for the party congress coming early in 1986. The document was not published in the Soviet Union. Later, a copy was made available in Moscow to the British newspaper *Guardian*'s correspondent, Martin Walker, and published abroad. According to Walker, its authors represent the 'maximalist wing' of Soviet reformers.[1]

The Leningrad manifesto was an attempted leadership act aimed at fostering systemic change in the USSR. It diagnosed the Soviet situation as grave and proposed steps to rescue the country from its impasse. Measures 'of a revolutionary nature' were needed, it said, in the economy and in the polity.

On the economic side, the manifesto attacked the disregard of 'general economic laws' inherent in ending Lenin's NEP and in collectivization. It said that 80 per cent of the collective farms are unprofitable and exist at state expense, resulting in 1984 in the import of 50 million tons of grain, a quarter of the country's needs. Enterprises should be made fully self-supporting on the basis of expanded rights. State planning and economic administration should be decentralized and wages made dependent on output. Private initiative should be allowed in the service trades and consumer-goods production, as under the NEP. Soviet citizens should be permitted to rent farm machines and land for cultivation and repay the state with a part of their produce. Such a reform, we may note, would mean not simply a return to the *prodnalog* but, in effect, de-collectivization.

According to the manifesto's authors, the crisis of the Soviet economic order is linked with a political crisis involving the state's fundamental constitutional principles of freedom of speech, press and assembly, personal immunity, privacy of correspondence and telephone conversations, and freedom to join organizations. The message was that these principles, proclaimed in the Soviet Constitution, are not observed in practice. The political measures needed would comprise: the creation of a press independent of the party and state; no more persecution of people for political or religious beliefs; a guarantee of freedom of expression; and the provision of constitutional conditions for the forming of 'alternative political organizations'. After discussion of some advantages of a multi-party system, such as bringing new ideas into the polity and helping to combat inertia and abuse of power, the manifesto opted for a socialist state system short of that. The 'different political organizations' would share the aim of building a socialist society and compete in advancing policy programmes in the interests of the workers, peasants and intelligentsia and for the right to represent these groups in governmental organs.

These maximalist reformers are Soviet loyalists. As such they find in Lenin, whom they cite copiously, their authority figure. They tell us that Lenin said in a draft resolution on press freedom that every group of citizens of a certain size, say 10,000, should be granted paper supplies and printing facilities; that 'it is ridiculous to speak of democracy' without *glasnost*, that 'Every citizen must be given the opportunity to participate in discussing the laws of the state, electing his representatives, and putting state laws into practice'; that freedom of capitalist development (this said in 1921) 'is not something for socialism to fear so long as transport and industry remain in the proletariat's hands'; and that it is necessary 'to limit much more precisely the functions of the party (and its secret service) and to increase Soviet officials' and institutions' responsibility. . .'.

The manifesto is a reform document in the sense of this book in so far as it proposes to bring Soviet political and juridical practice into line with articles of the Soviet Constitution that proclaim freedoms of expression and person. But the reformers go beyond this to assert the need to legitimate pluralism by allowing different political organizations that share socialist goals to compete for citizen allegiance.

Is this idea Leninist? The authors' selective citations from Lenin suggest an affirmative answer. But their document is rather forthright in acknowledging that what was valid in Lenin's time is so no longer:

The single-party system in operation in the country was established by Lenin as the proletarian dictatorship's political embodiment for destroying the old socio-political order, suppressing the remnants of exploiting classes and building a new socialist society in Russia. Having secured the complete and final victory of socialism, the proletarian dictatorship has fulfilled its historic mission from the standpoint of internal development and ceased to be necessary in the USSR.

The manifesto's authors thus cautiously affirm that the time has come in Soviet Russia's development to go beyond the Leninist legacy by introducing open political pluralism into single-party rule.

But they did not address a more fundamental question to which such a change relates: what, in terms of political culture, distinguishes the forms of constitutional statehood that emerged from the great Western revolutions—England's, France's and America's? It is that no one, be it a ruling person, a government in power or a ruling party, may act on the principle *L'Etat, c'est moi*. For the state is the body of citizens, together with the collectively self-accepted system of laws by which they are governed and which centre in the constitution.

The result is a disjunction between loyalty to the state and agreement with the policies of a particular government in power or acceptance of that government as a desirable one for the nation. The citizen may openly oppose and criticize the government's policies and officials or disapprove of its presence in power without exposing himself or herself to a charge of disloyalty, much less criminality. That, it seems, is the essence of constitutionalism as a political culture; open plurality of political groups or parties is an institutional derivative of this disjunction. Where constitutionalism does not exist, even though a constitutional charter may have been formally proclaimed, the authorities treat disagreement with the given government's or ruling party's policies, or disapproval of the government itself, as disloyalty to the state. In effect, they say: *L'Etat, c'est nous.*

Under Lenin's aegis the Russian Revolution yielded a political system of the latter kind. It did so because of belief in a creed that made this outcome appear politically progressive. Believing as he and fellow Bolsheviks did in Marxism as revealed truth, and the Communist Party as the vehicle of future history's unfolding by virtue of its commitment to Marxist truth, its members' mastery of it and dedication to creating and spreading socialism in accordance with it, Lenin presided over the rise in post-1917 Russia of a party-state that had, as we have noted in chapter one, a significant similarity (no less real for Lenin's unawareness of it) to traditional church-states. In them a body of theology is the revealed truth, the ruling orthodoxy from which it is heretical for a subject to deviate in his thinking and speaking. In the Leninist party—state it was and is an ideology. The fact that tsarist Russia had a state religion in Orthodox Christianity doubtless contributed something to the way in which the new orthodoxy developed in this land then mainly populated by devout peasants. The Bolsheviks' 'anti-religious' campaign on behalf of 'scientific atheism' was in fact a campaign to replace one state-sponsored belief system or state religion, Orthodox Christianity, by another, orthodox Leninist Marxism.

Notwithstanding the statements that the Leningrad manifesto selectively cites from the Lenin corpus, which in the latest, fifth edition fills 55 volumes of his (still incomplete) *Complete*

Works, he fathered a new orthodox form of statehood in Russia. Lest that seem a fanciful metaphor, let us recall that it was Lenin who introduced the term 'deviation' (*uklon*) into the party's lexicon when he drafted and put through, at its Tenth Congress, the resolution declaring anarchism and syndicalism an heretical departure from Marxist truth, something that no party member had a right to espouse. It remained for the one-time theology-school student Stalin to become the party–state's Grand Inquisitor who condemned those found guilty of deviation—a notion broadened to include any hint of a critical attitude toward Stalin—not only to expulsion from the party, if they were members, but to death or concentration camp as traitors.

The question of the Leninist legacy must, in the end, be confronted in these terms. To bring open political pluralism into the system, even if within the framework of single-party rule (as the manifesto's loyalist authors allow), the orthodoxy-heterodoxy problem will have to be faced and resolved in a secularizing way. Marxism-Leninism will have to be disenthroned as party orthodoxy from which it is heretical to deviate, and those who happen at any one time to be in authority will have to recognize for all citizens the legitimacy of diversity in viewpoints on policy issues and, indeed, on matters of fundamental conviction.

The disenthronement here in view should not be taken to mean that the ruling party would renounce guidance by the ideas of Marx and Lenin, although it would have to recognize that the corpus of their writings does not contain solutions to all the problems of socialism and the present-day world and that other thinkers, socialist or not, have had and do have notable contributions of their own. The disenthronement would also mean acceptance of the fact that the Marxian thought world itself is pluralistic, containing a current (hitherto disallowed or discouraged by the official custodians of orthodoxy in Moscow's Institute of Marxism-Leninism) that finds enduringly valuable the younger Karl Marx who formulated his philosophy of history as a moral story of humanity's estrangement from its human nature and ultimate recovery of it in a future of freedom from both want and the drive to accumulate material wealth. It would mean recognition of the fact that to

Marx, both younger and older, future 'communism' did not mean a new economic system, but rather the end of economics in a society where humanity, freed from much of the necessity to labour, would realize its creative nature aesthetically in a life of leisure.[2] Such recognition would compel Soviet Marxists to face the fact that the statist system erected in the Soviet period, particularly during Stalin's long reign, has title to the designation 'Petrine socialism' but not to Marx's idea of what socialism might mean, nor to Lenin's.

A century ago or more, no few of the tsar's educated subjects 'believed that Russia could not be governed by a strong hand alone, that the country had to be heard and in some way involved in running its own affairs.'[3] The Leningrad manifesto's authors, like those of such earlier *samizdat* statements as Fedor Zniakov's, are of the same mind now and with greater justification because development in the seven decades since 1917 has produced a more numerous educated citizenry with a substantial middle class of professional people of various kinds, from engineers and managers to creative artists. From the point of view of many of these people, Soviet Russia has outgrown the need, to the extent that it once existed, for the paternalism inherent in Lenin's Bolshevism as a party-taught, party-led culture-building culture, a society in which a party of the Marxist elect has a valid claim to guide change toward socialism and communism. In Lenin's Bolshevism, as we saw earlier, the party was conceived as a collective tutor for the worker-peasant masses of the people. Now, graduation time should be coming in Lenin's school of communism—at a minimum, in the sense of freedom for different socialist-minded political organizations to compete for public support in a Soviet Russia of Leninist lineage.

Such a transcending of the Bolshevik Revolution's legacy is no part of the programme for cultural renovation that Gorbachev has enunciated. Although he has spoken of the need for 'revolutionary transformations', he is no revolutionary as conceptualized in chapter two of this book; he would preserve the one-party system established under Lenin's aegis. He is a classic exemplar of the leader for reform who wants to make the existing order successful by effecting changes in it and who recognizes that they must be gradual because they involve the outgrowing of culturally patterned ways of thinking and acting that have been formed over decades.

Yet, this judgement must be qualified by the realization that 'Marxism-Leninism' is not at present a rigidly defined set of dogma that allows no scope for differences of interpretation on matters of importance, as it was earlier on. Gorbachev is propounding his own version of it while recognizing—and deploring—that far from all his party comrades share it. Thus he takes his ideological cues from the NEP Lenin who wanted the Soviet regime to deal with its worker—peasant constituency by means of persuasion, who thought that socialism meant a less bureaucratic and more just form of society, who showed some growing awareness of the role of legality in the Soviet polity, and who envisaged a steady rise of meaningful popular participation in economic and political life under a unified single party's guidance. There are, in other words, different ways of adhering to party doctrine in the Soviet Russia of Gorbachev's time.

The reform enterprise should not be discounted as of small significance on the ground that its goals are as circumscribed as they are. Gradual change with limited goals can be more enduring, and more likely to pave the way for further change in the same direction, than rapid and radical change is. Such non-revolutionary change was Sakharov's prescription in the *samizdat* memorandum whose publication abroad in 1968 made him world-famous—and started him down the road to becoming an outcast in Brezhnev's Russia. He said in it that he was not 'one of those who consider the multi-party system to be an essential stage in the development of the socialist system or, even less, a panacea for all ills. . .'. And what he concretely proposed was a law on press and information that would end 'irresponsible and irrational censorship', the repeal of all anti-constitutional laws and decrees violating human rights; amnesty for political prisoners, and carrying through the exposure of Stalin to the end.[4] The fact that some of these things have started to happen, at long last, may help to explain why Sakharov, on returning to Moscow unbroken by seven years of detention in Gorky, voiced support for Gorbachev.

While gradual change, or the fight for it, is going on, the existing Soviet Russia of the party—state, with some form of

Marxism—Leninism as its offical creed, is the one with which the rest of the world has to deal, and the question arises in conclusion: Would it be in the non-Communist West's best interests, or not, for Gorbachev's reform course to succeed? This issue can best be approached by looking into the relation between the *perestroika* and the Gorbachev-sponsored 'new thinking' in international affairs that has been summarized in chapter seven.

The thesis I wish to present is that the Gorbachev who has shown himself to be a leader for reform within his country is likewise a would-be reform leader in world affairs. He has revealed this in many of his statements and some of his actions during his first two years in power, and also by using his talismanic term in reference to the need for new policies in inter-state relations. Addressing a congress of Soviet trade unions on February 25, 1987, the anniversary of his report to the Twenty-Seventh Party Congress, he called for a qualitatively new approach to the tasks facing humanity at the end of the second millenium. These were fundamentally two: to save the world from a nuclear catastrophe and to place at humankind's service the enormous potential of knowledge and material resources that it now possesses. The new Soviet moves towards arms-control agreements, he went on, were aimed 'at giving an impulse to a *perestroika* in state-to-state relations as well, at bringing them into accord with the real tasks and demands of our time'.[5]

To interpret Gorbachev as a leader for reform internationally may seem to contravene the portrayal of him in these pages as one who takes Lenin as his authority figure in politics. But the Lenin to whose authority he appeals in internal policy is the NEP Lenin who preached the need for a reformist rather than a revolutionary course in fostering change toward socialism in Soviet Russia. As there is no comparably reformist Lenin in international policy, Gorbachev grounds his call for reform in the international sphere not on ideological texts but on the existence of historically unprecedented 'real tasks', namely, those of saving mankind from nuclear self-annihilation and from succumbing to global environmental, demographic and other problems that in our time are getting out of hand. And here lies the link between the internal *perestroika* of which

Gorbachev has become the champion and the 'new thinking' that faces the need to address global problems of a supra-class nature and recognizes that security in the nuclear age 'can only be mutual'.

A final consideration is in order. When the government of a great power has come to recognize that its country faces an internal crisis situation calling for deep-seated reform of its economic, social, cultural and political way of life, that government loses the need that there was in the past to conjure up for its citizens the image of a relatively intractable external enemy and danger on which energy and attention need to be focused as a matter of highest priority, normally by increasing the country's military strength still further. The willingness openly to confront the existence of profound internal problems and seek to solve them by changing the society frees the government to become less combative and more cooperative in external relations. In the two years during which Gorbachev has been Soviet Russia's foremost leader, there have been many signs of such a shift in the posture of its regime.

In my view, therefore, the world has a stake in the success of this new Soviet leader's reform enterprise and his incipient efforts to develop new approaches in international affairs. Apart from the changes in past Soviet foreign policy that such new approaches would involve, a Soviet Russia that comes through reform to enjoy a greater measure of general welfare, that grows more open and pluralist within its present political structure, and lives in greater harmony with itself than it has for a very long time, will be abler and readier to work with other interested states to construct a desperately needed cooperative regime of war prevention and deal effectively with global problems that pose a mounting menace to humanity's long-term future.

'Russia is where the true belief is', Berdyaev has been quoted in these pages as saying. A recurring theme throughout the book is that Russia has been, in various ways, a society of believers, its culture a belief culture. So it was with old orthodox Russia, and so again with Soviet Russia under Lenin. So then, in a macabre way, it was under Stalin, who tried through terror to transform the belief system inherited from

Lenin's time into one in which he himself, the most villainous ruler in Russia's history, figured as an object of reverential belief for his people. Khrushchev shattered that belief without managing to restore the belief culture on a new foundation, as he tried to do.

Stalin not only terrorized Russia through the nearly two decades of his despotic rule; he deeply corrupted it as well. Especially did he corrupt in large measure the bureaucratic serving class that he elevated to its privileged position in the society; it learned to live by hypocrisy. Brezhnev and his assistants kept that privileged class in place for nearly two decades while the corruption grew more and more widespread and took on more and more blatant forms. The corrosion of belief among the people continued too, although there was a recovery of belief in diverse dissident forms in a small-scale heterodox movement that was heavily repressed. And now, in Gorbachev's time, elements of the elite, along with members of the intelligentsia and others, are seeking to bring about a kind of reformation in the society.

Is a revival of belief possible? The issue, in the final analysis, is whether a reform administration under the able leadership of a man who appears to combine a genuine streak of idealism with pragmatism in his political makeup can succeed over time in regenerating a meaningful relationship between contemporary Soviet Russian society and what there was of humanistic ideals in the Revolution of 1917. If the official reform effort falters and fails, as Gorbachev in speeches of early 1987 feared that it might, that will mean something more serious than the failure of a particular reform leader. It will indicate that Stalin's tyranny hurt the country so deeply and pervasively that there is little hope for success of a reform movement aimed at socialism as the Soviet project.

And if the reform movement succeeds? Then we shall see belief reemerging, particularly among a younger generation from which the world has yet to hear. But this reformed Soviet Russia will not be a reprise of the Red Russia of Lenin's early period in power. Although professing some form of Marxist and Leninist ideas, it will be a Russia that has learned to live at home with a mixed economy, a non-repressive polity, and an unregimented cultural life. It will be a Russia tolerant of diversity in its neighbouring sphere of influence and one whose international efforts are directed to working with willing governments and other constructive political forces abroad to check the present global drift to environmental disaster, contain the threat of war, and sustain a world fit for the generations yet to come. In other words, a Russia worth believing in.

NOTES

1. Martin Walker, 'The party men who looked west and saw the warning', *The Manchester Guardian Weekly*, 27 July 1986. For an edited version of the document's text in English translation, see *The Guardian*, 22 July 1986. For the full text in Russian, see *Novoye Russkoye Slovo*, 6, 7 and 8 August 1986.
2. For this interpretation of Marx, see Robert C. Tucker, *The Marxian Revolutionary Idea* (New York and London, 1969), chs. 1 and 7.
3. Hans Rogger, *Russia in the Age of Modernisation and Revolution, 1881-1917* (London and New York, 1983), 9.
4. Andrei Sakharov, *Progress, Coexistence and Intellectual Freedom* (New York, 1968), 83, 87.
5. *Izvestia*, 26 February 1987.

Index